WordPress®

FOR

DUMMIES®

A Wiley Brand

7th Edition

by Lisa Sabin-Wilson

Foreword by Matt Mullenweg
Cofounder of WordPress

WordPress® For Dummies®, 7th Edition

Published by: **John Wiley & Sons, Inc.,** 111 River Street, Hoboken, NJ 07030-5774, www.wiley.com

Copyright © 2015 by John Wiley & Sons, Inc., Hoboken, New Jersey

Published simultaneously in Canada

For general information on our other products and services, please contact our Customer Care Department within the U.S. at 877-762-2974, outside the U.S. at 317-572-3993, or fax 317-572-4002. For technical support, please visit www.wiley.com/techsupport.

Wiley publishes in a variety of print and electronic formats and by print-on-demand. Some material included with standard print versions of this book may not be included in e-books or in print-on-demand. If this book refers to media such as a CD or DVD that is not included in the version you purchased, you may download this material at http://booksupport.wiley.com. For more information about Wiley products, visit www.wiley.com.

Library of Congress Control Number: 2015944209

ISBN 978-1-119-08857-8 (pbk); ISBN 978-1-119-08873-8 (ebk); ISBN 978-1-119-08855-4 (ebk)

Manufactured in the United States of America

10 9 8 7 6 5 4 3 2

Contents at a Glance

Table of Contents

Foreword

. . . .

*T*here used to be a program from Microsoft called FrontPage that was the first visual interface for creating websites that I saw. It worked like Word or Publisher, so with very little knowledge, I was able to hack together the world's worst website in just a few hours without worrying about what was going on under the hood.

Years later when I look back at that website, I cringe, but at the time it was incredibly empowering. The software, though crude, helped me publish something anybody in the entire world could see. It opened up a world I had never imagined before.

Now, using software like WordPress, you can have a blog or website light years beyond my first one in both functionality and aesthetics. However, just as my first web experience whetted my appetite for more, I hope that your experience entices you to explore the thousands of free plugins, themes, and customizations possible with WordPress, many of which are explained in this book.

WordPress is more than just software; it is a community, a rapidly evolving ecosystem, and a set of philosophies and opinions about how to create the best web experience. When you embrace it, you'll be in good company. WordPress users include old media organizations such as CNN, *The New York Times*, and *The Wall Street Journal*, along with millions of personal bloggers like myself for whom a WordPress blog is a means of expression.

Matt Mullenweg
Cofounder of WordPress

Introduction

• •

*I*t was 2003 when I discovered the WordPress blogging software. Way back then (and in Internet years, that's actually quite a lot of time) I used Movable Type as my blogging platform. My friend Chelle introduced me to the WordPress software. "Try it," she said. "You'll really like it."

As a creature of habit, I felt reluctant to make the change. But I haven't looked back. I've been with WordPress ever since.

WordPress started out a tool for blogging. Authors, students, parents, business owners, academics, journalists, hobbyists — you name it — use blogs as a matter of course. Over the past decade, WordPress has emerged as the premier content management system available on the Internet today. WordPress software currently powers 25 percent of the websites you see on the World Wide Web — that means 1 in every 4 websites you run across are powered by WordPress.

Today, WordPress is so much more than a blogging tool. Individuals, organizations, and corporations are using WordPress to build their entire web presence. WordPress has grown into a valuable solution for everything from selling products on the Internet to membership sites, blogging, media — pretty much anything you think you can do with your website can be accomplished with WordPress.

To a brand-new user, some aspects of WordPress can seem a little bit intimidating. After you take a look under the hood, however, you begin to realize how intuitive, friendly, and extensible the software is.

This book presents an insightful look at WordPress and covers managing and maintaining your WordPress-powered website through the use of plugins, themes, and using the intuitive WordPress Dashboard to manage your content. If you're interested in taking a detailed look at the website-building tool provided by WordPress, you happen to have just the right book in your hands.

About This Book

This book covers all the important aspects of WordPress that new users need to know to begin using the software for their own website. In this book, I cover the software package available at https://wordpress.org by highlighting all the important topics, such as these:

- Locating good hosting services for the software
- Installing and setting up the WordPress software
- Navigating the WordPress Dashboard
- Adding media files to your website
- Finding and installing free themes to use in your WordPress website
- Using basic coding to design your own WordPress theme or modify the one you're using
- Using templates and tags in WordPress
- Installing, activating, and managing WordPress plugins
- Choosing to use the multiple-site WordPress Network option to host a network of multiple websites on your domain
- Discovering the potential pitfalls associated with WordPress
- Understanding the challenges you face when running a WordPress-powered site, such as dodging comment and trackback spam
- Exploring RSS feed syndication and integration with social media like Twitter and Facebook
- Migrating your existing website to WordPress (if you are using a different platform, such as Drupal, Movable Type, or Expression Engine)
- Discovering the power of WordPress as a content management system (CMS) to create a full-service website
- Upgrading your WordPress website and staying up to date and informed about ongoing WordPress software development
- Finding support, tips, and resources for using the WordPress software

With WordPress, you can truly tailor a website to your own tastes and needs. All the tools are out there. Some of them are packaged with the WordPress software; others are third-party plugins and add-ons created by members of the WordPress user community. It takes a little research, knowledge, and time on your part to put together a blog that suits your needs and gives your readers an exciting experience that keeps them coming back for more.

Foolish Assumptions

I'll never know what assumptions you've made about me at this point, but I can tell you a few things that I already assume about you:

- ✔ You know what a computer is. You can turn it on, and you understand that if you spill coffee on your keyboard, you'll have to run out and get a replacement.

- ✔ You understand how to hook yourself into the Internet and know the basics of using a web browser to surf websites.

- ✔ You have a basic understanding of what websites and blogs are, and you're interested in using WordPress to start your own. Or you already have a website, are already using WordPress, and want to understand the program better so that you can do more cool stuff and stop bugging your geeky best friend whenever you have a question about something. Or, even better, you already have a website on another platform and want to move your website to WordPress.

- ✔ You know what email is. You know what an email address is. You actually have an email address, and you send and receive email on a semi-regular basis.

Icons Used in This Book

Icons emphasize a point to remember, a danger to be aware of, or information that I think you may find helpful. Those points are illustrated as such:

Tips are little bits of information that you may find useful.

I use this icon to point out dangerous situations.

All geeky stuff goes here. I don't use this icon very often, but when I do, you know you're about to encounter technical mumbo-jumbo.

When you see this icon, read the text next to it two or three times to brand it into your brain so that you remember whatever it was that I think you need to remember.

Beyond the Book

I've put a ton of information between the covers of this book, but you'll find even more information at www.dummies.com, such as the following:

✔ I provide you with a Cheat Sheet at www.dummies.com/cheatsheet/wordpress that lists

  • The best places to find WordPress support online.

  • The basic sections of the WordPress Dashboard.

  • How to locate a reliable web-hosting provider.

  • Where to find some great WordPress resources online.

✔ You'll also find helpful online articles at www.dummies.com/extras/wordpress that discuss

  • Setting up a WordPress.com account.

  • Changing your WordPress Dashboard layout to create your own unique work space.

  • Avoiding unsafe WordPress themes.

  • Great examples of ten sites that use WordPress as a full-blown content management system (as opposed to just a blog).

Where to Go from Here

This book is a veritable smorgasbord of WordPress information, ideas, concepts, tools, resources, and instruction. Some of it will apply directly to what you want to do with your WordPress blog. Other parts may deal with topics that you're only mildly curious about, so feel free to skim (or skip) those pages.

For example, if you already have WordPress installed on your web server, you can skip Chapter 3. If you aren't interested in digging into the code of a WordPress template, and don't want to find out how to apply CSS or HTML to enhance your design, you can skip Chapters 9–12. If you have no interest in running more than one website with WordPress, you can skip Chapter 13.

I don't intend for you to read this book from cover to cover (unless you're my mother — then I won't forgive you if you don't). Rather, scan the Table of Contents and the Index of this book to find the information you need.

Long story short: Take what you need and leave the rest.

Part I
Introducing WordPress

getting started
with

WordPress

In this part. . .

- ✔ Explore all WordPress has to offer.
- ✔ Discover the basic concepts about publishing a website with WordPress.
- ✔ Understand the different versions of WordPress and choose the right one for you.
- ✔ Get ready to use WordPress for your online publishing.

Chapter 1

What WordPress Can Do for You

In This Chapter

▶ Seeing how WordPress can benefit you

▶ Participating in the WordPress community

▶ Understanding the different versions of WordPress

*I*n a world in which technology advances in the blink of an eye, WordPress really does make building websites easy — and free! How else can you get your content out to a potential audience of millions worldwide and spend exactly nothing? There may be no such thing as a free lunch in this world, but you can bet your bottom dollar that there are free websites and blogs. WordPress serves them all up in one nifty package.

The software's free price tag, its ease of use, and the speed at which you can get your blog up and running are great reasons to use WordPress to power your personal blog or business website. An even greater reason is the incredibly supportive and passionate WordPress community. In this chapter, I introduce you to the WordPress software so that you can begin to discover how effective it is as a tool for creating your blog or website.

Discovering the Benefits of WordPress

I work with first-time website owners all the time — folks who are new to the idea of publishing content on the Internet. One of the questions I'm most frequently asked is "How can I run a website? I don't even know how to code or create websites."

Enter WordPress. You no longer need to worry about knowing the code because the WordPress software does the code part for you. When you log in to your website, you have to do only two simple things to publish your thoughts and ideas:

1. Write your content.

2. Click a button to publish your content.

That's it!

WordPress offers the following competitive advantages as the most popular content management tool on the market:

- ✔ **Diverse options:** Two versions of WordPress are available to suit nearly every type of website owner:

  - *WordPress.com:* A hosted turnkey solution; primarily used for blogging

  - *WordPress.org:* A self-hosted version to install on the web server of your choice; used for building blogs and websites

  I go into detail about each of these versions later in this chapter, in the "Choosing a WordPress Platform" section.

- ✔ **Ease of use:** WordPress setup is quick and the software is easy to use.

- ✔ **Extensibility:** WordPress is extremely extensible, meaning that you can easily obtain plugins and tools that let you customize it to suit your purposes.

- ✔ **Strong community of users:** WordPress has a large and loyal members-helping-members community via public support forums, mailing lists, and websites geared to the use of WordPress.

The following sections fill in a few details about these features and point you to places in the book where you can find out more about them.

Getting set up the fast and easy way

WordPress is one of the only platforms that can brag about a 5-minute installation — and stand behind it! Both versions of WordPress take you approximately the same amount of time to sign up.

Mind you, five minutes is an *approximate* installation time. It doesn't include the time required to obtain domain registration and web-hosting services or to set up the options in the Dashboard. (You can find information on web-hosting services in Chapter 3.)

When you complete the installation, however, the world of WordPress awaits you. The Dashboard is well organized and easy on the eyes. Everything is clear and logical, making it easy for even a first-time user to see where to go to manage settings and options.

The WordPress software surely has enough meat on it to keep the most experienced developer busy and happy. At the same time, however, it's friendly enough to make a novice user giddy about how easy it is to get started. Each time you use WordPress, you can find out something exciting and new.

Extending WordPress's capabilities

I've found that the most exciting and fun part of running a WordPress website is exploring the flexibility of the software. Hundreds of plugins and *themes* (designs) are available to let you create a blog that functions the way *you* need it to.

If you think of your website as a vacuum cleaner, plugins are the attachments. The attachments don't function alone. When you add them to your vacuum cleaner, however, you add to the functionality of your vacuum, possibly improving its performance.

All WordPress websites are pretty much the same at their core, so by using plugins, you can truly individualize your website by providing additional features and tools that benefit you and your readers. When you come upon a WordPress website that has some really different and cool functions, 98 percent of the time you can include that function on your own website by using a WordPress plugin. If you don't know what plugin that website is using, try dropping the website owner an email or leave a comment. WordPress website owners usually are eager to share the great tools they discover.

Most plugins are available at no charge. You can find out more about WordPress plugins and where to get them in Chapter 7. Chapter 15 lists my top ten choices for popular WordPress plugins available for download.

In addition to using plugins, you can embellish your WordPress blog with templates and themes. WordPress comes with a very nice default theme to get you started. Figure 1-1 shows the default Twenty Fifteen theme, created by the team from WordPress, which is displayed by default after you install and set up your blog for the first time.

The theme's default style is a minimal, with a handy application built in to the preferences that allows you to change the colors and insert an image to use as a header image. (You can find more about tweaking WordPress themes in Chapters 9–12.)

The Twenty Fifteen theme (shown in Figure 1-1) includes all the basic elements that you need when starting a new WordPress blog. You can extend your WordPress blog in a hundred ways with plugins and themes released by members of the WordPress community, but this default theme is a nice place to start.

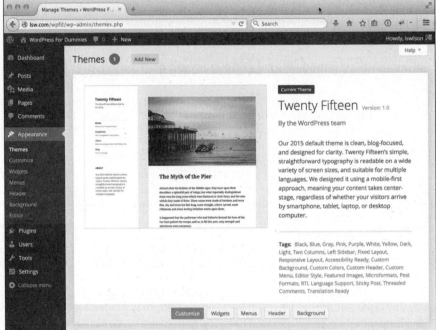

Figure 1-1:
Start a new
WordPress
website
with a
theme.

Using some of the thousands of plugins and themes available, you can truly manage many different kinds of content on your website. WordPress is not just for blogging anymore (although it does still excel at it!). Although WordPress became well known as a blogging platform, you can use it to power diverse and dynamic websites that allow you to do things like develop an e-commerce site (selling products online), create a members-only site where your content is curated only for those who have registered and become members of your site, or create a large corporate business site like the one you can see on the Microsoft News Center at `http://news.microsoft.com`.

Using WordPress as a CMS — content management system — frees you from running only a blog on the platform. (See Chapter 12 for more about the technique of designing for WordPress as a CMS.)

Taking part in the community

Allow me to introduce you to the fiercely loyal folks who make up the user base, better known as the vast WordPress community. This band of merry ladies and gentlemen comes from all around the globe, from California to Cairo, Florida to Florence, and all points in between and beyond.

In March 2005, Matt Mullenweg of WordPress proudly proclaimed that the number of WordPress downloads had reached 900,000 — an amazing landmark in the history of the software. But the real excitement occurred in August 2006, when WordPress logged more than 1 million downloads, and in 2007, when the software had more than 3 million downloads. The number of WordPress downloads has broken the ceiling since 2007 (over 5 million downloads by the end of 2013), and the number of WordPress users has climbed to the tens of millions and is growing daily. WordPress is easily the most popular content management system available on the web today. It currently powers approximately 25 to 30 percent of all the websites you see on the Internet in 2015 — that's roughly 1 in every 4 websites you encounter on the World Wide Web.

Don't let the sheer volume of users fool you: WordPress also has bragging rights to the most helpful blogging community on the web. You can find users helping other users in the support forums at `https://wordpress.org/support`. You can also find users contributing to the very helpful WordPress Codex (a collection of how-to documents) at `http://codex.wordpress.org`. Finally, across the Internet, you can find multiple blogs about WordPress itself, with users sharing their experiences and war stories in the hope of helping the next person who comes along.

You can subscribe to various mailing lists, too. These lists offer you the opportunity to become involved in various aspects of the WordPress community as well as in the ongoing development of the software.

Joining the WordPress community is easy: Simply start your own website by using one of the two WordPress software options. If you're already publishing on a different platform, such as Blogger or Movable Type, WordPress enables you to easily migrate your current data from that platform to a new WordPress setup. (See Chapter 14 for information about migrating your existing website to WordPress.)

Choosing a WordPress Platform

One of the realities of running a website today is choosing among the veritable feast of software platforms to find the one that performs the way you need. You want to be sure that the platform you choose has all the options you're looking for. WordPress is unique in that it offers two versions of its software, each designed to meet various needs:

- The hosted version at WordPress.com: `https://wordpress.com`.
- The self-installed and self-hosted version available at WordPress.org. (This book focuses on this version.)

Every WordPress website setup has certain features available, whether you're using the self-hosted software from WordPress.org or the hosted version at WordPress.com. These features include (but aren't limited to)

✔ Quick and easy installation and setup

✔ Full-featured blogging capability, letting you publish content to the web through an easy-to-use web-based interface

✔ Topical archiving of your blog posts, using categories

✔ Monthly archiving of your posts, with the ability to provide a listing of those archives for easy navigation through your site

✔ Comment and trackback tools

✔ Automatic spam protection through Akismet

✔ Built-in gallery integration for photos and images

✔ Media Manager for video and audio files

✔ Great community support

✔ Unlimited number of static pages, letting you step out of the blog box and into the sphere of running a fully functional website

✔ RSS (Really Simple Syndication) capability with RSS 2.0, RSS 1.0, and Atom support (see Chapter 2 for more information on RSS)

✔ Tools for importing content from different blogging systems (such as Blogger, Movable Type, and LiveJournal)

Table 1-1 compares the two WordPress versions.

Table 1-1	Exploring the Differences Between the Two Versions of WordPress	
Feature	*WordPress.org*	*WordPress.com*
Cost	Free	Free
Software download	Yes	No
Software installation	Yes	No
Web hosting required	Yes	No
Custom CSS* control	Yes	$99/year
Template access	Yes	No
Sidebar widgets	Yes	Yes
RSS syndication	Yes	Yes
Access to core code	Yes	No

Feature	WordPress.org	WordPress.com
Ability to install plugins	Yes	No
Theme installation**	Yes	Yes
Multiauthor support	Yes	Yes
Unlimited number of website setups with one account	Yes	Yes
Community-based support forums	Yes	Yes

*CSS = Cascading Style Sheets

**Limited selection on WordPress.com

Choosing the hosted version from WordPress.com

WordPress.com is a free service. If downloading, installing, and using software on a web server sound like Greek to you — and like things you'd rather avoid — the WordPress folks provide a solution for you at WordPress.com.

WordPress.com is a *hosted solution,* which means it has no software requirement, no downloads, and no installation or server configurations. Everything's done for you on the back end, behind the scenes. You don't even have to worry about how the process happens; it happens quickly, and before you know it, you're making your first blog post using a WordPress.com blog solution.

WordPress.com has some limitations, though. You cannot install plugins or custom themes, for example, and you cannot customize the base code files, nor are you able to sell advertising or monetize your blog at all on WordPress.com. Also, WordPress.com will display advertisements on your blog posts to users who are not logged into the WordPress.com network (`https://en.support.wordpress.com/no-ads/`). But even with its limitations, WordPress.com is an excellent starting point if you're brand new to blogging and a little intimidated by the configuration requirements of the self-installed WordPress.org software.

If you don't want or need to create a full website for your business or service and just want to create an online diary of sorts, you would typically use WordPress.com because it excels at allowing you to get a simple blog up and running quickly. As I mentioned previously, however, if you want to use the thousands of plugins and themes available for WordPress — or if you want to customize your own theme for your website, you are limited on the WordPress.com-hosted service.

The good news is this: If you ever outgrow your WordPress.com-hosted blog and want to make a move to the self-hosted WordPress.org software, you can. You can even take all the content from your WordPress.com-hosted blog with you and easily import it into your new setup with the WordPress.org software.

Self-hosting with WordPress.org

The self-installed version from WordPress.org that is covered in this book requires you to download the software from the WordPress website and install it on a web server. Unless you own your own web server, you need to lease one — or lease space on one.

Using a web server is typically referred to as *web hosting,* and unless you know someone who knows someone, hosting generally isn't free. That being said, web hosting doesn't cost a whole lot, either. You can usually obtain a good web-hosting service for anywhere from $5 to $20/month, depending on your needs (Chapter 3 gives you the important details you need to know about obtaining a web host.)

You need to make sure, however, that any web host you choose to work with has the required software installed on the web server. Currently, the minimum software requirements for WordPress include

- ✔ PHP version 5.2.4 or greater
- ✔ MySQL version 5.0 or greater

After you have WordPress installed on your web server (see the installation instructions in Chapter 3), you can start using it to blog to your heart's content. With the WordPress software, you can install several plugins that extend the functionality of the blogging system, as I describe in Chapter 7.

You also have full control of the core files and code that WordPress is built on. So if you have a knack for PHP and knowledge of MySQL, you can work within the code to create your own themes and plugins that you think would be good for you and your website. Find information about PHP and MySQL in Chapter 2.

You don't need design ability to make your website look great. Members of the WordPress community have created more than 3,000 WordPress themes, and you can download them for free and install them on your WordPress blog.

(See Chapter 8.) Additionally, if you're creatively inclined, like to create designs on your own, and know CSS, you'll be glad to know that you have full access to the template system within WordPress and can create your own custom themes. (See Part IV.)

The self-hosted WordPress.org software lets you run an unlimited number of blogs on one installation of its software platform, on one domain. When you configure the Network options within WordPress to enable a multisite interface, you become administrator of a network of blogs. All the options remain the same, but with the Network options configured, you can have additional websites and domains and allow registered users of your website to host their own website within your network, as well. You can find out more about the WordPress Multisite feature in Chapter 13.

Sites that use the Network options within WordPress include the following:

- **Best Buy** (`http://stores.bestbuy.com/577`): Blog networks can have more than 150 blogs. The popular electronics retail store, Best Buy, uses WordPress to power 1,050 local store blogs.

- **_The New York Times_** (`www.nytimes.com/interactive/blogs/directory.html`): Newspapers, magazines, and universities use WordPress to manage the blog sections of their websites. Another example is the Harvard Law School blog at `http://news.harvard.edu/gazette/`.

- **Microsoft Windows** (`http://blogs.windows.com`): Niche-specific blog networks use WordPress to manage the content they publish through various channels on their website about the Windows software — in multiple languages.

Chapter 2

WordPress Basics

In This Chapter

▶ Considering website types

▶ Finding out what WordPress technology can do for you

▶ Outlining your initial website plan

A lot happens behind the scenes to make your WordPress blog or website function. The beauty of it is that you don't have to worry about what's happening on the back end to manage and maintain a WordPress site — unless you really want to. In this chapter, I delve a little bit into the technology behind the WordPress platform, including a brief look at PHP and MySQL, two software components required to run WordPress.

This chapter also covers some of the various technologies that help you on your way to running a successful website, such as the use of comments and RSS feed technology, as well as information about combating spam.

Shining the Spotlight on WordPress

Publishing content and blogging is an evolutionary process, and blogs have evolved beyond personal diaries and journals. Undoubtedly, a blog is a fabulous tool for publishing your personal diary of thoughts and ideas; however, blogs also serve as excellent tools for business, editorial journalism, news, and entertainment. Sometimes, you will find standalone blogs where that is all the website has to offer; other times you will find a full website that contains a blog, but has other offerings as well (products for sale, memberships, newsletters, forums, and so on). Here are some ways that people use blogs and websites powered by WordPress:

✔ **Personal:** This type of blogger creates a blog as a personal journal or diary. You're considered a personal blogger if you use your blog mainly to discuss topics that are personal to you or your life — your family, your cats, your children, or your interests (for example, technology, politics, sports, art, or photography). My blog, which you can find at `http://lisasabin-wilson.com`, is an example of a personal blog.

✔ **Business:** This type of blogger uses the power of blogs to promote a company's business services, products on the Internet, or both. Blogs are very effective tools for promotion and marketing, and business blogs usually offer helpful information to readers and consumers, such as tips and product reviews. Business blogs also let readers provide feedback and ideas, which can help a company improve its services. ServerBeach is a good example of a business that keeps a blog on the hosted WordPress.com service at `https://serverbeach.wordpress.com`.

✔ **Media/journalism:** More and more popular news outlets, such as Fox News, MSNBC, and CNN, have added blogs to their websites to provide information on current events, politics, and news on regional, national, and international levels. These news organizations often have editorial bloggers as well. *Reader's Digest* is an example of such a publication — its WordPress-powered site can be found at `www.rd.com`.

✔ **Citizen journalism:** The emergence of citizen journalism coincided with the swing from old media to new media. In old media, the journalists and news organizations direct the conversation about news topics.

With the popularity of blogs and the millions of bloggers who exploded onto the Internet, old media felt a change in the wind. Average citizens, using the power of their voices on blogs, changed the direction of the conversation. Citizen journalists often fact-check traditional media news stories and expose inconsistencies, with the intention of keeping the media or local politicians in check. An example of citizen journalism is the Power Line blog at `www.powerlineblog.com`.

✔ **Professional:** This category of blogger is growing every day. Professional bloggers are paid to blog for individual companies or websites. Blog networks, such as Scientific American (`http://blogs.scientificamerican.com`), have a full network of staff blogs. Also, several services match advertisers with bloggers so that the advertisers pay bloggers to make blog posts about their products. Is it possible to make money as a blogger? Yes, and making money at blogging has become common these days. If you're interested in this type of blogging, check out Darren Rowse's ProBlogger blog at `www.problogger.net`. Darren is considered the grandfather of all professional bloggers.

Dipping into WordPress Technologies

The WordPress software is a personal publishing system that uses a PHP and MySQL platform. This platform provides everything you need to create your own website and publish your own content dynamically, without having to know how to program those pages yourself. In short, all your content is stored in a MySQL database in your hosting account.

PHP (which stands for *PHP: Hypertext Preprocessor* — and PHP itself originally stood for *personal home page,* as named by its creator, Rasmus Lerdorf) is a server-side scripting language for creating dynamic web pages. When a visitor opens a page built in PHP, the server processes the PHP commands and then sends the results to the visitor's browser. MySQL is an open source relational database management system (RDBMS) that uses Structured Query Language (SQL), the most popular language for adding, accessing, and processing data in a database. If all that sounds like Greek to you, just think of MySQL as a big filing cabinet in which all the content on your blog is stored.

Every time a visitor goes to your website to read your content, he makes a request that's sent to a host server. The PHP programming language receives that request, obtains the requested information from the MySQL database, and then presents the requested information to your visitor through his web browser.

In using the term *content* as it applies to the data that's stored in the MySQL database, I'm referring to your posts, pages, comments, and options that you set up in the WordPress Dashboard. The theme (design) you choose to use for your website — whether it's the default theme, one you create for yourself, or one that you have custom designed — isn't part of the content, or data, stored in the database assigned to your website. Those files are part of the file system and aren't stored in the database. So create and keep a backup of any theme files that you're using. See Part IV for further information on WordPress theme management.

When you look for a hosting service, choose one that provides daily backups of your site so that your content/data won't be lost in case something happens. Web-hosting providers that offer daily backups as part of their services can save the day by restoring your site to its original form. You can find more information on choosing a hosting provider in Chapter 3.

Archiving your publishing history

Packaged within the WordPress software is the capability to maintain chronological and categorized archives of your publishing history, automatically. WordPress uses PHP and MySQL technology to sort and organize everything you publish in an order that you, and your readers, can access by date and category. This archiving process is done automatically with every post or page you publish to your website.

When you create a post on your WordPress website, you can file that post under a category that you specify. This feature makes for a very nifty archiving system in which you and your readers can find articles or posts that you've placed within a specific category. The Archives page on my personal blog (see it at http://lisasabin-wilson.com/archives) contains an Archives by Subject section, where you find a list of categories I've created for my blog posts. Clicking a link below the Archives by Subject heading takes you to a listing of posts that I wrote on that topic. See Figure 2-1.

WordPress lets you create as many categories as you want for filing your content and posts by topic. I've seen sites that have just one category and sites that have up to 1,800 categories — WordPress is all about preferences and options for organizing your content. On the other hand, using WordPress categories is your choice. You don't have to use the category feature.

Interacting with your readers through blog comments

One of the most exciting and fun aspects of blogging with WordPress is getting feedback from your readers the moment you make a post to your blog. Feedback, referred to as *blog comments,* is akin to having a guestbook on

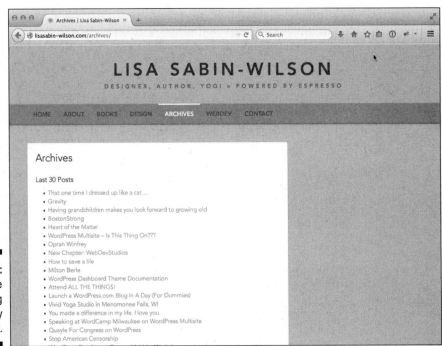

Figure 2-1:
An archive
of my blog
posts by
subject.

your blog. People can leave notes for you that are published to your site, and you can respond and engage your readers in conversation about the topic at hand. See Figures 2-2 and 2-3 for examples. Having this function in your blog creates the opportunity to expand the thoughts and ideas that you presented in your blog post by giving your readers the opportunity to add their two cents.

In the WordPress Dashboard, you have full administrative control over who can and can't leave comments. In addition, if someone leaves a comment with questionable content, you can edit the comment or delete it. You're also free to choose not to allow any comments on your blog. Chapter 5 has the information you need about setting up your preferences for comments on your blog.

Some blog users say that a blog without comments isn't a blog at all. This belief is common in the blogging community because experiencing visitor feedback through the use of comments is part of what has made blogging so popular. It's a personal choice, though. Allowing comments on your blog invites your audience members to actively involve themselves in your blog by creating a discussion and dialog about your content. By and large, readers find commenting to be a satisfying experience when they visit blogs because comments make them part of the discussion.

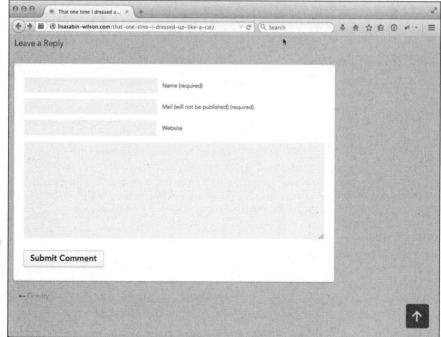

Figure 2-2:
Readers use the form to leave their comments.

Feeding your readers

An RSS (Really Simple Syndication) feed is a standard feature that website visitors have come to expect. The Introduction to RSS page on the resource site WebReference.com (`www.webreference.com/authoring/languages/xml/rss/intro`) defines RSS as "a lightweight XML format designed for sharing headlines and other Web content. Think of it as a distributable 'What's New' for your site."

Readers can use feed readers to download your feed — that is, their feed readers automatically discover new content (such as posts and comments) from your blog. Readers can then download that content for their consumption. Table 2-1 lists some of the most popular feed readers on the market today.

For your readers and website visitors to stay updated with the latest and greatest content you publish to your site, they need to subscribe to your RSS feed. Most platforms allow the RSS feeds to be *autodiscovered* by the various feed readers — that is, the blog reader needs to enter only your site's URL, and the program will automatically find your RSS feed.

Table 2-1	Popular RSS Feed Readers	
Reader	**Source**	**Description**
Digg Reader	`http://digg.com`	Digg Reader is a free online service for searching, subscribing to, and sharing different types of feeds, like RSS and Twitter feeds. You have no software to download or install; Digg Reader is all web-based. You need to sign up for an account to use this service.
FeedDemon	`http://feeddemon.com`	Although discontinued in 2013, this free service continues to work for you and requires that you download the RSS reader application to your own computer.
Feedly	`http://feedly.com`	With Feedly, you can keep up with your favorite blogs and websites that have syndicated (RSS) content. You have no software to download or install to use this service, but optional applications are available for your use.

 Most browser systems today alert visitors to the RSS feed on your site by displaying the universally recognized orange RSS feed icon, shown in the margin.

WordPress has built-in RSS feeds in several formats. Because the feeds are built in to the software platform, you don't need to do anything to provide your readers an RSS feed of your content. Check out Chapter 5 to find out more about using RSS feeds within the WordPress program.

Tracking back

The best way to understand trackbacks is to think of them as comments, except for one thing: *Trackbacks* are comments that are left on your blog by other blogs, not by actual people. Sounds perfectly reasonable, doesn't it? Actually, it does.

A trackback happens when you make a post on your blog, and within that post, you provide a link to a post made by another blogger in a different blog.

When you publish that post, your blog sends a sort of electronic memo to the blog you've linked to. That blog receives the memo and posts an acknowledgment of receipt in a comment to the post that you linked to. Chapter 10 gives you information on how to use HTML to create links on your blog.

That memo is sent via a *network ping* — a tool used to test, or verify, whether a link is reachable across the Internet — from your site to the site you link to. This process works as long as both blogs support trackback protocol.

Sending a trackback to a blog is a nice way of telling the blogger that you like the information she presented in her blog post. All bloggers appreciate the receipt of trackbacks to their posts from other bloggers.

Trackbacks aren't really as popular as they were years ago, but they do still exist and are a tool that some people like to take advantage of. There is an option in WordPress that allows you to turn trackbacks off if you want to; you can find more information in Chapter 5.

Dealing with comment and trackback spam

Ugh. The absolute bane of every blogger's existence is comment and trackback spam. When blogging became the "it" thing on the Internet, spammers saw an opportunity. Think of the email spam you've received — comment and trackback spam is similar and just as frustrating.

Before blogs came onto the scene, you often saw spammers filling Internet guestbooks with their links but not leaving any relevant comments. The reason is simple: Websites receive higher rankings in the major search engines if they have multiple links coming in from other sites. Enter blog software, with comment and trackback technologies — prime breeding ground for millions of spammers.

Because comments and trackbacks are published to your site publicly — and usually with a link to the commenters' websites — spammers get their site links posted on millions of blogs by creating programs that automatically seek websites with commenting systems and then hammering those systems with tons of comments that contain links back to their own sites.

No blogger likes spam. As a matter of fact, blogging services such as WordPress have spent untold hours in the name of stopping these spammers in their tracks, and for the most part, they've been successful. Every once in a while, however, spammers sneak through. Many spammers are offensive, and all of them are frustrating because they don't contribute to the ongoing conversations.

All WordPress systems have one very major, very excellent thing in common: Akismet, which kills spam dead. Chapter 7 tells you more about Akismet, which is brought to you by Automattic, the makers of WordPress.com.

Using WordPress as a Content Management System

You hear something like the following a lot if you browse different websites that publish articles about WordPress: "WordPress is more than a blogging platform; it's a full content management system." A *content management system* (CMS) is a platform that gives you the capability to run a full website on your domain. This means that in addition to hosting a blog, you can build pages and have additional features built into your website that have nothing to do with the content on your blog.

Exploring the difference between a website and a blog

A website and a blog are really two different things. Although a website can contain a blog, a blog doesn't and can't contain a full website. I know it sounds confusing, but after you read this section and explore the difference between the two, you'll have a better understanding.

A *blog* is a chronological display of content, most often posts or articles written by the blog author. Those posts (or articles) are published and, usually, categorized into topics and archived by date. Blog posts can have comments activated, which means that readers of a blog post can leave their feedback and the blog post author can respond, thereby creating an ongoing dialog between author and reader about the blog post.

A *website* is a collection of published pages and sections that offer the visitor a variety of experiences or information. Part of the website can be a blog that enhances the overall visitor experience, but it usually includes other sections and features that might include things such as the following:

✔ **Photo galleries:** This specific area of your website houses albums and galleries of uploaded photos, allowing your visitors to browse through and comment on the photos you display.

✔ **E-commerce store:** This feature is a fully integrated shopping cart through which you can upload products for sale, and your visitors can purchase your products via your online store.

✔ **Discussion forums:** This area of your website allows visitors to join, create discussion threads, and respond back and forth to one another in specific threads of conversation.

✔ **Social community:** This section of your website allows visitors to become members, create profiles, become friends with other members, create groups, and aggregate community activity.

✔ **Portfolio of work:** If you're a photographer or web designer, for example, you can display your work in a specific section of your site.

✔ **Feedback forms:** You can have a page on your website with a contact form that visitors can fill out to contact you via email.

✔ **Static pages such as a Bio, FAQ (Frequently Asked Questions), or Services page:** These pages don't change as often as a blog page does. Blog pages change each time you publish a new post. Static pages contain content that doesn't change very often.

Viewing examples: Blog versus website

I include a couple of figures in this section to further illustrate the difference between a blog and a website. Figure 2-4 shows the front page of my personal blog located at `http://lisasabin-wilson.com`. Notice that the site displays a chronological listing of the most recent blog posts I've made. On my personal site, I use WordPress primarily as a blogging tool.

In contrast, my business website, located at `http://webdevstudios.com`, uses WordPress as a CMS to publish a full website. This site includes a static front page of information that acts as a portal into the rest of the site, where you find a blog, a portfolio of work, a contact form, an order form, and various static pages used to tell my visitors more about the business. The static pages include services, FAQ, Terms of Service, Privacy Policy, and more.

Check out Figure 2-5 for a look at the front page of my business site at WebDevStudios and notice how it's quite different from my personal blog site, shown in Figure 2-4.

Using WordPress as a CMS means that you're using it to create not just a blog but an entire website full of sections and features that offer a different experience for your visitors.

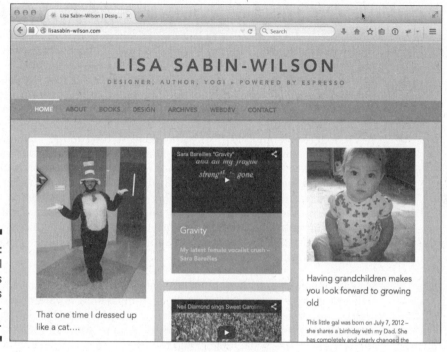

Figure 2-4:
My personal blog uses WordPress as a blogging tool.

Figure 2-5:
My business website uses WordPress as a CMS.

Moving On to the Business of Publishing

Before getting started with publishing, you need to take a long look at your big plans for your website. A word of advice: Organize your plan of attack before you start. Have a good idea of what types of information you want to publish, how you want to present and organize that information, and what types of services and interaction you want to provide your audience.

Ask this question out loud: "What am I going to blog about?" or "Am I going to have a blog on my website at all?" Go ahead — ask it. Do you have an answer? Maybe you do, and maybe not — either way, it's all right. There's no clear set of ground rules you must follow. Having an idea of what you expect to write about in your blog makes planning your attack a little easier. You may want to write about your personal life. Maybe you plan to share only some of your photography and provide very little commentary to go along with it. Or maybe you're a business owner and want to blog about your services and the current news within your industry.

Having an idea of your subject matter helps you determine how you want to deliver that information. My design blog, for example, is where I write about web design projects, client case studies, and news related to design and blogging. You won't find pictures of my cats there, but you will find those pictures on my personal blog. I keep the two blogs separate, in much the same way as most people like to keep a distinct line of separation between their personal and professional lives, no matter what industry they work in.

When you have your topic and plan of delivery in mind, you can move forward and adjust your blog settings to work with your plan.

Part II
Setting Up WordPress

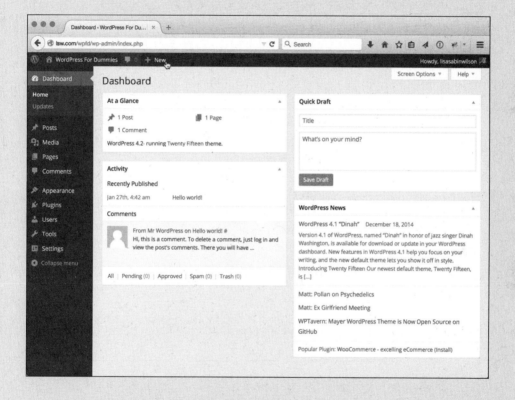

Learn how to set up a WordPress.com user account at www.dummies.com/extras/wordpress.

In this part. . .

- ✔ Discover everything you need to know about the WordPress software version found on `https://wordpress.org`.

- ✔ Set up your website base camp by registering a domain and getting set up with a web-hosting provider.

- ✔ Install WordPress on your own hosted server and begin configuring the settings and options to personalize your site the way you want it.

- ✔ Establish your own publishing routine by discovering and using the tools that WordPress provides.

Chapter 3

Setting Up Blogging Base Camp

In This Chapter

▶ Finding and buying a domain name

▶ Finding web hosting

▶ Brushing up on FTP

▶ Installing WordPress

*B*efore you can start using WordPress, you have to set up your base camp. Doing so involves more than simply downloading and installing the WordPress software. You also need to establish your *domain* (your website address) and your *web-hosting service* (the place that houses your website). Although you initially download your WordPress software onto your hard drive, your web host is where you install it.

Obtaining a web server and installing software on it are much more involved projects than simply obtaining an account with the hosted version of WordPress that's available at WordPress.com (covered in Chapter 1). You need to consider many factors in this undertaking, as well as cope with a learning curve, because setting up your website through a hosting service involves using some technologies that you may not feel comfortable with at first.

This chapter takes you through the basics of those technologies, and by the last page of this chapter, you'll have WordPress successfully installed on a web server with your own domain name.

Establishing Your Domain

You've read all the hype. You've heard all the rumors. You've seen the flashy websites on the web powered by WordPress. But where do you start?

The first steps toward installing and setting up a WordPress website are deciding on a domain name and then purchasing the registration of that name through a domain registrar. A *domain name* is the *unique* web address that you type in a web browser's address bar to visit a website. Some examples of domain names are WordPress.org and Google.com.

I emphasize the word "unique" because no two domain names can be the same. If someone else has registered the domain name you want, you can't have it. With that in mind, it sometimes takes a bit of time to find a domain that isn't already in use and is available for you to use.

Understanding domain name extensions

When registering a domain name, be aware of the *extension* that you want. The .com, .net, .org, .info, .me, .us, or .biz extension that you see tacked onto the end of any domain name is the *top-level domain extension.* When you register your domain name, you're asked to choose the extension you want for your domain (as long as it's available, that is).

A word to the wise here: Just because you have registered your domain as a .com doesn't mean that someone else doesn't, or can't, own the very same domain name with a .net. So if you register MyDogHasFleas.com, and it becomes a hugely popular site among readers with dogs that have fleas, someone else can come along and register MyDogHasFleas.net and run a similar site to yours in the hope of riding the coattails of your website's popularity and readership.

You can register your domain name with all available extensions if you want to avert this problem. My own website, for example, has the domain name lisasabin-wilson.com; however, I also own lisasabin-wilson.net.

Domain names: Do you own or rent?

When you "buy" a domain name, you don't really own it. Rather, you're purchasing the right to use that domain name for the period of time specified in your order. You can register a domain name for one year or up to ten years. Be aware, however, that if you don't renew the domain name when your registration period ends, you lose it — and most often, you lose it right away to someone who preys on abandoned or expired domain names. Some people keep a close watch on expiring domain names, and as soon as the buying window opens, they snap up the names and start using them for their own websites in the hope of taking full advantage of the popularity that the previous owners worked so hard to attain for those domains.

Considering the cost of a domain name

Registering a domain costs you anywhere from $3 to $30/year depending on what service you use for a registrar and what options (such as privacy options and search-engine submission services) you apply to your domain name during the registration process.

When you pay the domain registration fee today, you need to pay another registration fee when the renewal date comes up again in a year, or two, or five — however many years you chose to register your domain name for. (See the previous "Domain names: Do you own or rent?" sidebar.) Most registrars give you the option of signing up for a service called Auto Renew to automatically renew your domain name and bill the charges to the credit card you set up on that account. The registrar sends you a reminder a few months in advance, telling you it's time to renew. If you don't have Auto Renew set up, you need to log in to your registrar account before it expires and manually renew your domain name.

Registering your domain name

Domain registrars are certified and approved by the Internet Corporation for Assigned Names and Numbers (ICANN). Although hundreds of domain registrars exist today, those in the following list are popular because of their longevity in the industry, competitive pricing, and variety of services they offer in addition to domain name registration (such as web hosting and website traffic builders):

- **Go Daddy:** https://www.godaddy.com
- **Name.com:** https://www.name.com
- **Network Solutions:** www.networksolutions.com
- **Register.com:** www.register.com

No matter where you choose to register your domain name, here are the steps you can take to accomplish this task:

1. **Decide on a domain name.**

   Doing a little planning and forethought here is necessary. Many people think of a domain name as a *brand* — a way of identifying their websites or blogs. Think of potential names for your site, then you can proceed with your plan.

2. **Verify the domain name's availability.**

   In your web browser, enter the URL of the domain registrar of your choice. Look for the section on the registrar's website that lets you enter the domain name (typically, a short text field) to see whether it's available. If the domain name isn't available as a .com, try .net or .info.

3. **Purchase the domain name.**

   Follow the domain registrar's steps to purchase the name using your credit card. After you complete the checkout process you'll receive an email confirming your purchase, so use a valid email address during the registration process.

The next step is obtaining a hosting account, which I cover in the next section.

Some of the domain registrars have hosting services that you can sign up for, but you don't have to use those services. Often you can find hosting services for a lower cost than most domain registrars offer. It just takes a little research.

Finding a Home for Your Website

When you have registered your domain, you need to find a place for it to live: a web host. Web hosting is the second piece of the puzzle that you need before you begin working with the WordPress software.

A *web host* is a business, group, or individual that provides web server space and bandwidth for file transfer to website owners who don't have it. Usually, web-hosting services charge a monthly or annual fee — unless you're fortunate enough to know someone who's willing to give you server space and bandwidth for free. The cost varies from host to host, but you can obtain web-hosting services starting at $5 to $20/month or more, depending on your individual needs.

Most web hosts consider WordPress to be a *third-party application*. What this means to you is that the host typically won't provide technical support on the use of WordPress (or any other software application) because support isn't included in your hosting package. To find out whether your chosen host supports WordPress, always ask first. As a WordPress user, you can find WordPress support in the official forums at https://wordpress.org/support.

Several web-hosting providers also have WordPress-related services available for additional fees. These services can include technical support, plugin installation and configuration, and theme design services.

Web-hosting providers generally provide (at least) these services with your account:

- ✔ Hard drive space
- ✔ Bandwidth (transfer)
- ✔ Domain email with web mail access
- ✔ File Transfer Protocol (FTP) access
- ✔ Comprehensive website statistics
- ✔ MySQL database(s)
- ✔ PHP

Because you intend to run WordPress on your web server, you need to look for a host that provides the minimum requirements needed to run the software on your hosting account, which are

- ✔ PHP version 5.2.4 (or greater)
- ✔ MySQL version 5.0 (or greater)

The easiest way to find out whether a host meets the minimum requirements for running the WordPress software is to check the FAQ (Frequently Asked Questions) section of the host's website, if it has one. If not, find the contact information for the hosting company and fire off an email requesting information on exactly what it supports.

Getting help with hosting WordPress

The popularity of WordPress has given birth to services on the web that emphasize the use of the software. These services include WordPress designers, WordPress consultants, and — yes — web hosts that specialize in using WordPress.

Many of these hosts offer a full array of WordPress features, such as an automatic WordPress installation included with your account, a library of WordPress themes, and a staff of support technicians who are very experienced in using WordPress.

Here is a list of some of those providers:

- ✔ **Bluehost:** www.bluehost.com
- ✔ **GoDaddy:** https://www.godaddy.com
- ✔ **HostGator:** www.hostgator.com

✔ **Page.ly:** `https://page.ly`

✔ **WP Engine:** `http://wpengine.com`

A few web-hosting providers offer free domain name registration when you sign up for hosting services. Research this topic and read their terms of service, because that free domain name may come with conditions. Many of my clients have gone this route only to find out a few months later that the web-hosting provider has full control of the domain name, and they aren't allowed to move that domain off the host's servers either for a set period (usually a year or two) or for eternity. It's always best to have the control in *your* hands, not someone else's, so try to stick with an independent domain registrar, such as Network Solutions.

Dealing with disk space and bandwidth

Web-hosting services provide two very important things with your account:

✔ Disk space

✔ Bandwidth transfer

Think of your web host as a garage that you pay to park your car in. The garage gives you the place to store your car (disk space). It even gives you the driveway so that you, and others, can get to and from your car (bandwidth). It won't, however, fix your rockin' stereo system (WordPress or any other third-party software application) that you've installed — unless you're willing to pay a few extra bucks for that service.

Managing disk space

Disk space is nothing more complicated than the hard drive on your computer. Each hard drive has the capacity, or space, for a certain number of files. An 80GB (gigabyte) hard drive can hold 80GB of data — no more. Your hosting account provides you a limited amount of disk space, and the same concept applies. If your web host provides you 80GB of disk space, that's the limit on the file size that you're allowed to have. If you want more disk space, you need to upgrade your space limitations. Most web hosts have a mechanism in place for you to upgrade your allotment.

Starting out with a small WordPress blog doesn't take much disk space at all. A good starting point for disk space is between 10 and 20GB of storage space. If you need additional space, contact your hosting provider for an upgrade.

The larger your website, the more space you will need. Also, the more visitors and traffic your website has, the more bandwidth you will require (see the next section).

Choosing the size of your bandwidth "pipe"

Bandwidth refers to the amount of data that is carried from point A to point B within a specific period (usually, only a second or two). I live out in the country — pretty much the middle of nowhere. I get my water from a private well that lies buried in the backyard somewhere. Between my house and the well are pipes that bring the water into my house. The pipes provide a free flow of water to our home so that everyone can enjoy their long, hot showers while I labor over dishes and laundry, all at the same time. Lucky me!

The very same concept applies to the bandwidth available with your hosting account. Every web-hosting provider offers a variety of bandwidth limits on the accounts it offers. When I want to view your website in my browser window, the bandwidth is essentially the "pipe" that lets your data flow from your "well" to my computer and appear on my monitor. The bandwidth limit is kind of like the pipe connected to my well: It can hold only a certain amount of water before it reaches maximum capacity and won't bring the water from the well any longer. Your bandwidth pipe size is determined by how much bandwidth your web host allows for your account — the larger the number, the bigger the pipe. A 50MB bandwidth limit makes for a smaller pipe than does a 100MB limit.

Web hosts are pretty generous with the amount of bandwidth they provide in their packages. Like disk space, bandwidth is measured in gigabytes (GB). Bandwidth provision of 10 to 50GB is generally a respectable amount to run a website with a blog.

Websites that run large files — such as video, audio, or photo files — generally benefit from more disk space (compared with sites that don't have large files). Keep this point in mind when you're signing up for your hosting account: If your site requires big files, you need more space. Planning now will save you a few headaches down the road.

Understanding FTP Concepts

The ability to use File Transfer Protocol (FTP) with your hosting account is a given for almost every web host on the market today. FTP offers two ways of moving files from one place to another:

- ✔ **Uploading:** Transferring files from your local computer to your web server

- ✔ **Downloading:** Transferring files from your web server to your local computer

You can do several other things with FTP, including the following, which I discuss later in this chapter:

- ✔ **View files:** After you log in via FTP, you can see all the files that are located on your web server.

- ✔ **View date modified:** You can see the date a file was last modified, which can sometimes be helpful when trying to troubleshoot problems.

- ✔ **View file size:** You can see the size of each file on your web server, which is helpful if you need to manage the disk space on your account.

- ✔ **Edit files:** Almost all FTP clients allow you to open and edit files through the client interface, which is a convenient way to get the job done.

- ✔ **Change permissions:** Commonly referred to as CHMOD, an acronym for Change Mode, it controls what type of read/write/execute permissions the files on your web server have.

FTP is a convenient utility that gives you access to the files located on your web server, which makes managing your WordPress website a bit easier.

SFTP (Secret File Transfer Protocol) is also a method of FTP. SFTP provides an additional layer of security because it uses SSH (Secure Shell) and encrypts sensitive information, data, and passwords from being clearly transferred within the hosting network. Encrypting the data ensures that anyone monitoring the network is not able to read the data freely — and therefore, cannot obtain information that should be secured, such as passwords and usernames. I highly recommend using SFTP over FTP if it is available from your hosting provider.

Setting up FTP on your hosting account

Many web hosts today offer FTP as part of their hosting packages, so just confirm that your hosting provider makes FTP available to you for your account. cPanel is by far the most popular hosting account management software used by hosts on the web, eclipsing other popular tools such as Plesk and NetAdmin. It is within the hosting account management interface that you can set up the FTP account for your website.

In this chapter, I use cPanel as the example. If your hosting provider gives you a different interface to work with, the concepts are still the same, but you'll need to refer to your hosting provider for the specifics to adapt these directions to your specific environment.

Mostly, the FTP for your hosting account is set up automatically. Figure 3-1 shows you the FTP Accounts page in cPanel. Follow these steps to get to this page and set up your FTP account:

1. **Log in to cPanel for your hosting account.**

   Typically, you'll browse to `http://yourdomain.com/cpanel` to bring up the login screen for your cPanel. Enter your specific hosting account username and password in the login fields and then click OK.

2. **Browse to the FTP Accounts page.**

   Click the FTP Accounts link or icon in your cPanel to open the FTP Accounts page shown in Figure 3-1.

3. **View the existing FTP account.**

   If your hosting provider automatically sets you up with an FTP account, you will see it listed in the Account Management section. Ninety-nine percent of the time, the default FTP account uses the same username and password combination as your hosting account or the login information you used to log in to your cPanel in Step 1.

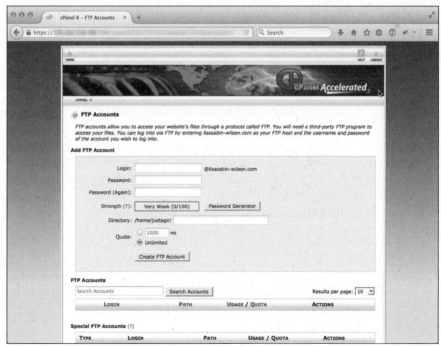

Figure 3-1:
The FTP Accounts page within cPanel.

If the FTP Accounts page doesn't display a default FTP user in the Account Management section, you can easily create one in the Add FTP Account section:

1. **Type your desired username in the Login field.**

   This creates the username of *username@yourdomain*.com (where *username* is the desired username you typed and *yourdomain*.com is your specific domain name).

2. **Type your desired password in the Password field.**

   You can choose to type in your own password or click the Password Generator button to have the server generate a secure password for you. Retype the password in the Password (Again) field to validate it.

3. **Check the Strength indicator.**

   The server tells you if your password is Very Weak, Weak, Good, Strong, or Very Strong. (Refer to Figure 3-1.) You want to have a very strong password for your FTP account that's difficult for hackers and malicious Internet users to guess and crack.

4. **(Optional) Type the directory access for this FTP user.**

   cPanel will fill this in for you and it will look something like this: public_html/user (the user, in this case, is the same username you entered in Step 1). Leaving this field as is gives this new FTP user access to only a folder with their username. For the purposes of installing WordPress, you want this account to have access to the public_html folder, so remove the /user portion of the directory access so that the field contains only public_html.

5. **Indicate the space limitations in the Quota field.**

   Because you're the site owner, leave the radio button selection set to Unlimited. (In the future, if you add a new FTP user, you can limit the amount of space, in megabytes [MB], by selecting the radio button to the left of the text field and typing the numeric amount in the text box; for example, 50MB.)

6. **Click the Create FTP Account button.**

   A new screen appears with a message that the account was created successfully. Additionally, the settings for this new FTP account appear, which you should copy and paste into a blank text editor window (such as Notepad for PC or TextEdit for Mac users). The settings for the FTP account are the connection details you need to connect to your web server via FTP.

7. **Save the following settings:**

   FTP Username, Password, and FTP Server are specific to your domain and the information you entered in the preceding steps.

- FTP Username: *username@yourdomain*.com

- Password: *yourpassword*

- FTP Server: ftp.*yourdomain*.com

- FTP Server Port: 21

- Quota: Unlimited MB

Typically, the FTP Server Port will be 21. Be sure to double-check your FTP settings to make sure that this is the case. However, if you are setting up an SFTP account instead (Secure FTP), the port will need to be set to 22. Check with your hosting provider for specific port number assignment.

Connecting to the web server via FTP

For the purposes of this chapter, I use the FileZilla FTP client (http://sourceforge.net/projects/filezilla) because it's very easy to use, and the cost is free ninety-nine (that's open source geek-speak for free!).

Figure 3-2 shows a FileZilla client that's not connected to a server. By default, the left side of the window displays a directory of files and folders on the local computer.

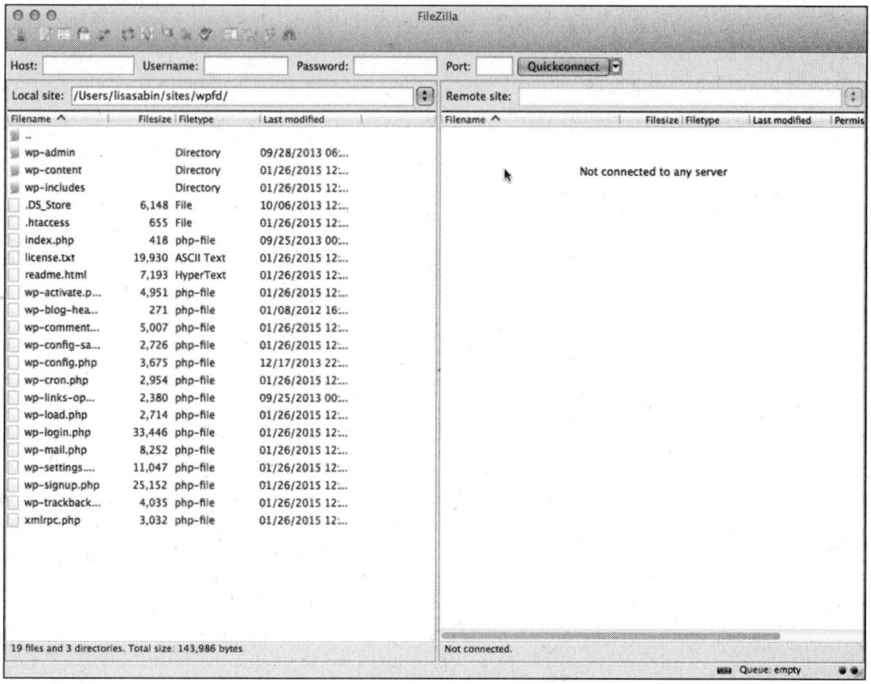

Figure 3-2:
Mozilla
FileZilla FTP
client soft-
ware.

The right side of the window displays content when the FileZilla client is connected to a web server; specifically, it shows directories of the web server's folders and files.

If you use a different FTP client software than FileZilla, the steps and look of the software will differ, and you will need to adapt your steps and practice for the specific FTP client software you're using.

Connecting to a web server is an easy process. Remember the FTP settings you saved from Step 7 in the previous section? As a reminder, here they are again:

FTP Username: *username@yourdomain*.com

Password: *yourpassword*

FTP Server: ftp.*yourdomain*.com

FTP Server Port: 21

Quota: Unlimited MB

This is where you need that information. To connect to your web server via the FileZilla FTP client, follow these few steps:

1. **Open the FTP client software on your local computer.**

   Locate the program on your computer and click (or double-click) the program icon to launch the program.

2. **Choose File ⇨ Site Manager to open the Site Manager utility.**

   The Site Manager utility appears, as shown in Figure 3-3.

3. **Click the New Site button.**

4. **Type a name for your site that helps you identify the site.**

   This site name can be anything you want it to be because it isn't part of the connection data you add in the next steps. (In Figure 3-4, you see *My Site* — original, I know.)

5. **Enter the FTP server in the Host field.**

   Host is the same as the FTP server information provided to you when you set up the FTP account on your web server. In the example, the FTP server is ftp.*yourdomain*.com, so that's entered in the Host field, as shown in Figure 3-4.

6. **Enter the FTP port in the Port field.**

   Typically, in most hosting environments, FTP uses port 21, and this never changes. However, double-check your port number and enter it in the Port field, as shown in Figure 3-4.

7. Select the server type.

FileZilla asks you to select a server type (as do most FTP clients). Choose FTP - File Transfer Protocol from the Protocol drop-down menu, as shown in Figure 3-4.

8. Select the encryption type.

By default, Filezilla has this set to Use plain FTP. You can leave this as is, unless your hosting provider has instructed you to use a different setting here.

9. Select the logon type.

FileZilla gives you several different logon types to choose from (as do most FTP clients). Choose Normal from the Logon Type drop-down menu.

10. Enter your username in the User field.

This is the username given to you in the FTP settings. In the example, the username is *User*.

11. Type your password in the Password field.

This is the password given to you in the FTP settings.

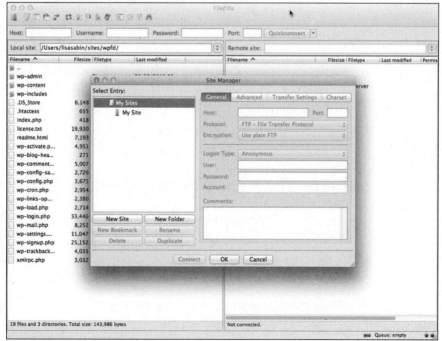

Figure 3-3:
The Site Manager utility in the FileZilla FTP client software.

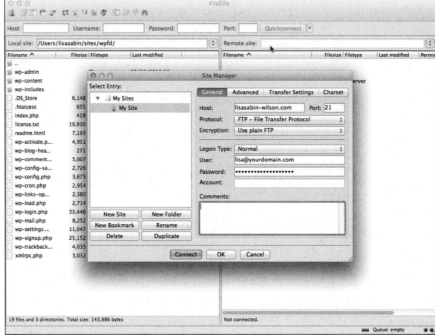

Figure 3-4:
The FileZilla
Site
Manager
utility with
FTP account
information
filled in.

12. Click the Connect button.

This step connects your computer to your web server. The directory of folders and files from your local computer display on the left side of the FileZilla FTP client window, and the directory of folders and files on your web server display on the right side, as shown in Figure 3-5.

Now you can take advantage of all the tools and features FTP has to offer you!

Transferring files from point A to point B

Now that your local computer is connected to your web server, transferring files between the two couldn't be easier. Within the FTP client software, you can browse the directories and folders on your local computer on the left side and browse the directories and folders on your web server on the right side.

FTP clients make it easy to transfer files from your computer to your hosting account by using a drag-and-drop method.

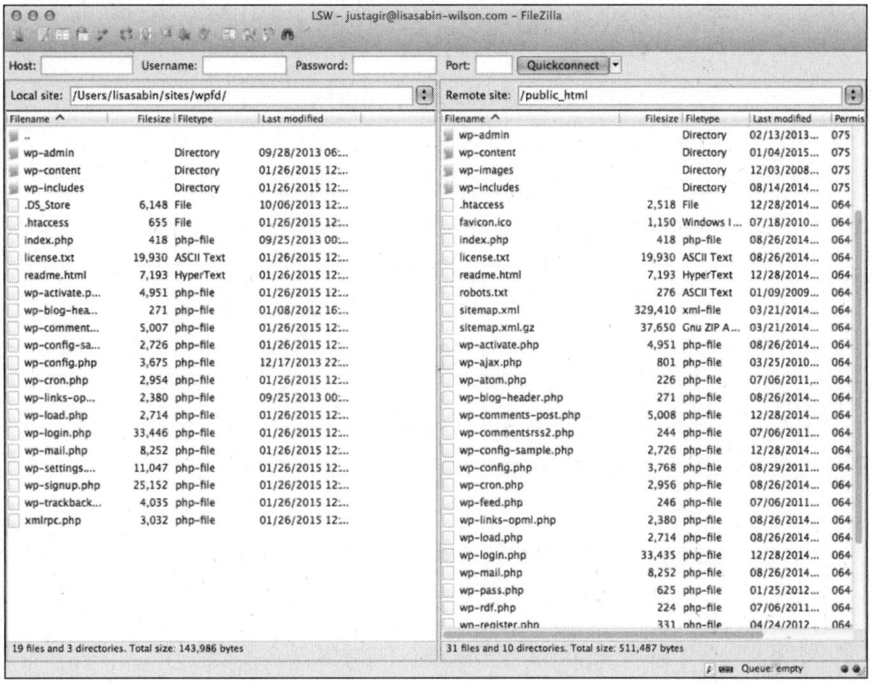

Figure 3-5:
FileZilla
displays
local files on
the left and
server files
on the right.

Two methods of transferring files are

✔ **Uploading:** Generally, transferring files from your local computer to your web server. To upload a file from your computer to your web server, click the file you want to transfer from your local computer and drag and drop it onto the right side (the web server side).

✔ **Downloading:** Transferring files from your web server to your local computer. To download a file from your web server to your local computer, click the file you want to transfer from your web server and drag and drop it onto the left side (the local computer side).

Downloading files from your web server is an efficient, easy, and smart way of backing up files to your local computer. It's always a good idea to keep your files safe, especially things like theme files and plugins, which are covered in Part IV of this book.

Editing files using FTP

You will run into situations where you need to edit certain files that live on your web server. You can use the methods described in the preceding section to download a file, open it, edit it, save it, and then upload it to your web server. That is one way to do it. Another way is to use the built-in edit feature that exists in most FTP client software, by following these steps:

1. **Connect the FTP client to your web server.**

2. **Locate the file you want to edit.**

3. **Open the file using the internal FTP editor.**

   Right-click the file and choose View/Edit. (Remember I'm using FileZilla; your FTP client may use different labels, such as Open or Edit.) FileZilla, like most FTP clients, uses a program (such as Notepad for a PC or TextEdit for Mac) designated for text editing that already exists on your computer. In some rare cases, your FTP client software may have its own internal text editor.

4. **Edit the file to your liking.**

5. **Save the changes you made to the file.**

   Click the Save icon or choose File⇨Save.

6. **Upload the file to your web server.**

   After you save the file, FileZilla alerts you that the file has changed and asks whether you want to upload the file to the server. Click Yes; the newly edited file replaces the old one.

That's all there is to it. Use the FTP edit feature to edit, save, and upload files as needed.

When you edit files using the FTP edit feature, you're editing files in a "live" environment, meaning that when you save the changes and upload the file, the changes take effect immediately and affect your live website. For this reason, I strongly recommend downloading a copy of the original file to your local computer before making changes. That way, if you happen to make a typo on the saved file and your website goes haywire, you have a copy of the original file to upload to restore it to its original state.

Changing file permissions

Every file and folder on your web server has a set of assigned attributes, called *permissions,* that tells the web server three things about the folder or file. On a very simplistic level, these permissions include:

✔ **Read:** This setting determines whether the file/folder is readable by the web server.

✔ **Write:** This setting determines whether the file/folder is writable by the web server.

✔ **Execute:** This setting determines whether the file/folder is executable by the web server.

Each set of permissions has a numeric code assigned to it, identifying what type of permissions are assigned to that file or folder. There are a lot of them, so here are the most common ones that you run into when running a WordPress website:

✔ **644:** Files with permissions set to 644 are readable by everyone and writable only by the file/folder owner.

✔ **755:** Files with permissions set to 755 are readable and executable by everyone, but they're writable only by the file/folder owner.

✔ **777:** Files with permissions set to 777 are readable, writable, and can be executed by anyone. For security reasons, you should not use this set of permissions on your web server unless absolutely necessary.

Typically, folders and files within your web server are assigned permissions of either 644 or 755. Usually, you'll see PHP files, or files that end with the .php extension, with permissions set to 644 if the web server is configured to use PHP Safe Mode.

This is a very basic look at file permissions because, usually, you will not need to mess with file permissions on your web server. In case you do need to dig further, you can find a great reference on file permissions from Elated. com at www.elated.com/articles/understanding-permissions.

You may run across a situation where you're asked to edit and change the file permissions on a particular file on your web server. With WordPress sites, this usually happens when dealing with plugins or theme files that require files or folders to be writable by the web server. This practice is referred to as *CHMOD*, an acronym for Change Mode. When someone says, "You need to CHMOD that file to 755," you'll know what he is talking about.

Here are some easy steps for using your FTP program to CHMOD a file, or edit its permissions on your web server:

1. **Connect the FTP client to your web server.**

2. **Locate the file you want to CHMOD.**

3. **Open the file attributes for the file.**

   Right-click the file on your web server and choose File Permissions. (If your client is not FileZilla, it may use different terminology.)

   The Change File Attributes window appears, as shown in Figure 3-6.

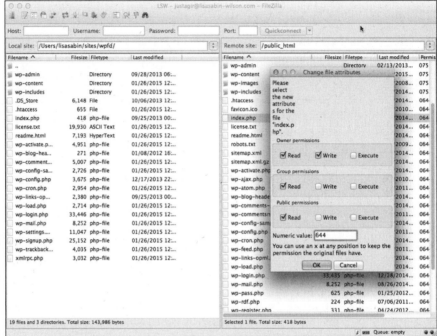

Figure 3-6:
The
Change File
Attributes
window.

4. Type the correct file permissions number in the Numeric Value field.

This is the number assigned to the permissions you want to give the file. Most often, the plugin or theme developer tells you which permissions number to assign to the file or folder; typically, it will be either 644 or 755. (The permissions in Figure 3-6 are assigned the value of 644.)

5. Click OK to save the file.

Installing WordPress

By the time you're finally ready to install WordPress, you should have done the following things:

- ✔ Purchased the domain name registration for your account
- ✔ Obtained a hosting service on a web server for your blog
- ✔ Established your hosting account's username, password, and FTP address
- ✔ Acquired an FTP client for transferring files to your hosting account

If you missed doing any of these items, you can go back to the beginning of this chapter to read the portions you need.

Some hosting providers have their own WordPress installers that can make installing WordPress an easier process by providing things like a step-by-step wizard or an easy interface to make it happen. Check with your hosting provider to see if they provide a WordPress installer for you to use.

Installing WordPress manually

If you have to install WordPress manually, here's where the rubber meets the road — that is, you're putting WordPress's famous five-minute installation to the test. Set your watch and see whether you can meet that five-minute mark.

The famous five-minute installation includes the time it takes to install the software only. It doesn't include the time to

- ✔ Register a domain name.
- ✔ Obtain and set up your web-hosting service.
- ✔ Download, install, configure, and learn how to use the FTP software.

Without further ado, go get the latest version of the WordPress software at `https://wordpress.org/download`.

WordPress gives you two compression formats for the software: `zip` and `tar.gz`. I recommend getting the `.zip` file because it's the most common format for compressed files.

Download the WordPress software to your computer and decompress (unpack or unzip) it to a folder on your computer's hard drive. These steps are the first in the installation process for WordPress. Having the program on your own computer isn't enough, however; you also need to *upload* (transfer) it to your web server account (the one you obtained in "Finding a Home for Your Website," earlier in this chapter).

Before installing WordPress on your web server, make sure that you have a MySQL database set up and ready to accept the WordPress installation. The next section tells you what you need to know about MySQL.

Setting up the MySQL database

The WordPress software is a personal publishing system that uses a PHP-and-MySQL platform, which provides everything you need to create your own website and publish your own content dynamically without having to know how to program those pages yourself. In short, all your content (options, posts, comments, and other pertinent data) is stored in a MySQL database in your hosting account.

Every time visitors go to your blog to read your content, they make a request that's sent to your server. The PHP programming language receives that request, obtains the requested information from the MySQL database, and then presents the requested information to your visitors through their web browsers.

Every web host is different in how it gives you access to set up and manage your MySQL database(s) for your account. In this section, I use cPanel, a popular hosting interface. If your host provides a different interface, the same basic steps apply; just the setup in the interface that your web host provides may be different.

To set up the MySQL database for your WordPress website with cPanel, follow these steps:

1. **Log in to the administration interface with the username and password assigned to you by your web host.**

   I'm using the cPanel administration interface, but your host may provide NetAdmin or Plesk, for example.

2. **Locate the MySQL Database Administration section.**

   In cPanel, click the MySQL Databases icon.

3. **Choose a name for your database and enter it in the Name text box.**

   Note the database name because you'll need it during the installation of WordPress later.

   For security reasons, make sure that your password isn't something that sneaky hackers can easily guess. Usually, I give my database a name that I will easily recognize later. This practice is especially helpful if you're running more than one MySQL database in your account. If I name this database something like *WordPress* or *wpblog,* I can be reasonably certain — a year from now, when I want to access my database to make some configuration changes — that I know exactly which one I need to deal with.

4. **Click the Create Database button.**

   You get a message confirming that the database has been created.

5. **Click the Go Back link or the Back button on your browser toolbar.**

6. **Choose a username and password for your database, enter them in the Add New User text boxes, and then click the Create User button.**

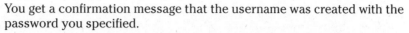

You get a confirmation message that the username was created with the password you specified.

Make absolutely sure that you note the database name, username, and password that you set up during this process. You *will* need them in the next section before officially installing WordPress on your web server. Jot them down on a piece of paper, or copy and paste them into a text-editor window; either way, just make sure that you have them immediately handy.

7. **Click the Go Back link or the Back button on your browser toolbar.**

8. **In the Add Users to Database section, choose the user account you just set up from the User drop-down menu; then choose the new database from the Database drop-down menu.**

   The MySQL Account Maintenance, Manage User Privileges page appears in cPanel.

9. **Assign user privileges by selecting the All Privileges check box.**

   Because you're the administrator (owner) of this database, you need to assign all privileges to the new user account you just created.

10. **Click the Make Changes button.**

    A page opens with a confirmation message that you've added your selected user to the selected database.

11. **Click the Go Back link.**

    You go back to the MySQL Databases page.

Uploading the WordPress files

To upload the WordPress files to your host, return to the folder on your computer where you unpacked the WordPress software that you downloaded earlier. You'll find all the files you need (shown in Figure 3-7) in a folder called /wordpress.

Using your FTP client, connect to your web server and upload all these files to your hosting account into the root directory.

If you don't know what your root directory is, contact your hosting provider and ask, "What is my root directory for my account?" Every hosting provider's setup is different. On my web server, my root directory is the public_html folder; some of my clients have a root directory in a folder called httpdocs. The answer really depends on what type of setup your hosting provider has. When in doubt, ask!

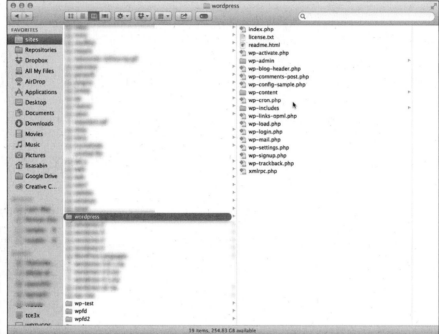

Figure 3-7:
WordPress
software
files to be
uploaded
to your web
server.

Here are a few things to keep in mind when you're uploading your files:

- ✔ **Upload the *contents* of the /wordpress folder to your web server —
  not the folder itself.** Most FTP client software lets you select all the files
  and drag and drop them to your web server. Other programs have you
  highlight the files and click a Transfer button.

- ✔ **Choose the correct transfer mode.** File transfers via FTP have two different forms: ASCII and binary. Most FTP clients are configured to autodetect the transfer mode. Understanding the difference as it pertains to
  this WordPress installation is important so that you can troubleshoot
  any problems you have later:

    - *Binary transfer mode* is how images (such as .jpg, .gif, .bmp,
      and .png files) are transferred via FTP.

    - *ASCII transfer mode* is for everything else (text files, PHP files,
      JavaScript, and so on).

  For the most part, it's a safe bet to make sure that the transfer mode of
  your FTP client is set to autodetect. But if you experience issues with
  how those files load on your site, retransfer the files using the appropriate transfer mode.

✔ **You can choose a different folder from the root.** You aren't required to transfer the files to the root directory of your web server. You can make the choice to run WordPress on a subdomain, or in a different folder, on your account. If you want your blog address to be http://*yourdomain*.com/blog, you transfer the WordPress files into a folder named /blog.

✔ **Choose the right file permissions.** *File permissions* tell the web server how these files can be handled on your server — whether they're files that can be written to. As a general rule, PHP files need to have a permission (CHMOD) of 644, whereas file folders need a permission of 755. Almost all FTP clients let you check and change the permissions on the files if you need to. Typically, you can find the option to change file permissions in the menu options of your FTP client.

Some hosting providers run their PHP software in a more secure format called *safe mode.* If this is the case with your host, you need to set the PHP files to 644. If you're unsure, ask your hosting provider what permissions you need to set for PHP files.

Last step: Running the install script

The final step in the installation procedure for WordPress is connecting the WordPress software you uploaded to the MySQL database. Follow these steps:

1. **Type this URL in the address window of your browser, replacing** *yourdomain*.com **with your own domain name:**

   ```
   http://yourdomain.com/wp-admin/install.php
   ```

   If you chose to install WordPress in a different folder from the root directory of your account, make sure you indicate this fact in the URL for the install script. If you transferred the WordPress software files to a folder called /blog, for example, you would point your browser to the following URL to run the installation: http://*yourdomain*.com/blog/wp-admin/imstall.php.

   Assuming that you did everything correctly (see Table 3-1 for help with common installation problems), you see the box shown in Figure 3-8.

2. **Select your preferred language.**

   WordPress is currently available in 47 different languages. Select the one you prefer and then click Continue.

3. **Click the Let's Go button.**

   WordPress presents you with a message welcoming you to WordPress and gives you a few details about what you need to proceed with the installation, such as your database information.

Table 3-1	Common WordPress Installation Problems	
Error Message	*Common Cause*	*Solution*
`Error Connecting to the Database`	The database name, username, password, or host was entered incorrectly.	Revisit your MySQL database to obtain the database name, username, and password, and re-enter that information.
`Headers Already Sent Error Messages`	A syntax error occurred in the `wp-config.php` file.	Open the `wp-config.php` file in a text editor. The first line should contain only this line: `<?php`. The last line should contain only this line: `?>`. Make sure that those lines contain nothing else — not even white space. Save the file changes.
`500: Internal Server Error`	Permissions on PHP files are set incorrectly.	Try setting the permissions (`CHMOD`) on the PHP files to 666. If that doesn't work, set them to 644. Each web server has different settings for how it lets PHP execute on its servers.
`404: Page Not Found`	The URL for the login page is incorrect.	Double-check that the URL you're using to get to the login page is the same as the location of your WordPress installation (such as `http://yourdomain.com/wp-login.php`).
`403: Forbidden Access`	An `index.html` or `index.htm` file exists in the WordPress installation directory.	WordPress is a PHP application, so the default home page is `index.php`. Look in the WordPress installation folder on your web server. If there is an `index.html` or `index.htm` file in there, delete it.

4. **Dig out the database name, username, and password that you saved earlier, and use that information to fill in the following fields (shown in Figure 3-9):**

   • *Database Name:* Type the database name you used when you created the MySQL database before this installation. Because hosts differ in configurations, enter either the database name or the database name with your hosting account username appended.

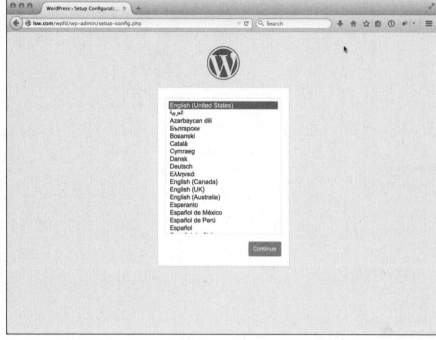

Figure 3-8:
The first
time you
run the
installation
script for
WordPress,
you see
this box to
select your
preferred
language.

If you named your database *wordpress,* for example, you would enter that in this text box. Or if your host requires you to append the database name with your hosting account username, you would enter **username_wordpress***,* substituting your hosting username for *username.* My username is *lisasabin,* so I would enter **lisasabin_wordpress**.

- *User Name:* Type the username you used when you created the MySQL database before this installation. Depending on what your host requires, you may need to append this username to your hosting account username.

- *Password:* Type the password you used when you set up the MySQL database. You don't need to append the password to your hosting account username here.

- *Database Host:* Ninety-nine percent of the time, you'll leave this field set to *localhost.* Some hosts, depending on their configurations, have different hosts set for the MySQL database server. If *localhost* doesn't work, you need to contact your hosting provider to find out the MySQL database host.

- *Table Prefix:* Leave this field set to *wp_,* although you can change the table prefix to something completely random to increase security for your site, such as xyz123_.

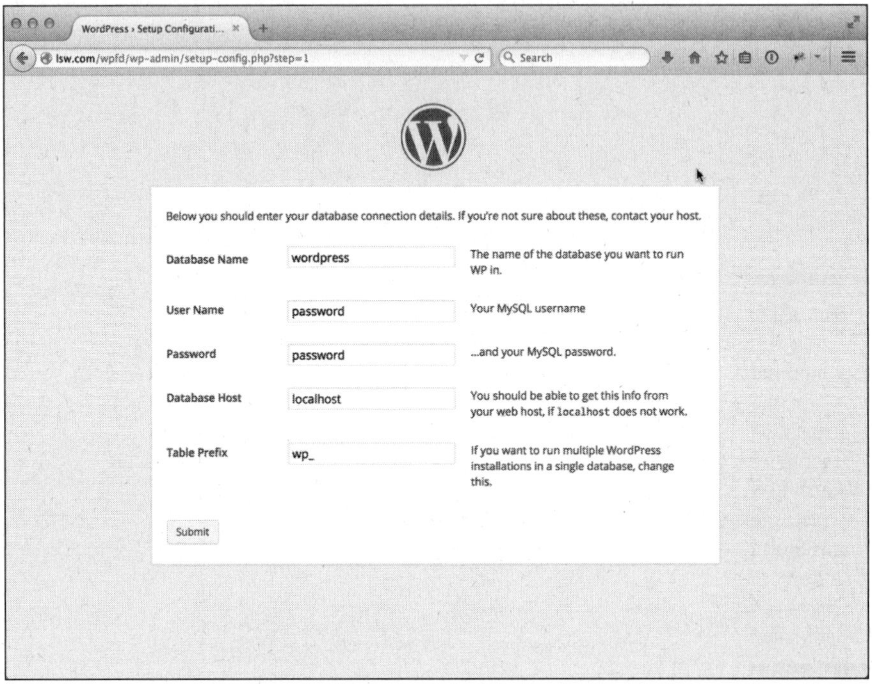

Figure 3-9:
At this
step of the
WordPress
installation,
enter the
database
name, user-
name, and
password.

5. When you have all that information filled in, click the Submit button.

You see a message that says `All right, sparky! You've made it through this part of the installation. WordPress can now communicate with your database. If you're ready, time now to run the install!`

6. Click the Run the Install button.

You see another welcome page with a message welcoming you to the famous five-minute WordPress installation process.

7. Enter or possibly change this information (shown in Figure 3-10):

- *Site Title:* Enter the title you want to give your blog. The title you enter isn't written in stone; you can change it later.

- *Username:* This is the name you will use to log in to WordPress. By default, the username is admin, and you can leave it that way. However, for security reasons, it's recommended practice to change your username to something unique to you.

- *Password:* Type your desired password in the first text box. Then type it again in the second text box to confirm that you've typed it correctly. If the two versions of your password don't match, WordPress alerts you with an error message. If you don't enter a password, one will automatically be generated for you.

Figure 3-10:
Information
needed to
finish the
WordPress
installation.

For security reasons (and so that other people can't make a lucky guess), passwords should be at least seven characters long and use as many different characters in as many combinations as possible. Use a mixture of uppercase and lowercase letters, numbers, and symbols (such as ! " ? $ % ^ &).

- *Your Email:* Enter the email address you want to use to be notified of administrative information about your blog. You can change this address later, too.

- *Allow search engines to index this site:* By default, this check box is selected, which lets the search engines index the content of your website and include your website in search results. To keep your blog private and out of the search engines, deselect this check box.

8. Click the Install WordPress button.

The WordPress installation machine works its magic and creates all the tables within the database that contain the default data for your blog. WordPress displays the login information you need to access the

WordPress Dashboard. Make note of this username and password before you leave this page. Scribble it down on a piece of paper or copy it into a text editor such as Notepad.

After you click the Install WordPress button, you'll receive an email with the login information and login URL. This information is handy if you're called away during this part of the installation process. So go ahead and let the dog out, answer the phone, brew a cup of coffee, or take a 15-minute power nap. If you somehow get distracted away from this page, the email sent to you contains the information you need to successfully log in to your WordPress website.

9. Click the Log In button to log in to WordPress.

If you happen to lose this page before clicking the Log In button, you can always find your way to the login page by entering your domain followed by the call to the login file (for example, `http://yourdomain.com/wp-login.php`).

You know that you're finished with the installation process when you see the login page, as shown in Figure 3-11. Refer to Table 3-1 if you experience any problems during this installation process; it covers some of the common problems users encounter.

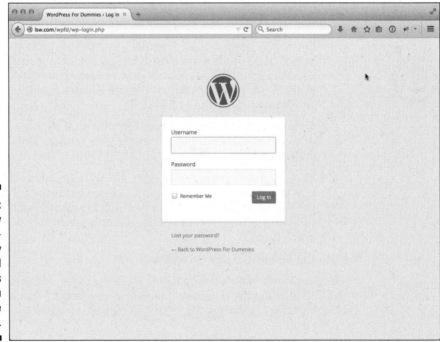

Figure 3-11:
You know you've successfully installed WordPress when you see the login page.

So do tell — how much time does your watch show for the installation? Was it five minutes? Stop by my blog sometime (`http://lisasabin-wilson.com`) and let me know whether WordPress stood up to its famous five-minute-installation reputation. I'm a curious sort.

The good news is — you're done! Were you expecting a marching band? WordPress isn't that fancy . . . yet. Give them time, though; if anyone can produce it, the folks at WordPress can.

Let me be the first to congratulate you on your newly installed WordPress blog! When you're ready, log in and familiarize yourself with the Dashboard, which I describe in Chapter 4.

Chapter 4

Understanding the WordPress.org Dashboard

*W*ith WordPress.org successfully installed, you can explore your new website software. This chapter guides you through the preliminary setup of your new WordPress site using the Dashboard.

When you create a website with WordPress, you spend a lot of time in the Dashboard, which is where you make all the exciting, behind-the-scenes stuff happen. In this panel, you find all the settings and options that enable you to set up your site just the way you want it. (If you still need to install and configure WordPress, check out Chapter 3.)

Feeling comfortable with the Dashboard sets you up for a successful entrance into the WordPress world. Expect to tweak your WordPress settings several times throughout the life of your website. In this chapter, as I go through the various sections, settings, options, and configurations available to you, understand that nothing is set in stone. You can set options today and change them at any time.

Logging In to the Dashboard

I find that the direct approach (also known as jumping in) works best when I want to get familiar with a new software tool. To that end, just follow these steps to log in to WordPress and take a look at the guts of the Dashboard:

1. **Open your web browser and type the WordPress login-page address (or URL) in the address box.**

   The login-page address looks something like this (exchange that `.com` for an `.org` or a `.net` as needed):

   ```
   http://www.yourdomain.com/wp-login.php
   ```

   If you installed WordPress in its own folder, include that folder name in the login URL. If you installed WordPress in a folder ingeniously named `wordpress`, the login URL becomes

   ```
   http://www.yourdomain.com/wordpress/wp-login.php
   ```

2. **Type your username in the Username text box and your password in the Password text box.**

   In case you forget your password, WordPress has you covered. Click the *Lost Your Password?* link (located near the bottom of the page), enter your username or email address, and then click the *Get New Password* button. WordPress resets your password and emails the new password to you.

   After you request a password, you receive an email from your WordPress installation. The email contains a link that you need to click to reset your password.

3. **Select the Remember Me check box if you want WordPress to place a cookie in your browser.**

   The cookie tells WordPress to remember your login credentials the next time you show up. The cookie set by WordPress is harmless and stores your WordPress login on your computer. Because of the cookie, WordPress remembers you the next time you visit. Also, because this option tells the browser to remember your login, I don't advise checking this option on public computers. Avoid selecting Remember Me when you're using your work computer or a computer at an Internet café.

   Note: Before you set this option, make sure that your browser is configured to allow cookies. (If you aren't sure how to do this, check the help documentation of the Internet browser you're using.)

4. **Click the Log In button.**

   After you log in to WordPress, you see the Dashboard page.

Navigating the Dashboard

You can consider the Dashboard to be a Control Panel of sorts because it offers several quick links and areas that provide information about your website, starting with the actual Dashboard page shown in Figure 4-1.

You can change how the WordPress Dashboard looks by changing the order of the modules that appear on it (for example, At a Glance and Activity). You can expand (open) and collapse (close) the individual modules by clicking the small gray arrow to the right of its title. This feature is really nice because you can use the Dashboard for just those modules that you use regularly.

The concept is simple: Keep the modules you use all the time open and close the ones that you use only occasionally — you can open those modules only when you really need them. You save space and can customize your Dashboard to suit your own needs. WordPress will remember the way you set your Dashboard, so if you close certain modules today, they will remain closed every time you visit the Dashboard until you open them again.

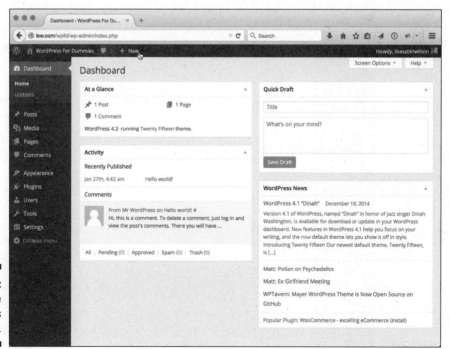

Figure 4-1:
Log in to the
WordPress
Dashboard.

When you view your Dashboard for the first time, all the modules appear in the expanded (open) position by default (refer to Figure 4-1).

The navigation menu in the WordPress Dashboard appears on the left side of your browser window. When you need to get back to the main Dashboard page, click the *Dashboard* link at the top of the navigation menu found on any of the pages within your WordPress Dashboard.

In the following sections, I cover the Dashboard page as it appears when you log in to your WordPress Dashboard for the very first time; later in this chapter, I show you how to configure the appearance of your Dashboard so that it best suits how you use the available modules.

At a Glance

The At a Glance module in the Dashboard shows some details of what is going on in your website right now, right this very second! Figure 4-2 shows the expanded At a Glance module in my brand-spanking-new WordPress site.

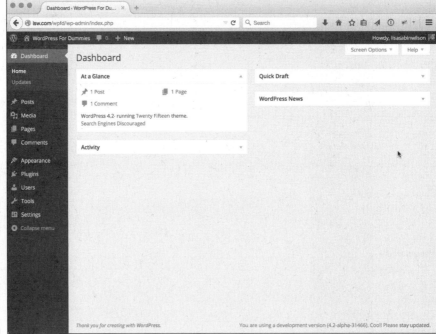

Figure 4-2:
The At a Glance module in the Dashboard expanded to see the available features.

The At a Glance module shows the following by default:

- **The number of posts you have:** This number reflects the total number of posts you have in your WordPress site; I have one post on my site. The number is blue, which means it's a link that you can click. When you do, you go to the Edit Posts page, where you can edit the posts on your blog. I cover editing posts in Chapter 5.

- **The number of pages:** This is the number of pages on your website, which will change as you add or delete pages. (*Pages,* in this context, refer to the static pages you have created in your blog.) Figure 4-2 shows that my site has one page.

  Clicking this link takes you to the Edit Pages page, where you can view, edit, and delete your pages. (Find the difference between WordPress posts and pages in Chapter 5.)

- **The number of comments:** This is the total number of comments on your blog. Figure 4-2 shows that I have only one comment, which makes sense since this is a brand new WordPress installation.

  Clicking the comments link takes you to the Edit Comments page, where you can manage the comments on your blog. I cover the management of comments in the "Comments" section, later in this chapter.

The last section of the Dashboard's At a Glance module shows the following information:

- **The version of WordPress you're using:** Figure 4-2 shows that I'm using WordPress version 4.2. This version announcement changes if you are using an older version of WordPress. When WordPress software is upgraded, this statement tells you that you're using an outdated version of WordPress and encourages you to upgrade to the latest version.

- **Which WordPress theme you're using:** Figure 4-2 shows that I'm using the theme Twenty Fifteen. The theme name is a link that takes you to the Manage Themes page, where you can view and activate themes on your blog.

- **Search Engines Discouraged:** This is displayed only if you have indicated that you would like to block your blog from search engines in the privacy settings, covered later in this chapter.

Activity

Within the next module, called Activity, you find these sections:

- **Recently Published:** This area lists your most recently published posts and displays the date and title of the post. Clicking the title of the post takes you to the Edit Post screen in the Dashboard.

- **Most recent comments published to your blog:** WordPress displays a maximum of five comments in this area (in Figure 4-1 you see only one comment because that is a screenshot of a brand new installation).

- **The author of each comment:** The name of the person who left the comment appears above it. This section also displays the author's picture (or avatar), if she has one (if she doesn't, the default avatar appears).

- **A link to the post the comment was left on:** The post title appears to the right of the commenter's name. Click the link and you go to that post in the Dashboard.

- **An excerpt of the comment:** This is a snippet of the comment this person left on your blog.

- **Comment management links:** When you hover your mouse pointer over the comment, five links appear underneath the comment. These links give you the opportunity to manage those comments right from your Dashboard: The first link is Unapprove, which appears only if you have comment moderation turned on. (Find out more about moderating comments in the "Comments" section, later in this chapter.) The other four links are Reply, Edit, Spam, and Trash.

- **View links:** These links appear at the bottom of the Recent Comments module, where you can click All, Pending, Approved, Spam, or Trash.

You find even more information on managing your comments in the "Comments" section, later in this chapter.

Quick Draft

The Quick Draft module is a handy form that allows you to write, save, and publish a blog post right from your WordPress Dashboard. The options are similar to the ones I cover in the section on writing posts in Chapter 5.

If you're using a brand new WordPress blog and this is a new installation, the Drafts list in the Quick Draft module does not appear. That's because you haven't written any posts that are set to "Draft" status. As time goes on, however, and you've written a few posts in your blog, you may save some of those posts as Drafts — to be edited and published at a later date. Those drafts show up in the Drafts sections of the Quick Draft module.

WordPress displays up to five drafts and displays the title of the post and the date it was last saved. Click the post title to go to the Edit Post page where you can view, edit, and manage the draft post. Check out Chapter 5 for more information.

WordPress News

When you first install WordPress, the WordPress News module is by default populated with the five most recent updates from the official WordPress news blog at `http://planet.wordpress.org`. You see the title of the last post, the date it was published, and a short excerpt of the post. Click a title and you go directly to that post.

Following the updates of the WordPress news blog is very useful, and I highly recommend it because every single time you log in to your WordPress Dashboard, a glance at this section informs you about any news, updates, or alerts from the makers of WordPress. You can find out about any new versions of the software, security patches, or other important news regarding the software you are using to power your blog.

Arranging the Dashboard to Your Tastes

You can arrange the order of the modules in your Dashboard to suit your tastes. WordPress places a great deal of emphasis on user experience, and a big part of that effort results in your ability to create a Dashboard that you find most useful. Happily, changing the modules that are displayed, and the order in which they're displayed, is easy.

In the following steps, I show you how to move the At a Glance module so that it displays on the right side of your Dashboard page:

1. **Hover your mouse over the title bar of the At a Glance module.**

   When hovering over the box title, your mouse cursor changes to the Move cursor (a cross with arrows on a PC or the hand cursor on a Mac).

2. **Click and hold your mouse button and drag the At a Glance module to the right side of the screen.**

   As you drag the box, a light gray line with a dotted border appears on the right side of your screen. That gray line is a guide that shows you where you should drop the module. See Figure 4-3.

3. **Release the mouse button when you have the At a Glance module in place.**

   The At a Glance module is now positioned on the right side of your Dashboard page, at the top.

   The other modules on the left shift up to fill the space left by the At a Glance module, and the modules on the right side shift down to make room for the At a Glance module.

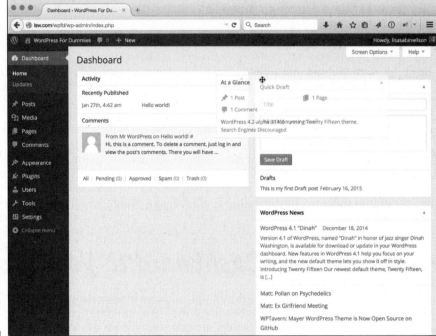

Figure 4-3:
A light gray line appears as a guide when dragging and dropping modules in the WordPress Dashboard.

4. (Optional) Click the gray arrow to the right of the At a Glance title.

The module collapses. Click the arrow again, and the module expands. You can keep that module opened or closed based on your own preference.

Repeat these steps with each module you see in the Dashboard by dragging and dropping them so that they appear in the order you prefer.

When you navigate away from the Dashboard, WordPress remembers the changes you've made. When you return, you still see your customized Dashboard and you don't need to redo these changes.

If you find that your Dashboard contains a few modules you just never use, you can get rid of them altogether by following these steps:

1. Click the Screen Options button at the top of the Dashboard.

The Screen Options menu opens, displaying the title of each module with check boxes to the left of each title.

2. Deselect the module you want to hide in your Dashboard.

The check mark is removed from the box, and the module disappears from your Dashboard. Figure 4-4 shows my customized Dashboard, where I've removed the Quick Draft module and moved the At a Glance module to the top right.

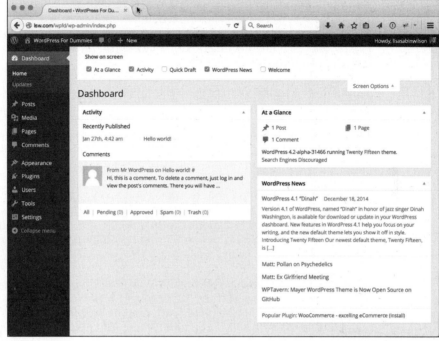

If you remove a module in the Screen Options panel and later find that you want it back, you can always revisit the Screen Options panel and re-enable the module by selecting the check box next to the name of the module you want to show in your Dashboard.

Finding Inline Documentation and Help

One thing I really appreciate about the WordPress software is the time and effort put in by the developers to provide users with tons of inline documentation that provides you with several tips and hints right inside the Dashboard. You can generally find inline documentation for just about every WordPress feature you use.

Inline documentation are those small sentences and/or phrases that you see alongside, or underneath, a feature in WordPress that give a short but very helpful explanation of what the feature is and serve as guiding tips that correspond with each feature. These tips sometimes even provide basic, recommended settings.

In addition to the inline documentation that you see scattered throughout the Dashboard, you'll find a helpful tab in the upper-right corner of your Dashboard labeled Help. Click this tab and a panel drops down that contains a lot of text providing documentation relevant to the page you are currently viewing in your Dashboard.

For example, if you're viewing the General Settings page, the Help tab drops down documentation relevant to the General Settings page, as shown in Figure 4-5. Likewise, if you're viewing the Add New Post page, clicking the Help tab drops down documentation with topics relevant to the settings and features you find on the Add New Post page within your Dashboard. Just click the Help tab again to close the Help panel when you're done reading it.

The inline documentation and the topics and text you find under the Help tab exist to assist and support you as you experience the WordPress platform to help make it as easy to understand as possible. You can also find help and support for WordPress on the WordPress Support Forums at `https://wordpress.org/support`.

Throughout the different pages of your WordPress Dashboard, you can apply the customization features that I cover for the main Dashboard page earlier in this chapter. Every section of the WordPress Dashboard is customizable with drag-and-drop modules, screen options, and inline help and documentation.

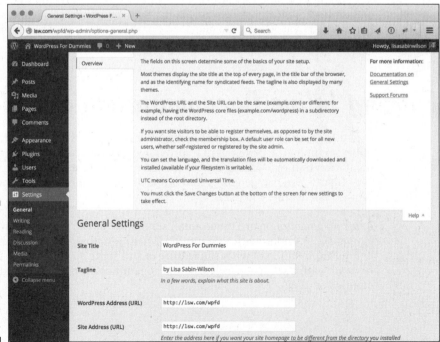

Figure 4-5: Help documentation shown on the General Settings page in the Dashboard.

Have a look at Figure 4-6, which displays the Posts page in the WordPress Dashboard (the Posts page is covered in greater detail in Chapter 5). In the figure, the Screen Options menu shows your options for customization, including the following:

✔ Check boxes that you can select to display the Author, Categories, Tags, Comments, and Date of the posts listed on the Posts page

✔ A text field for you to input the number of posts you want displayed on the Posts page

Figure 4-7 displays the Help topics on the Posts page when you click the Help tab at the top of the screen to display the inline documentation for the page.

Another helpful feature in the Help menu on each page of the WordPress Dashboard is the links that lead you to other areas on the Internet that contain additional help, support topics, and resources for you to learn more about the various WordPress features.

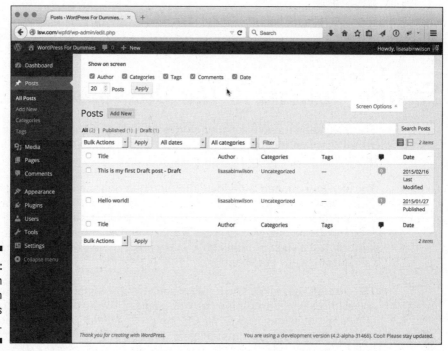

Figure 4-6:
Screen
Options on
the Posts
page.

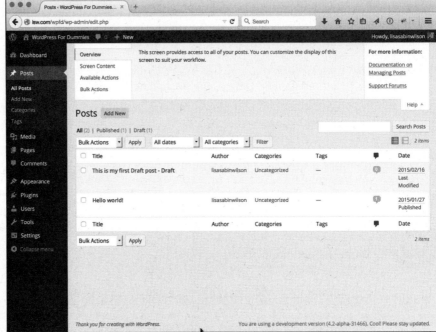

Figure 4-7:
Click the
Help tab on
the Posts
page to
display
inline docu-
mentation.

Setting Options in the Dashboard

The navigation menu is located on the left side of every page within the WordPress Dashboard. You find it there everywhere you go; like a loyal friend, it's always there for you when you need it!

The navigation menu is divided into nine different menus (not counting the Dashboard menu, mentioned previously). Hover your mouse over a menu, and another menu flies out to the right to reveal the submenu of items. The submenu items take you to areas within your Dashboard that allow you to perform tasks such as publishing a new post, configuring your site settings, or managing your comments.

The settings that allow you to personalize your blog are the first ones that I cover in the next part of this chapter. Some of the menu items, such as creating and publishing new posts, are covered in detail in other chapters, but they're well worth a mention here as well so that you know what you're looking at. (Sections with additional information contain a cross-reference telling you where you can find more in-depth information on that topic in this book.)

Configuring the Settings

At the bottom of the navigation menu is the Settings menu. Hover over the Settings link, and a submenu appears to the right that contains the following links, which I discuss in the sections that follow:

- ✔ General
- ✔ Writing
- ✔ Reading
- ✔ Discussion
- ✔ Media
- ✔ Permalinks

General

After you install the WordPress software and log in, you can put a personal stamp on your blog by giving it a title and description, setting your contact email address, and identifying yourself as the author of the blog. You take care of these and other settings on the General Settings page.

To begin personalizing your blog, start with your general settings by following these steps:

1. Click the General link in the Settings menu.

The General Settings page appears. See Figure 4-8.

2. Enter the name of your website in the Site Title text box.

The title you enter here is the one that you've given your website to identify it as your own. In Figure 4-8 I gave my new blog the title *WordPress For Dummies,* which appears on the site as well as in the title bar of the viewer's web browser.

Give your blog an interesting and identifiable name. You can use *Fried Green Tomatoes,* for example, if your website covers that topic of Fried Green Tomatoes; the book, or the movie, or even anything remotely related to the lovely Southern dish.

3. In the Tagline text box, enter a five- to ten-word phrase that describes your blog.

Figure 4-8 shows that my tagline is *by Lisa Sabin-Wilson.* So my website displays my site title followed by the tagline: *WordPress For Dummies by Lisa Sabin-Wilson.*

The general Internet-surfing public can view your website title and tagline, which various search engines (such as Google, Yahoo!, and MSN) grab for indexing, so choose your words with this fact in mind.

4. **In the WordPress Address (URL) text box, enter the location where you installed your WordPress software.**

    Be sure to include the `http://` portion of the URL and the entire path to your WordPress installation — for example, `http://yourdomain.com`. If you installed WordPress in a folder in your directory — in a folder called `wordpress`, for example — you need to include it here. If I had installed WordPress in a folder called `wordpress`, the WordPress address would be `http://yourdomain.com/wordpress`.

5. **In the Site Address (URL) text box, enter the web address where people can find your blog by using their web browsers.**

    Typically, what you enter here is the same as your domain name (`http://yourdomain.com`). If you install WordPress in a subdirectory of your site, the WordPress installation URL is different from the blog URL. If you install WordPress at `http://yourdomain.com/word-press/` (WordPress URL), you need to tell WordPress that you want the blog to appear at `http://yourdomain.com` (the blog URL).

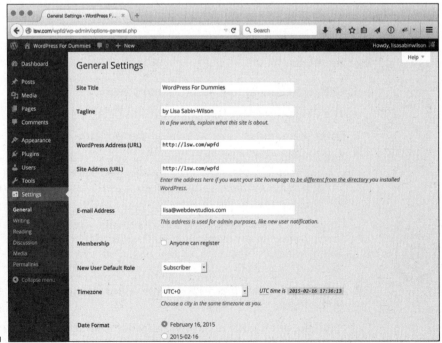

Figure 4-8: Personalize the settings of your WordPress blog on the General Settings page.

6. Enter your email address in the Email Address text box.

WordPress sends messages about the details of your website to this email address. When a new user registers for your site, for example, WordPress sends you an email alert.

7. Select a Membership option.

Select the Anyone Can Register check box if you want to keep registration on your site open to anyone who wants to register. Keep the check box deselected if you'd rather not have open registration on your website.

8. From the New User Default Role drop-down menu, choose the role that you want new users to have when they register for user accounts in your website.

You need to understand the differences among the user roles because each user role is assigned a different level of access to your website, as follows:

- *Subscriber:* Subscriber is the default role. Assigning this role to new users is a good idea, particularly if you don't know who's registering. Subscribers are given access to the Dashboard page and they can view and change the options in their profiles on the Your Profile and Personal Options page. (They don't have access to your account settings, however — only to their own.) Each user can change his username, email address, password, bio, and other descriptors in his user profile. Subscribers' profile information is stored in the WordPress database, and your site remembers them each time they visit so that they don't have to complete the profile information each time they leave comments on your website.

- *Contributor:* In addition to the access Subscribers have, Contributors can upload files and write, edit, and manage their own posts. Contributors can write posts, but they can't publish the posts; the administrator reviews all Contributor posts and decides whether to publish them. This setting is a nice way to moderate content written by new authors.

- *Author:* In addition to the access Contributors have, Authors can publish and edit their own posts.

- *Editor:* In addition to the access Authors have, Editors can moderate comments, manage categories, manage links, edit pages, and edit other Authors' posts.

- *Administrator:* Administrators can edit all the options and settings in the WordPress website. Simply put, Administrators have access to everything, so use caution when handing out Administrator access to your website.

9. In the Timezone section, choose your UTC time from the drop-down menu.

This setting refers to the number of hours that your local time differs from Coordinated Universal Time (UTC). This setting ensures that all your posts and comments left on your blog are time-stamped with the correct time. If you're lucky enough, like me, to live on the frozen tundra of Wisconsin, which is in the Central time zone (CST), you would choose –6 from the drop-down menu because that time zone is six hours off UTC. WordPress also gives you the names of some of the major cities across the world to make it easier. Just select the name of the major city you live closest to, and chances are, you're in the same time zone as that city.

If you're unsure what your UTC time is, you can find it at the Greenwich Mean Time website (`wwp.greenwichmeantime.com`). GMT is essentially the same thing as UTC.

10. **In the Date Format text box, enter the format in which you want the date to be displayed in your website.**

    This setting determines the style of the date display. The default format is already selected and displayed for you: **F j, Y** (F = the full month name; j = the two-digit day; Y = the four-digit year), which gives you the date output. This default date format displays the date like this: February 16, 2015.

    Select a different format by clicking the circle to the left of the option. You can also customize the date display by selecting the Custom option and entering your preferred format in the text box provided. If you're feeling adventurous, you can find out how to customize the date format by clicking the Documentation on Date and Time Formatting link between the date and time options, which takes you to this page in the WordPress Codex: `http://codex.wordpress.org/Formatting_Date_and_Time`.

11. **In the Time Format text box, enter the format in which you want the time to be displayed in your website.**

    This setting is the style of the time display. The default format is already inserted for you: **g:i a** (g = the two-digit hour; i = the two-digit minute; a = lowercase as a.m. or p.m.), which gives you the output of 12:00 a.m.

    Select a different format by clicking the circle to the left of the option. You can also customize the date display by selecting the Custom option and entering your preferred format in the text box provided; find out how at `http://codex.wordpress.org/Formatting_Date_and_Time`.

    You can format the time and date in several ways. Go to `http://us3.php.net/manual/en/function.date.php` to find potential formats at the PHP website.

12. **From the drop-down menu, choose the day the week starts in your calendar.**

    Displaying a calendar in the sidebar of your website is optional. If you choose to display a calendar, you can select the day of the week you want your calendar to start with.

13. Set your site language preference.

The Site Language drop-down menu gives you several different language options to choose from. The default setting is English; however, the WordPress software is available in approximately 45 different languages. If your website should be in Spanish, then use the drop-down menu here to change it from English to Spanish.

Click the Save Changes button at the bottom of any page where you set new options. If you don't click Save Changes, your settings aren't saved, and WordPress reverts to the preceding options. Each time you click the Save Changes button, WordPress reloads the current page, displaying the new options that you just set.

Writing

Click the Writing link in the Settings menu; the Writing Settings page opens. See Figure 4-9.

This page lets you set some basic options for writing your posts. Table 4-1 gives you some information on choosing how your posts look and how WordPress handles some specific conditions.

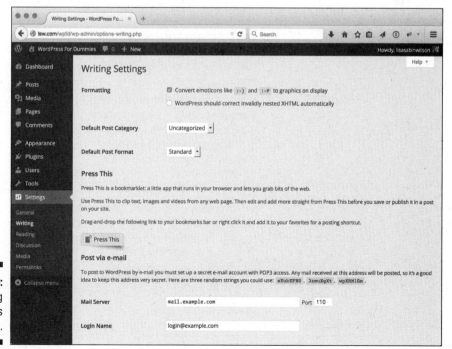

Figure 4-9:
The Writing
Settings
page.

Table 4-1	Writing Settings Options	
Option	**Function**	**Default**
Formatting	Determines whether WordPress converts emoticons to graphics and whether WordPress corrects invalidly nested XHTML automatically. In general, I recommend selecting this option. (You can find more information about valid XHTML code at `http://validator.w3.org/docs/#docs_all`.)	Convert emoticons is selected. XHTML is deselected.
Default Post Category	Lets you select the category that WordPress defaults to any time you forget to choose a category when you publish a post.	Uncategorized
Default Post Format	Lets you select the post format that WordPress defaults to any time you publish a post to your blog.	Standard
Press This	A small application to use in your browser that lets you post information and content you find on the web to your website in a quick and easy fashion. Just drag and drop the Press This button to your browser's bookmark toolbar to use.	N/A
Post via E-mail	Lets you publish posts from your email account by letting you enter the email and server information for the account you'll be using to send posts to your WordPress website.	N/A
Update Services **Note:** This option is available only if your website is made public in the Privacy settings.	Lets you indicate which ping service you want to use to notify the world that you've made updates, or published new posts. These update services include `blogrolling.com` and `weblogs.com`. The default, `rpc.pingomatic.com`, updates all the popular services simultaneously.	`rpc.pingomatic.com`

After you set your options, be sure to click the Save Changes button; otherwise, the changes won't take effect.

Go to `http://codex.wordpress.org/Update_Services` for comprehensive information on update services.

Reading

The third link in the Settings menu is Reading (see Figure 4-10).

You can set the following options in the Reading Settings page:

- ✔ **Front Page Displays:** Choose what you want to display on the front page of your website: your latest posts or a static page. You can find detailed information about using a static page for your front page in Chapter 12.

- ✔ **Blog Pages Show at Most:** Type the maximum number of posts you want to display on each content page. The default is set to 10.

- ✔ **Syndication Feeds Show the Most Recent:** In the Posts box, type the maximum number of posts you want to show in your RSS feed at any time. The default is set to 10.

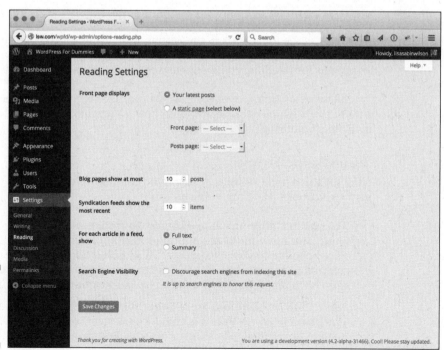

Figure 4-10: The Reading Settings page.

✔ **For Each Article in a Feed, Show:** Select either Full Text or Summary. Full Text publishes the entire post to your RSS feed, whereas Summary publishes only an excerpt. By default, Full Text is selected. (Check out Chapter 5 for more information on WordPress RSS feeds.)

✔ **Search Engine Visibility:** By default, the Discourage Search Engines from Indexing This Site option is not checked. If you are one of those rare bloggers who *doesn't* want search engines to be able to visit and index your website in their search directories, check the Discourage Search Engines from Indexing This Site option.

Generally, you want search engines to be able to find your website. However, if you have special circumstances, you may want to enforce your privacy settings. I would block search engines, for example, because the site I'm using for the figures in this book is one that I don't want search engines to find. On the main Dashboard, in the At a Glance box, is a note that says Search Engines Discouraged. This note exists only when you have your privacy settings set to block search engines. When you have Search Engine Visibility selected, search engines and other content bots can't find your website.

Be sure to click the Save Changes button when you've set all your options in the Reading Settings page to make the changes take effect.

Discussion

Discussion is the fourth link in the Settings menu; click it to open the Discussion Settings page (see Figure 4-11). The sections on this tab let you set options for handling comments and publishing posts to your blog.

The following sections cover the options available to you in the Discussion Settings page, which deals mainly with how comments and trackbacks are handled in your blog.

Default Article Settings

In the Default Article Settings section, you can tell WordPress how to handle post notifications. Here are your options:

✔ **Attempt to Notify Any Blogs Linked To from the Article:** Select this check box and your blog sends a notification (or *ping*) to any site you have linked to in your blog posts. This notification is also commonly referred to as a *trackback* (I discuss trackbacks in Chapter 2). Deselect this check box if you don't want these notifications to be sent.

✔ **Allow Link Notifications from Other Blogs (Pingbacks and Trackbacks):** By default, this check box is selected and your blog is open to be notified via a ping or trackback from another blog that has linked to yours. Any trackbacks or pings sent to your blog are listed on your site in the comments section of the blog post. If you deselect this check box, your blog won't accept pings or trackbacks from other blogs.

✔ **Allow People to Post Comments on New Articles:** By default, this check box is selected, and people can leave comments on your blog posts. If you deselect this check box, no one can leave comments on your blog. (You can override these settings for individual articles — find more information about this in Chapter 5.)

Other Comment Settings

The Other Comment Settings tell WordPress how to handle comments:

✔ **Comment Author Must Fill Out Name and E-mail:** Enabled by default, this option requires all commenters on your blog to fill in the Name and E-mail field when leaving a comment. This option is very helpful in combating comment spam. (See Chapters 2 and 7 for information on comment spam.) Deselect this check box to disable this option.

✔ **Users Must Be Registered and Logged In to Comment:** Not enabled by default, this option allows you to accept comments on your blog from only those people who have registered and are currently logged in as a user on your blog. If the user is not logged in, he sees a message that says `You must be logged in in order to leave a comment.`

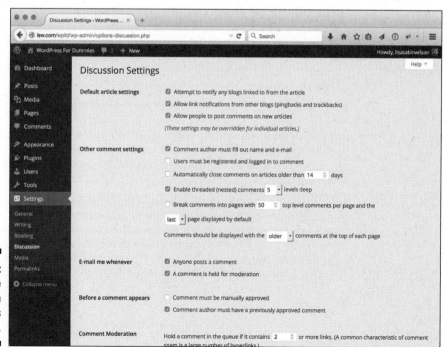

Figure 4-11:
The Discussion Settings page.

✔ **Automatically Close Comments on Articles Older Than _X_ Days:** Select the check box next to this option to tell WordPress that you want comments on older articles to be automatically closed. Fill in the text box with the number of days you want to wait before WordPress closes comments on older articles.

This feature is a very effective anti-spam technique that many bloggers use to keep down the comment and trackback spam on their blogs.

✔ **Enable Threaded (Nested) Comments _X_ Levels Deep:** The drop-down menu allows you to choose the level of threaded comments you'd like to have on your blog. The default is 5; you can choose up to 10 levels. Instead of all comments being displayed on your blog in chronological order (as they are by default), nesting them allows you and your readers to reply to comments within the comment itself.

✔ **Break Comments into Pages with _X_ Top Level Comments Per Page and the Last/First Page Displayed by Default:** Fill in the text box with the number of comments you want to display on one page. This is very helpful for blogs that receive a large number of comments. It enables you to break the long string of comments into several pages, which makes those comments easier to read and helps speed up the load time of your site because the page isn't loading such a large number of comments at one time. Also, select from the drop-down menu whether you want the first or last page displayed by default.

✔ **Comments Should Be Displayed with the Older/Newer Comments at the Top of Each Page:** Use the drop-down menu to select Older or Newer. Selecting Older displays the comments on your blog in the order of oldest to newest. Selecting Newer does the opposite: displays the comments on your blog in the order of newest to oldest.

E-mail Me Whenever

The two options in the E-mail Me Whenever section are enabled by default:

✔ **Anyone Posts a Comment:** This option lets you receive an email notification whenever anyone leaves a comment on your blog. Deselect the check box if you don't want to be notified by email about every new comment.

✔ **A Comment Is Held for Moderation:** This option lets you receive an email notification whenever a comment is awaiting your approval in the comment moderation queue. (See Chapter 5 for more information about the comment moderation queue.) Deselect this check box if you don't want this notification.

Before a Comment Appears

The two options in the Before a Comment Appears section tell WordPress how you want WordPress to handle comments before they appear in your blog:

- **Comment Must Be Manually Approved:** Disabled by default, this option keeps every single comment left on your blog in the moderation queue until you, the administrator, log in and approve it. Select this check box to enable this option.

- **Comment Author Must Have a Previously Approved Comment:** Enabled by default, this option requires comments posted by all first-time commenters to be sent to the comment moderation queue for approval by the administrator of the blog. After comment authors have been approved for the first time, they remain approved for every comment thereafter. WordPress stores their email addresses in the database, and any future comments that match any stored emails are approved automatically. This feature is another measure that WordPress has built in to combat comment spam.

Comment Moderation

In the Comment Moderation section, you can set options to specify what types of comments are held in the moderation queue to await your approval.

To prevent spammers from spamming your blog with a *ton* of links, select the Hold a Comment in the Queue If It Contains *X* or More Links check box. The default number of links allowed is 2. Give that setting a try and if you find that you're getting lots of spam comments with multiple links, you may want to revisit this page and increase that number. Any comment with a higher number of links goes to the comment moderation area for approval.

The large text box in the Comment Moderation section lets you type keywords, URLs, email addresses, and IP addresses in comments that you want to be held in the moderation queue for your approval.

Comment Blacklist

In this section, type a list of words, URLs, email addresses, and/or IP addresses that you want to flat-out ban from your blog. Items placed here don't even make it into your comment moderation queue; the WordPress system filters them as spam. Let me just say that the words I have placed in my blacklist are not family-friendly and have no place in a nice book like this.

Avatars and gravatars: How do they relate to WordPress?

An *avatar* is an online graphical representation of an individual. It's a small graphic icon that people use to visually represent themselves on the web in areas in which they participate in conversations, such as discussion forums and blog comments. *Gravatars* are globally recognized avatars; it's an avatar that you can take with you wherever you go. A gravatar appears alongside blog comments, blog posts, and discussion forums as long as the site you are interacting with is Gravatar-enabled.

In October 2007, Automattic, the core group behind the WordPress platform, purchased the Gravatar service and integrated it into WordPress so that all could enjoy and benefit from the service. Gravatars are not automatic; you need to sign up for an account with Gravatar before you can assign an avatar to yourself, via your email address. You can find out more about Gravatar by visiting `http://gravatar.com`.

Avatars

The final section of the Discussion Settings page is Avatars. (See the previous sidebar, "Avatars and gravatars: How do they relate to WordPress?" for information about avatars.) In this section, you can select different settings for the use and display of avatars on your site:

1. **In the Avatar Display section, select the Show Avatars option if you would like your site to display avatars beside comment authors' names.**

2. **In the Maximum Rating section, set the rating for the avatars that do display on your site.**

   This feature works similarly to the movie rating system you're used to. You can select G, PG, R, and X ratings for the avatars that appear on your site. If your site is family-friendly, you probably don't want it to display R- or X-rated avatars.

3. **Choose a default avatar in the Default Avatar section; see Figure 4-12:**
   - Mystery Person
   - Blank
   - Gravatar Logo
   - Identicon (Generated)
   - Wavatar (Generated)
   - MonsterID (Generated)
   - Retro (Generated)

4. **Click the Save Changes button.**

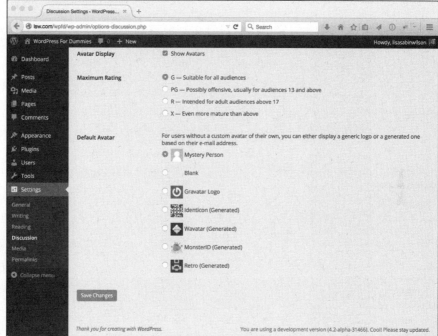

Figure 4-12:
Default ava-
tars you can
display in
your blog.

Avatars appear in a couple places:

✔ **The Comments page in the Dashboard:** In Figure 4-13, the comment displays the commenter's avatar next to it.

✔ **The comments on individual blog posts to your blog:** Figure 4-14 shows
a list of comments on my own personal blog.

To enable the display of avatars in comments on your blog, the Comments
Template (`comments.php`) in your active theme has to contain the code to
display them. Hop on over to Chapter 9 to find out how to do that.

Click the Save Changes button after you've set all your options on the
Discussion Settings page to put the changes into effect.

Media

The next link in the Settings menu is Media; click the Media link and the
Media Settings page opens. See Figure 4-15.

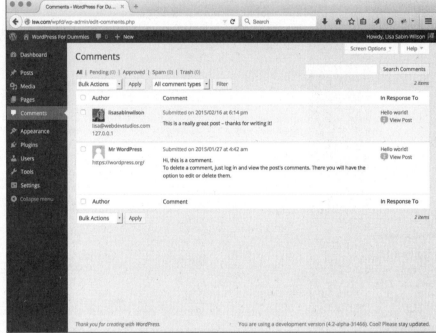

Figure 4-13:
Authors'
avatars
appear
in the
Comments
page in the
WordPress
Dashboard.

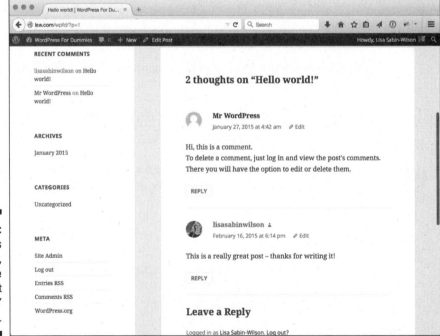

Figure 4-14:
Comments
on a post,
showing the
comment
authors'
avatars.

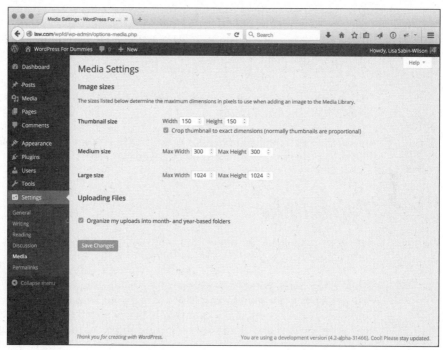

Figure 4-15:
The Media
Settings
page.

On the Media Settings page, you can configure the options for how your image files (graphics and photos) are resized for use in your website.

The first set of options on the Media Settings page deals with images. WordPress automatically resizes your images for you in three different sizes. The dimensions are referenced in pixels by width and then height. (For example, 150 x 150 means 150 pixels in width by 150 pixels in height.)

✔ **Thumbnail Size:** The default is 150 x 150; enter the width and height of your choice. Select the Crop Thumbnail to Exact Dimensions check box to resize the thumbnail exactly to the width and height you specified. Deselect this check box and WordPress resizes the image proportionally.

✔ **Medium Size:** The default is 300 x 300; enter the width and height numbers of your choice.

✔ **Large Size:** The default is 1024 x 1024; enter the width and height numbers of your choice.

Finally, the last set of options on the Media Settings page is the Uploading Files section. By default, the Organize My Uploads into Month- and Year-Based Folders check box is selected and WordPress organizes your uploaded files in folders by month and by year. Files you upload in February 2015, for example, would be in the following folder: `/wp-content/uploads/2015/02/`. Likewise, files you upload in December 2014 would be in `/wp-content/uploads/2014/12/`. Deselect this check box if you do not want WordPress to organize your files by month and year.

In Chapter 6, I go into much greater detail on how to insert images into your WordPress posts and pages.

Be sure to click the Save Changes button after you set all your options on the Privacy Settings page to make the changes take effect.

Permalinks

The next link on the Settings menu is Permalinks. Clicking this link loads the Permalink Settings page (see Figure 4-16).

Each of the posts you create on your blog has a unique URL called a *permalink,* which is a permanent link (URL) for all your website posts, pages, and archives. I cover permalinks extensively in Chapter 5 by explaining what they are, how you can use them, and how you set the options in this page.

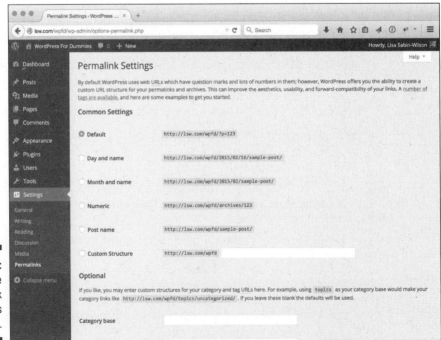

Figure 4-16: The Permalink Settings page.

Creating Your Personal Profile

The next place to visit to really personalize your blog is your profile page in your WordPress Dashboard.

To access your profile page, click the Your Profile link in the Users menu. You're taken to the Profile page. See Figure 4-17.

Here are the settings on this page:

- **Personal Options:** The Personal Options section is where you can set four preferences for your website:

  - *Visual Editor:* This selection enables you to use the Visual Editor when writing your posts. The Visual Editor gives you the formatting options you find in the Write Post page (discussed in detail in Chapter 5). By default, the Visual Editor is on. To turn it off, select the Disable the Visual Editor When Writing check box.

  - *Admin Color Scheme:* These options set the colors in your Dashboard. The default is a black and gray color scheme with blue as a highlight color; you can also select more colorful schemes for your Dashboard display, like Light, Blue, Coffee, Ectoplasm, Midnight, Ocean, and Sunrise.

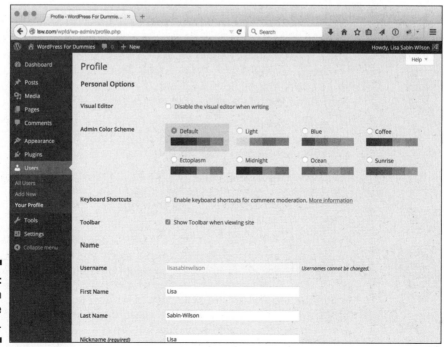

Figure 4-17: Establish your profile details here.

- *Keyboard Shortcuts:* This enables you to use keyboard shortcuts for comment moderation. To learn more about keyboard shortcuts, click the More Information link; you're taken to the Keyboard Shortcuts page (`http://codex.wordpress.org/Keyboard_Shortcuts`) in the WordPress Codex.

- *Toolbar:* The Toolbar displays at the top of your WordPress website, but it displays only to the user who is logged in to the site; it cannot be seen by regular viewers of your website. The Toolbar contains helpful links that allow you to get to different sections of your Dashboard quickly and easily with a single click. You can choose to display the Toolbar while you are viewing your site or the Dashboard, or both.

✔ **Name:** This section is where you can input personal information such as your first name, last name, and nickname, and specify how you want your name to be displayed publicly. Fill in the text boxes with the requested information and choose your display name from the drop-down list.

✔ **Contact Info:** In this section, you provide your email address and website URL to tell your visitors who you are and where they may find you on the web.

Note that your email address is the only required entry here. This is the address WordPress uses to notify you when you have new comments or new user registrations on your website. Make sure to use a real email address so that you get these notifications.

✔ **About Yourself:** This section is where you can provide a little bio about yourself and change the password for your website.

When your profile is published to your website, it not only can be viewed by anyone, but also gets picked up by search engines such as Yahoo! and Google. Always be careful with the information in your profile. Think hard about the information you want to share with the rest of the world!

- *Biographical Info:* Type a short bio in the Biographical Info text box. This information can be shown publicly if you are using a theme that displays your bio, so be creative!

- *New Password:* When you want to change the password for your website, type your new password in the first text box in the New Password section. To confirm your new password, type it again in the second text box.

Directly below the two text boxes is a little password helper. WordPress helps you create a secure password. It alerts you if the password you've chosen is too short or not secure enough by calling it *Very Weak, Weak,* or *Medium.* When creating a new password, use a combination of letters, numbers, and symbols to make it hard for anyone to guess (for example, `aty89!#4j`). When you create a password that WordPress thinks is a good one, it lets you know by calling it *Strong.*

Change your password frequently. I can't recommend this practice strongly enough. Some people on the Internet make it their business to attempt to hijack blogs for their own malicious purposes. If you change your password monthly, you lower your risk by keeping hackers guessing.

✔ **Log Out of All Other Sessions:** Click this button if you have logged into your website from another computer to ensure that you are logged out everywhere except for the current browser you are logged in with. This is an extra security measure to make sure no one else can access the Dashboard of your website from any other location.

When you finish setting all the options on the Profile page, don't forget to click the Update Profile button to save your changes.

Setting Your Site's Format

In addition to setting your personal settings in the Dashboard, you can manage the day-to-day maintenance of your website. This next section takes you through the links to these sections in the navigation menu, directly underneath the Dashboard link.

Posts

Hover your mouse over the Posts menu and a submenu appears with four links: All Posts, Add New, Categories, and Tags. Each link gives you the tools you need to publish content to your blog:

✔ **All Posts:** This link opens the Posts page, where you see a listing of all the saved posts you've written on your site. On this page, you can search for posts by date, category, or keyword. You can view all posts, only posts that have been published, or just posts that have been saved but not yet published (*drafts*). You can also edit and delete posts from this page. Check out Chapter 5 for more information on editing posts on your website.

✔ **Add New:** This link opens the Add New Post page, where you compose your posts, set the options for each post (such as assigning a post to a category, or making it a private or public post), and publish the post to your blog. You can find more information on posts, post options, and publishing in Chapter 5.

You can also get to the Add New Post page by clicking the Posts menu.

✔ **Categories:** This link opens the Categories page, where you can view, edit, add, and delete categories on your site. Find more information on categories in Chapter 5.

✔ **Tags:** This link opens the Tags page, where you can view, add, edit, and delete tags on your site. Chapter 5 provides you with more information about what tags are and why you use them on your website.

Media

Hover your mouse pointer over the Media menu link to expand the submenu of links for this section:

✔ **Library:** This link opens the Media Library page. On this page, you view, search, and manage all the media files you've ever uploaded to your WordPress site.

✔ **Add New:** This link opens the Upload New Media page, where you can use the built-in uploader to transfer media files from your computer to the media directory in WordPress. Chapter 6 takes you through the details of how to upload images, videos, audio, and other media files (such as Microsoft Word or PowerPoint documents) using the WordPress upload feature.

You can also get to the Upload New Media page by clicking the Media menu.

Pages

People use this feature to create pages on their sites such as an About Me or Contact Me page. Click the Pages menu to reveal the submenu links:

✔ **All Pages:** This link opens the Pages page, where you can search, view, edit, and delete pages in your WordPress site.

✔ **Add New:** This link opens the Add New Page page, where you can compose, save, and publish a new page on your blog. Table 4-2 describes the differences between a page and a post — it's subtle, but the two are very different from one another!

You can also get to the Add New Page page by clicking the Pages menu.

Table 4-2	The Differences Between a Page and a Post		
WordPress Options		**Page**	**Post**
Appears in blog post listings		No	Yes
Appears as a static page		Yes	No
Appears in category archives		No	Yes
Appears in monthly archives		No	Yes
Appears in Recent Posts listings		No	Yes
Appears in site RSS feed		No	Yes
Appears in search results		Yes	Yes

Comments

The Comments menu doesn't have a submenu of links. You simply click the Comments menu title to open the Comments page, where WordPress gives you the options to view:

- **All:** Shows all comments that currently exist on your blog. This includes approved, pending, and spam comments.

- **Pending:** Shows comments that are not yet approved by you but are pending in the moderation queue.

- **Approved:** Shows all comments that have been previously approved by you.

- **Spam:** Shows all the comments that are marked as spam.

- **Trash:** Shows comments that you have marked as Trash, but have not yet been deleted permanently from your blog.

You can find information in Chapter 2 about the purpose of comments. Also, in Chapter 5 I give you details on how to use the Comments section of your WordPress Dashboard.

Appearance

When you click the Appearance menu in the navigation menu, a submenu drops down with the following links to click:

- **Themes:** This link opens the Themes page, where you can manage the themes available on your website. Check out Chapter 9 to learn about using themes on your WordPress blog and how to manage those themes on this page.

✔ **Customize:** Some themes have a Customize page, where you can configure different settings for the theme, such as the default Twenty Fifteen theme. The Customize link appears under the Appearance menu only if the theme you're currently using has options available for configuration; if it doesn't, you won't see the Customize link here.

✔ **Widgets:** The Widgets page allows you to add, delete, edit, and manage the widgets you use on your blog.

✔ **Menus:** This link opens the Menus page, where you can build navigation menus to display on your site. Chapter 10 provides information on creating menus using this feature.

✔ **Header:** In the Custom Header page you can upload an image to use in the header (or top) of your WordPress website; however, this menu item and page exist only if you have the Twenty Fifteen theme activated, or any other theme that supports the Custom Header feature (more about that in Chapter 10). The Twenty Fifteen theme is activated by default on all new WordPress blogs, which is why I've included this menu item in this list. Not all WordPress themes use the Custom Header feature, so you don't see this menu item if your theme doesn't take advantage of that feature.

✔ **Background:** This link opens the Background Image page, where you can upload an image to use as the background of your WordPress website design; as with the Custom Header option, the Custom Background option exists in the Appearance menu only if you have the default Twenty Fifteen theme activated, or any other theme that supports the Custom Background feature. Not all WordPress themes use the Custom Background feature.

✔ **Editor:** This link opens the Theme Editor page, where you can edit your theme templates. Chapters 9–11 have extensive information on themes and templates.

Uploading header images and customizing the background of your site helps you to individualize the visual design of your website. You can find more information on tweaking and customizing your WordPress theme in Chapter 8. Chapter 9 gives you a great deal of information about how to use WordPress themes (including where to find, install, and activate them in your WordPress website) as well as detailed information on using WordPress widgets to display the content you want.

Part IV provides information about WordPress themes and templates. You can dig deep into WordPress template tags and tweak an existing WordPress theme by using Cascading Style Sheets (CSS) to customize your theme a bit more to your liking.

Plugins

The next menu in the navigation menu is Plugins. Click the Plugins menu to expand the submenu of links:

✔ **Installed Plugins:** This link opens the Plugins page, where you can view all the plugins currently installed on your website. On this page, you also have the ability to activate, deactivate, and delete plugins on your site.

✔ **Add New:** This link opens the Install Plugins page, where you can search for plugins from the official WordPress Plugin Directory by keyword, author, or tag. You can also install plugins directly to your site from the WordPress Plugin Directory.

✔ **Editor:** The Edit Plugins page allows you to edit the plugin files in a text editor. I strongly advise against editing plugin files unless you know exactly what you're doing — that is, you are familiar with PHP and WordPress functions.

See Chapter 7 for more on plugins.

Users

The Users menu has three links:

✔ **All Users:** Click this link to go to the Users page, where you can view, edit, and delete users on your WordPress website. Each user has a unique login name and password, as well as an email address assigned to her account. You can view and edit a user's information on the Users page.

✔ **Add New:** This link opens the Add New User page, where you can add new users to your WordPress site. Simply type the user's username, first name, last name, email (required), website, and a password into the fields provided and then click the Add User button. You can also select whether you want WordPress to send login information to the new user by email. If you like, you can also assign a new role for the new user. Turn to the earlier section, "General," for more info about user roles.

✔ **Your Profile:** Turn to the "Creating Your Personal Profile" section, earlier in this chapter, for more information about creating a profile page.

Tools

The last menu item in the navigation menu (and subsequently in this chapter!) is Tools. Click the Tools menu to drop down the submenu of links that includes:

- ✔ **Available Tools:** WordPress comes packaged with two extra features that you can use on your blog: Press This and Category/Tag Conversion.

- ✔ **Import:** WordPress gives you the ability to import from a different content management system. This feature is covered in depth in Chapter 14.

- ✔ **Export:** WordPress also allows you to export your content from WordPress so that you can import it into a different platform or another WordPress site. This information is also covered in Chapter 14.

Chapter 5

Establishing Your Publishing Routine

WordPress is a powerful publishing tool, especially when you use the full range of options available. With the basic settings configured (which I show you how to do in Chapter 4), now is the time to go forth and publish! You can skip to the "Writing Your First Entry" section in this chapter and jump right in to creating new posts for your website. Or you can stay right here and discover some of the options you can set to make your website a bit more organized and logical from the get-go.

Content on your website can become unwieldy and disorganized, requiring you to revisit these next few features sometime in the near future so that you can get the beast under control. So why not do a little planning and get the work over with now? I promise it won't take that long, and you'll thank me for it later.

Staying on Topic with Categories

In WordPress, a *category* is what you determine to be the main topic of an individual piece of content on your site. Through the use of categories, you can file your posts into topics by subject. To improve your readers' experiences in navigating your site, WordPress organizes posts by the categories you assign to them. Visitors can click the categories they're interested in to see the posts you've written on those particular topics.

You should know ahead of time that the list of categories you set up is displayed on your site in a few different places, including the following:

- ✔ **Body of the post:** In most WordPress themes, you see the title followed by a statement such as Filed In: *Category 1*, *Category 2*. The reader can click the category name to go to a page that lists all the posts you've made in that particular category. You can assign a single post to more than one category.

- ✔ **Sidebar of your theme:** You can place a full list of category titles in the sidebar. A reader can click any category and arrive at a page on your site that lists the posts you've made within that particular category.

Subcategories (also known as *category children*) can further refine the main category topic by listing specific topics related to the main (parent) category. In your WordPress Dashboard, on the Manage Categories page, subcategories are listed directly below the main category. Here's an example:

Books I Enjoy (main category)

Fiction (subcategory)

Nonfiction (subcategory)

Trashy romance (subcategory)

Biographies (subcategory)

For Dummies (subcategory)

Changing the name of a category

Upon installation, WordPress gives you one default category to get you started called *Uncategorized*. (See the Categories page shown in Figure 5-1.) That category name is pretty generic, so you'll definitely want to change it to one that's more specific to you. (On my site, I changed it to Life in General. Although that name's still a bit on the generic side, it doesn't sound quite so . . . well, uncategorized.)

The default category also serves as a kind of fail-safe. If you publish a post to your site and don't assign that post to a category, the post is automatically assigned to the default category, no matter what you name the category.

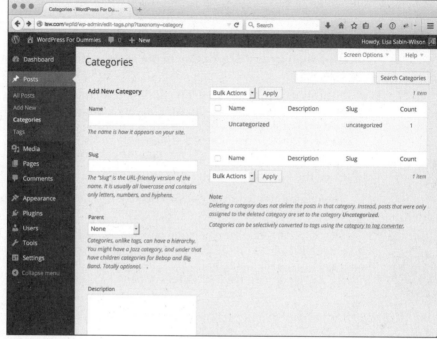

Figure 5-1:
The
Categories
page of a
brand-new
site shows
the default
Uncate-
gorized
category.

So how do you change the name of that default category? When you're logged in to your WordPress Dashboard, just follow these steps:

1. **Click the Categories link on the Posts Dashboard menu.**

   The Categories page opens, containing all the tools you need to set up and edit category titles for your blog.

2. **Click the title of the category you would like to edit.**

   To change the Uncategorized category, click the word Uncategorized, and you go to the Edit Category page. See Figure 5-2.

3. **Type the new name for the category in the Name text box.**

4. **Type the new slug in the Slug text box.**

   The term *slug* refers to the word(s) used in the web address for the specific category. For example, the Books category has a web address of `http://yourdomain.com/category/books`; if you change the slug to *Books I Like,* the web address is `http://yourdomain.com/category/books-i-like`. (WordPress automatically inserts a dash between the slug words in the web address.)

5. Choose a parent category from the Parent drop-down menu.

If you want this category to be a main category, not a subcategory, choose None.

6. (Optional) Type a description of the category in the Description text box.

Use this description to remind yourself what your category is about. Some WordPress themes display the category description right on your site, too, which can be helpful for your visitors. (See Chapter 9 for more about themes.) You'll know if your theme is coded in this way if your site displays the category description on the category page(s).

7. Click the Update button.

The information you just edited is saved, and the Categories page reloads, showing your new category name.

If you want to edit a category's name only, you can click the Quick Edit link underneath the name on the Category page, which you see when you hover your mouse over the Category name. Then you can do a quick name edit without having to load the Edit Category page.

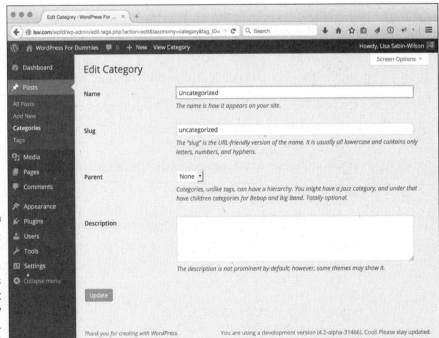

Figure 5-2:
Editing a category in WordPress on the Edit Category page.

Creating new categories and deleting others

Today, tomorrow, next month, next year — as your website grows in size and age, you'll continue adding new categories to further define and archive the history of your posts. You aren't limited in the number of categories and subcategories you can create.

Creating a new category is as easy as following these steps:

1. **Click the Categories link on the Posts Dashboard menu.**

   The Categories page opens.

2. **The left side of the Categories page displays the Add New Category section.**

   See Figure 5-3.

3. **Type the name of your new category in the Name text box.**

   Suppose that you want to create a category in which you file all your posts about the books you read. In the Name text box, type something like **Books I Enjoy**.

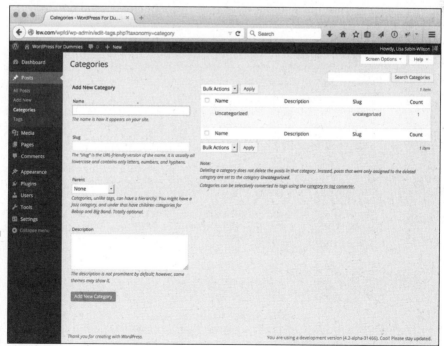

Figure 5-3:
Create
a new
category
on your
blog.

4. Type a name in the Slug text box.

The slug creates the link to the category page that lists all the posts you've made in this category. If you leave this field blank, WordPress automatically creates a slug based on the category name. If the category is Books I Enjoy, WordPress automatically creates a category slug like this: `http://yourdomain.com/category/books-i-enjoy`. If you want to shorten it, however, you can. Type **books** in the category Slug text box, and the link to the category becomes this: `http://yourdomain.com/category/books`.

5. Choose the category's parent from the Parent drop-down menu.

Choose None if you want this new category to be a parent (or top-level) category. If you'd like this category to be a subcategory of another category, choose the category you want to be the parent of this one.

6. (Optional) Type a description of the category in the Description text box.

Some WordPress templates are set up to display the category description directly beneath the category name (see Chapter 9). Providing a description helps you to further define the category intent for your readers. The description can be as short or as long as you like.

7. Click the Add New Category button.

That's it! You've added a new category to your blog. Armed with this information, you can add an unlimited number of categories to your blog.

You can delete a category on your blog by hovering your mouse over the title of the category you want to delete. Then click the Delete link that appears below the category title.

Deleting a category doesn't delete the posts and links in that category. Instead, posts in the deleted category are assigned to the Uncategorized category (or whatever you've named the default category).

If you have an established WordPress website with categories already created, you can convert some or all of your categories to tags. To do so, look for the Category to Tag Converter link on the right side of the Categories page in your WordPress Dashboard. Click it to convert your categories to tags. (See the following "What are tags, and how/why do I use them?" sidebar for more information.)

What are tags, and how/why do I use them?

Tags are not to be confused with categories, but a lot of people do confuse them. *Tags* are clickable, comma-separated keywords that help you microcategorize a post by defining the topics in it. In contrast to WordPress categories, tags do not have a hierarchy; there are no parent tags and child tags. If you write a post about your dog, for example, you can put that post in the Pets category — but you can also add some specific tags that let you get a whole lot more specific, such as `poodle` or `small dogs`. If someone clicks your `poodle`

tag, he finds all the posts you've ever made that contain the `poodle` tag.

Another reason to use tags: Search-engine spiders harvest tags when they crawl your site, so tags help other people find your site when they search for specific words.

You can manage your tags in the WordPress Dashboard by clicking the Tags link on the Posts menu. The Tags page opens where you can view, edit, delete, and add new tags.

Examining a Post's Address: Permalinks

Each WordPress post and page is assigned its own web page, and the address (or URL) of that page is called a *permalink*. Posts that you see in WordPress sites usually put their permalinks in any of four areas:

- ✔ The title of the blog post
- ✔ The Comments link below the post
- ✔ A separate permalink that appears (in most themes) below the post
- ✔ The titles of posts appearing in a Recent Posts sidebar

Permalinks are meant to be permanent links to your blog posts (which is where the *perma* part of that word comes from, in case you're wondering). Ideally, the permalink of a post never changes. WordPress creates the permalink automatically when you publish a new post.

By default, a permalink in WordPress looks like this:

```
http://yourdomain.com/?p=100/
```

The p stands for *post,* and 100 is the ID assigned to the individual post. You can leave the permalinks in this format if you don't mind letting WordPress associate each post with an ID number.

WordPress, however, lets you take your permalinks to the beauty salon for a bit of a makeover. I'll bet you didn't know that permalinks could be pretty, did you? They certainly can. Allow me to explain.

Making your post links pretty

Pretty permalinks are links that are more pleasing to the eye than standard links and, ultimately, more pleasing to search-engine spiders. (See Chapter 12 for an explanation of why search engines like pretty permalinks.) Pretty permalinks look something like this:

```
http://yourdomain.com/2015/02/02/pretty-permalinks/
```

Break down that URL and you see the date when the post was made, in year/month/day format. You also see the topic of the post.

To choose how your permalinks look, click Permalinks in the Settings menu. The Permalink Settings page opens, as shown in Figure 5-4.

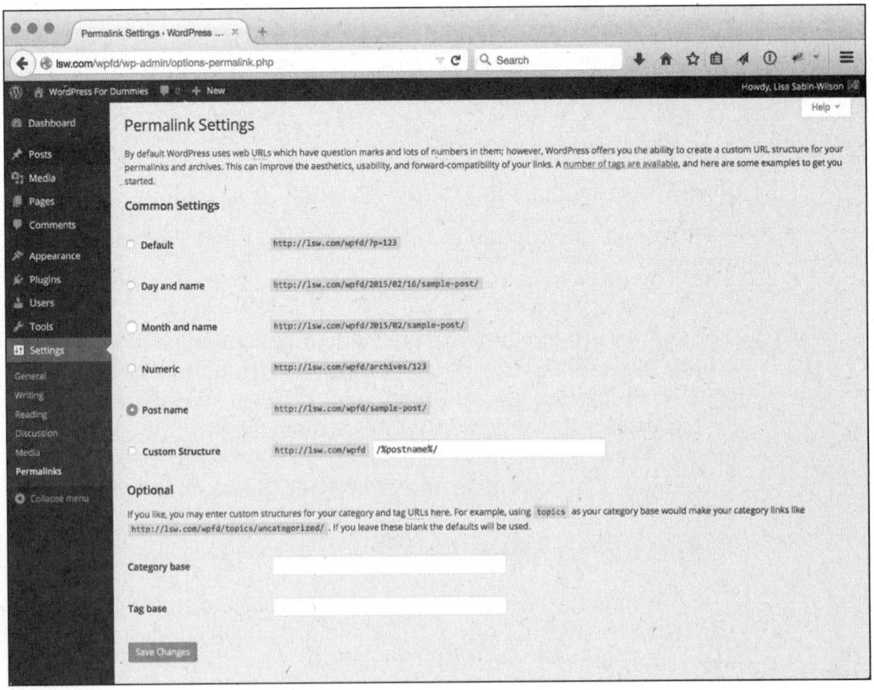

Figure 5-4:
Make your
permalinks
pretty.

On this page, you find several options for creating permalinks:

- **Default** (ugly permalinks): WordPress assigns an ID number to each post and creates the URL in this format: `http://yourdomain.com/?p=100`.

- **Day and Name** (pretty permalinks): For each post, WordPress generates a permalink URL that includes the year, month, day, and post slug/title: `http://yourdomain.com/2015/02/02/sample-post/`.

- **Month and Name** (also pretty permalinks): For each post, WordPress generates a permalink URL that includes the year, month, and post slug/title: `http://yourdomain.com/2015/02/sample-post/`.

- **Numeric** (not so pretty): WordPress assigns a numerical value to the permalink. The URL is created in this format: `http://yourdomain.com/archives/123`.

- **Post Name** (my preferred): WordPress takes the title of your post or page and generates the permalink URL from those words. For example, the name of the page that contains my bibliography of books is called simply *Books;* therefore, with this permalink structure, WordPress creates the permalink URL: `http://lisasabin-wilson.com/books`. Likewise, a post titled *WordPress is Awesome* gets a permalink URL like this: `http://lisasabin-wilson.com/wordpress-is-awesome`.

- **Custom Structure:** WordPress creates permalinks in the format you choose. You can create a custom permalink structure by using tags or variables, as I discuss in the next section.

To create a pretty-permalink structure, select the Post Name radio button; then click the Save Changes button at the bottom of the page.

Customizing your permalinks

A *custom permalink structure* is one that lets you define which variables you want to see in your permalinks by using the tags in Table 5-1.

If you want your permalink to show the year, month, day, category, and post name, select the Custom Structure radio button in the Permalink Settings page and type the following tags in the Custom Structure text box:

```
/%year%/%monthnum%/%day%/%category%/%postname%/
```

Table 5-1	Custom Permalinks
Permalink Tag	**Results**
`%year%`	4-digit year (such as `2015`)
`%monthnum%`	2-digit month (such as `02` for February)
`%day%`	2-digit day (such as `30`)
`%hour%`	2-digit hour of the day (such as `15` for 3:00 p.m.)
`%minute%`	2-digit minute (such as `45`)
`%second%`	2-digit second (such as `10`)
`%postname%`	Text — usually, the post name — separated by hyphens (such as `making-pretty-permalinks`)
`%post_id%`	The unique numerical ID of the post (such as `344`)
`%category%`	The text of the category name that you filed the post in (such as `books-i-read`)
`%author%`	The text of the post author's name (such as `lisa-sabin-wilson`)

Under this permalink format, the link for a post made on February 2, 2015, called WordPress For Dummies and filed in the Books I Read category, would look like this:

```
http://yourdomain.com/2015/02/02/books-i-read/wordpress-
      for-dummies/
```

Be sure to include the slashes (/) before tags, between tags, and at the very end of the string of tags. This format ensures that WordPress creates correct, working permalinks by using the correct `rewrite` rules located in the `.htaccess` file for your site. (See the following section for more information on `rewrite` rules and `.htaccess` files.)

Changing the structure of your permalinks in the future affects the permalinks for all the posts on your blog — new and old. Keep this fact in mind if you ever decide to change the permalink structure. An especially important reason: Search engines (such as Google and Yahoo!) index the posts on your site by their permalinks, so changing the permalink structure makes all those indexed links obsolete.

One nifty feature of WordPress is that it remembers when you change your permalink structure and automatically writes an internal redirect from the old permalink structure to the new one.

Don't forget to click the Save Changes button at the bottom of the Permalink Settings page; otherwise, your permalink changes won't be saved!

Making sure that your permalinks work with your server

After you set the format for the permalinks for your site by using any options other than the default, WordPress writes specific rules, or directives, to the .htaccess file on your web server. The .htaccess file in turn communicates to your web server how it should serve up the permalinks, according to the permalink structure you've chosen to use. To use an .htaccess file, you need to know the answers to two questions:

✔ Does your web server configuration use and give you access to the .htaccess file?

✔ Does your web server run Apache with the mod_rewrite module?

If you don't know the answers, contact your hosting provider to find out.

If the answer to both questions is yes, continue with the following steps. If the answer is no, skip to the "Working with servers that don't use Apache mod_rewrite" sidebar, later in this chapter.

You and WordPress work together in glorious harmony to create the .htaccess file that lets you use a pretty-permalink structure on your website. The file works like this:

1. **Locate the .htaccess file on your web server or create one and put it there.**

   If .htaccess already exists, you can find it in the root of your directory on your web server — that is, the same directory where you find your wp-config.php file. If you don't see it in the root directory, try changing the options of your FTP client to show hidden files. (Because the .htaccess file starts with a period [.], it may not be visible until you configure your FTP client to show hidden files.)

   If you need to create the file and put it on your web server, follow these steps:

   a. Using a plain-text editor (such as Notepad for Windows or TextEdit for a Mac), create a blank file and name it htaccess.txt.

   b. Upload htaccess.txt to your web server via FTP. (See Chapter 3 for more information about FTP.)

c. Rename the file .htaccess (notice the period at the beginning), and make sure that it is writable by the server by changing permissions to either 755 or 777. (See Chapter 3 for information on changing permissions on server files.)

2. **Create the permalink structure in the Permalink Settings page in your WordPress Dashboard.**

3. **Click the Save Changes button at the bottom of the Permalink Settings page.**

   WordPress inserts into the .htaccess file the specific rules necessary for making the permalink structure functional in your blog.

If you followed these steps correctly, you have an .htaccess file on your web server that has the correct permissions set so that WordPress can write the correct rules to it. Your pretty-permalink structure works flawlessly. Kudos!

If you open the .htaccess file and look at it now, you'll see that it's no longer blank. It should have a set of code in it called *rewrite rules,* which looks something like this:

```
# BEGIN WordPress
<IfModule mod_rewrite.c>
RewriteEngine On
RewriteBase /
RewriteCond %{REQUEST_FILENAME} !-f
RewriteCond %{REQUEST_FILENAME} !-d
RewriteRule . /index.php [L]
</IfModule>
# END WordPress
```

I could delve deeply into .htaccess and all the things you can do with this file, but I'm restricting this section to how it applies to WordPress permalink structures. If you'd like to unlock more mysteries about .htaccess, check out "Comprehensive Guide to .htaccess" at www.javascriptkit.com/howto/htaccess.shtml.

Through my experiences over the years, I have discovered that Yahoo! Hosting doesn't allow users access to the .htaccess file on its server, and it doesn't use mod_rewrite. So if you're hosting your domain on Yahoo!, use the custom permalink technique that I describe in the following sidebar, "Working with servers that don't use Apache mod_rewrite."

Working with servers that don't use Apache mod_rewrite

Using permalink structures requires that your web-hosting provider have a specific Apache module option called `mod_rewrite` activated on its servers. If your web-hosting provider doesn't have this item activated on its servers, or if you're hosting your site on a Windows server, the custom permalinks work only if you type **index.php** in front of any custom permalink tags.

For example, create the custom permalink tags like this:

```
/index.php/%year%/%monthnum%/
    %day%/%postname%/
```

This format creates a permalink like this:

```
http://yourdomain.com/
    index.php/2015/02/02/
    wordpress-for-dummies
```

You don't need an `.htaccess` file to use this permalink structure.

Discovering the Many WordPress RSS Options

In Chapter 2, you can read about RSS feed technology and why it's an important part of publishing content on the Internet. Allow me to quote myself from that chapter: For your readers to stay updated with the latest and greatest content you post to your site, they need to subscribe to your RSS feed.

RSS feeds come in different flavors, including RSS 0.92, RDF/RSS 1.0, RSS 2.0, and Atom. The differences among them lie within the base code that makes up the functionality of the syndication feed. What's important is that WordPress supports all versions of RSS — which means that anyone can subscribe to your RSS feed with any type of feed reader available.

I mention many times throughout this book that WordPress is very intuitive, and this section on RSS feeds is a shining example of a feature that WordPress automates. WordPress has a built-in feed generator that works behind the scenes to create feeds for you. This feed generator creates feeds from your posts, comments, and even categories.

The RSS feed for your posts is *autodiscoverable,* which means that almost all RSS feed readers and most browsers (Firefox, Chrome, Internet Explorer, and Safari, for example) automatically detect the RSS feed URL for a WordPress blog. Table 5-2 gives you some good guidelines on how to find the RSS feed URLs for the different sections of your blog.

Table 5-2	URLs for Built-In WordPress Feeds
Feed Type	*Example Feed URL*
RSS 0.92	`http://yourdomain.com/wp-rss.php` or `http://yourdomain.com/?feed=rss`
RDF/RSS 1.0	`http://yourdomain.com/wp-rss2.php` or `http://yourdomain.com/?feed=rdf`
RSS 2.0	`http://yourdomain.com/wp-rss2.php` or `http://yourdomain.com/?feed=rss2`
Atom	`http://yourdomain.com/wp-atom.php` or `http://yourdomain.com/?feed=atom`
Comments RSS	`http://yourdomain.com/?feed=rss&p=50` `p` stands for *post,* and `50` is the post ID. You can find the post ID in the Dashboard by clicking the Posts link. Locate a post and hover the mouse over the title to find the ID in the URL that displays in your browser status bar.
Category RSS	`http:// yourdomain.com/wp-rss2.php?cat=50` `cat` stands for *category,* and `50` is the category ID. You can find the category ID in the Dashboard by clicking the Categories link. Locate a category and hover the mouse over the title to find the ID in the URL that displays in your browser status bar.

If you're using custom permalinks (see the "Making your post links pretty" section, earlier in this chapter), you can simply add `/feed` to the end of any URL on your blog to find the RSS feed. Some of your links will look similar to these:

- ✔ `http://yourdomain.com/feed` — your main RSS feed

- ✔ `http://yourdomain.com/comments/feed` — your comments RSS feed

- ✔ `http://yourdomain.com/category/cat-name/feed` — RSS feed for a category

Try it with any URL on your site. Add `/feed` at the end and you'll have the RSS feed for that page.

RSS feeds are important parts of delivering content from your blog to your readers. RSS feeds are expected these days, so the fact that WordPress has taken care of everything for you — WordPress provides the feeds for you, is compliant with all RSS formats, and offers so many internal feeds — gives the software a huge advantage over any of the other content management systems.

Writing Your First Entry

It's finally time to write your first post on your new WordPress site! The topic you choose to write about and the writing techniques you use to get your message across are all on you; I have my hands full writing this book! I *can* tell you, however, how to write the wonderful passages that can bring you blog fame. Ready?

Composing your blog post

Composing a blog post is a lot like typing an email: You give it a title, you write the message, and you click a button to send your words into the world.

You can collapse or reposition all the modules on the Add New Post page to suit your needs. The only section on the Add New Post page that cannot be collapsed and repositioned is the section with the actual title and post box (where you write your post).

Follow these steps to write a basic post:

1. **Click the Add New link on the Posts Dashboard menu.**

   The Add New Post page opens, as shown in Figure 5-5.

2. **Type the title of your post in the Enter Title Here text field at the top of the Add New Post page.**

3. **Type the content of your post in the text box.**

   You can use the Visual Text Editor to format the text in your post. I explain the Visual Text Editor and the buttons and options after these steps.

4. **Click the Save Draft button in the Publish module, located at the top-right side of the Add New Post page.**

   The page refreshes with your post title and content saved but not yet published to your site.

By default, the area in which you write your post is in Visual Editing mode, as indicated by the Visual tab that appears above the text. Visual Editing mode is how WordPress provides WYSIWYG (What You See Is What You Get) options for formatting. Rather than have to embed HTML code in your post, you can simply type your post, highlight the text you want to format, and click the buttons (shown in Figure 5-5) that appear above the text box.

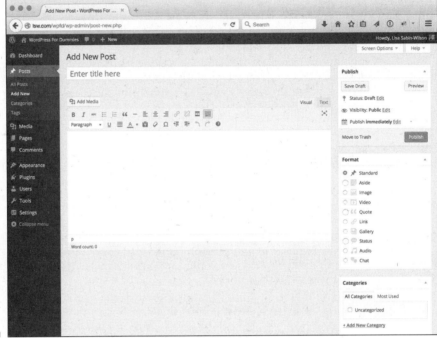

Figure 5-5:
This page is
where you
give your
post a title
and write
your post
body.

If you've ever used a word processing program, such as Microsoft Word, you'll recognize many of these buttons:

- **Bold:** Embeds the `<strong> </strong>` HTML tag to emphasize the text in bold. Example: **Bold Text.**

- **Italic:** Embeds the `<em> </em>` HTML tag to emphasize the text in italics. Example: *Italic Text.*

- **Strikethrough:** Embeds the `<strike> </strike>` HTML tag that puts a line through your text. Example: ~~Strikethrough Text~~.

- **Unordered List:** Embeds the `<ul><li> </li></ul>` HTML tags that create an unordered, or bulleted, list.

- **Ordered List:** Embeds the `<ol><li> </li></ol>` HTML tags that create an ordered, or numbered, list.

- **Blockquote:** Inserts the `<blockquote> </blockquote>` HTML tag that indents the paragraph or section of text you've selected.

- **Align Left:** Inserts the `<p align="left"> </p>` HTML tag that lines up the selected text against the left margin.

✔ **Align Center:** Inserts the `<p align="center"> </p>` HTML tag that positions the selected text in the center of the page.

✔ **Align Right:** Inserts the `<p align="right"> </p>` HTML tag that lines up the selected text against the right margin.

✔ **Insert/Edit Link:** Inserts the `<a href=" "> </a>` HTML tag around the text you've selected to create a hyperlink.

✔ **Unlink:** Removes the hyperlink from the selected text, if it was previously linked.

✔ **Insert More Tag:** Inserts the `<!--more-->` tag, which lets you split the display on your blog page. It publishes the text written above this tag with a Read More link, which takes the user to a page with the full post. This feature is good for really long posts.

✔ **Distraction-Free Writing Mode:** Lets you focus purely on writing, without the distraction of all the other options on the page. Click this button, and the post text box expands to fill the full height and width of your browser screen and displays only the barest essentials for writing your post. To bring the post text box back to its normal state, just click the Exit Fullscreen link.

✔ **Show/Hide Kitchen Sink:** I saw this button and thought, "Wow! WordPress does my dishes, too!" Unfortunately, the button's name is a metaphor that describes the advanced formatting options available with the Visual Text Editor. Click this button to make a new drop-down list that gives you options for underlining, font color, custom characters, undo and redo, and so on — a veritable kitchen sink full of text formatting options, such as:

  • *Paragraph:* Inserts the `<p> </p>` HTML tags around the text to indicate paragraph breaks.

  • *Address:* Inserts the `<address> </address>` HTML tags around the text to indicate the contact information for author or owner of a document.

  • *Preformatted:* Inserts the `<pre> </pre>` HTML tags around the text to indicate preformatted text and preserves both spaces and line breaks.

  • *Headings 1, 2, 3, 4, 5, 6:* Inserts header HTML tags such as `<H1> </H1>` around text to indicate HTML headings (H1 defines the largest, H6 defines the smallest; heading formats are usually defined in the CSS with font size and/or colors).

  • *Underline:* Inserts the `<u> </u>` HTML tags around the text to display it as underlined.

  • *Align Full:* Inserts the `<p style="text-align: justify"> </p>` HTML tag that lines up the selected text evenly between the left and right margins.

- *Text Color:* Displays the text in the color chosen.

- *Paste as Plain Text:* Useful if you copy text from another source, this option removes all formatting and special/hidden characters from the text and adds it to your post as unformatted text.

- *Paste from Word:* Useful if you're copying text from a Microsoft Word document, because Word inserts a lot of hidden HTML and characters that could make your post text look funny on your website. Use the Paste from Word feature to transfer posts from Word to WordPress to preserve formatting without the hidden mess.

- *Remove Formatting:* Removes all formatting inside the post.

- *Insert Custom Character:* If you click this option, a pop-up window appears, offering different characters such as $, %, &, and ©. In the pop-up window, click the symbol that you want to add to your post.

- *Outdent:* Moves text to the left one preset level with each click. This only works when the text has already been indented.

- *Indent:* Moves text to the right one preset level with each click.

- *Undo:* Click to undo your last formatting action.

- *Redo:* Click to redo your last formatting action.

- *Help:* Pops open a window with helpful information about using the text editor, including time-saving keyboard shortcuts.

You can turn off the Visual Text Editor by clicking the Your Profile link on the Users menu. Deselect the Use the Visual Editor When Writing box to turn off this editor if you'd rather insert the HTML code yourself in your posts.

If you'd rather embed your own HTML code and skip the Visual Text Editor, click the Text tab that appears to the right of the Visual tab. If you're planning to type HTML code in your post — for a table or video files, for example — you have to click the Text tab before you insert that code. If you don't, the Visual Text Editor formats your code, and it most likely will look nothing like you intended it to.

At this point, you can skip to the "Publishing your post" section in this chapter for information on publishing your post to your site, or continue with the following sections to discover how to refine the options for your post.

WordPress has a nifty, built-in autosave feature that saves your work while you're typing and editing a new post. If your browser crashes or you accidentally close your browser window before you've saved your post, it will be there for you when you get back. Those WordPress folks are so thoughtful!

Dressing up your posts with images, video, and audio

Directly above and to the left of the Visual Text Editor row of buttons is an Add Media area with a row of four icons. These icons let you insert images/photos, photo galleries, videos, and audio files into your posts. WordPress has an entire Media Library capability, which I describe in detail in Chapter 6.

Refining your post options

After you write the post, you can choose a few extra options before you publish it for the entire world to see. These settings apply to the post you're currently working on — not to any future or past posts. You can find these options below and to the right of the post text box (see Figure 5-6). Click the title of each option, and the settings for that specific option expand.

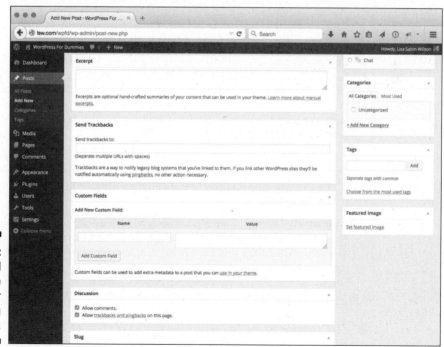

Figure 5-6:
Several options are available for your blog post.

If you do not see these options on the Add New Post page in your Dashboard, that most likely means you have not enabled them in the Screen Options (discussed in Chapter 4). Click the Screen Options tab at the top of the Add New Post page and enable the modules on this page that you would like to use.

You can reposition the different post option modules on the Add New Post page to fit the way you use this page.

Here are the options found underneath the post text box:

- **Excerpt:** Excerpts are short summaries of your posts. Many web publishers use snippets to show teasers of their posts, thereby encouraging the reader to click the Read More links to read the posts in their entirety. Type your short summary in the Excerpt box. Excerpts can be any length, in terms of words; however, the point is to keep it short and sweet and tease your readers into clicking the Read More link.

- **Send Trackbacks:** I discuss trackbacks in detail in Chapter 2. If you want to send a trackback to another site, enter the site's trackback URL in the Send Trackbacks To box. You can send trackbacks to more than one site; just be sure to separate trackback URLs with spaces.

- **Custom Fields:** Custom fields add extra data to your posts and are fully configurable.

- **Discussion:** Decide whether to let readers submit comments through the comment system by selecting the Allow Comments check box and allow trackbacks and pingbacks by selecting the Allow Trackbacks and Pingbacks on This Page check box. By default, the boxes are selected; deselect a check box to disallow comments and/or trackbacks and pingbacks on this post.

- **Slug:** By default, WordPress takes the title of your post and turns it into a permalink slug (see the "Examining a Post's Address: Permalinks" section earlier in this chapter). You can edit the permalink slug of your post in the Slug text field.

- **Author:** By default, WordPress assigns you as the author of the post. If you have multiple authors on your site, you can assign a different author to the post by selecting that person in the drop-down menu in the Author module.

Here are the options found to the right of the post text box:

- **Publish:** These are the publishing and privacy options for your post, which I cover in the upcoming "Publishing your post" section.

- **Format:** This module appears only when the theme that you're using on your site supports a WordPress feature called Post Formats (which I cover in detail in Chapter 12). In the Format module, you can select the type of format you want to use for the post you're publishing.

- **Categories:** You can file your posts in different categories to organize them by subject. (See more about organizing your posts by category in the "Staying on Topic with Categories" section at the start of this chapter.) Select the box to the left of the category you want to use. You can toggle between listing all categories and seeing just the categories you use the most by clicking the All Categories or Most Used links, respectively. Don't see the category you need listed here? Click the + Add New Category link, and you can add a category right there on the Add New Post page!

- **Tags:** Type your desired tags in the text box. Be sure to separate each tag with a comma so that WordPress knows where each tag begins and ends. Cats, Kittens, Felines represent three different tags, for example, but without the commas, WordPress would consider those three words to be one tag. Click the Add button to add the tags to your post. See the "What are tags, and how/why do I use them?" sidebar earlier in this chapter for more information on tags.

- **Featured Image:** Some WordPress themes are configured to use an image (photo) to represent each post that you have on your site. The image can display on the home/front page, blog page, archives, or anywhere within the content display on your website. If you're using a theme that has this option, you can easily define the post thumbnail by clicking the Set Featured Image link under the Featured Image module on the Add New Post page. Then you can assign an image that you've uploaded to your site as the featured image for a particular post.

When you finish setting the options for your post, don't navigate away from this page; your options have not yet been fully saved. The next section covers all the options you need for saving your post settings!

Publishing your post

You have given your new post a title and have written the content of your new post. Maybe you've even added an image or other type of media file to your blog post (see Chapter 6) and have configured the tags, categories, and other options. Now the question is, Publish? Or not publish (yet)?

WordPress gives you three options for saving or publishing your post when you're done writing it. The Publish module is located on the right side of the Add New (or Edit) Post page. Just click the title of the Publish module to expand the settings you need. Figure 5-7 shows the available options in the Publish module.

Figure 5-7:
The publish
status for
your blog
posts.

The Publish module has several options:

- **Save Draft:** Choose this option to save your post as a draft. The Edit Post page reloads with all your post contents and options saved; you can continue editing it now, tomorrow, or the next day. To access your draft posts, click the Edit link on the Posts menu.

- **Preview:** Click the Preview button to view your post in a new window, as it would appear on your live blog if you had published it. Previewing the post doesn't publish it to your site yet. It gives you the opportunity to view it on your site and check it for any formatting or content changes you'd like to make.

- **Status:** Click the Edit link to open the settings for this option. A drop-down menu appears, and you can select Draft or Pending Review:

  - Select *Draft* to save the post but not publish it to your site.

  - Select *Pending Review,* and the post shows up in your list of drafts next to a Pending Review header. This option lets the administrator of the blog know that contributors have entered posts that are waiting for administrator review and approval (helpful for sites with multiple authors).

  Click OK to save your settings.

- **Stick This Post to the Front Page:** Select this check box to have WordPress publish the post to your site and keep it at the very top of all blog posts until you change this setting.

This is otherwise known as a *sticky post*. Typically posts are displayed in chronological order on your blog, displaying the most recent post on top. If you make a post sticky, it remains at the very top no matter how many other posts you make after it. When you want to unstick the post, deselect the Stick This Post to the Front Page check box.

✔ **Password Protected:** By assigning a password to a post, you can publish a post to your blog that only you can see. You can also share the post password with a friend, who can see the content of the post after entering the password. But why would anyone want to do this? Imagine that you just ate dinner at your mother-in-law's house and she made the *worst* pot roast you've ever eaten. You can write all about it! Protect it with a password and give the password to your trusted friends so that they can read all about it without offending your mother-in-law.

✔ **Private:** Publish this post to your blog so that only you can see it — no one else will be able to see it, ever. You may want to do this for posts that are personal and private (if you're keeping a personal diary, for example).

✔ **Publish Immediately:** Click the Edit link and you can set the time stamp for your post. If you want the post to have the current time and date, ignore this setting.

If you'd like to future-publish this post, you can set the time and date for any time in the future. This feature has come in handy for me many times. For example, when I have a vacation planned and I don't want my blog to go without updates while I'm gone, I'll sit down and write a few posts and set the date for a time in the future. They're published to my site while I'm somewhere tropical, diving with the fishes.

✔ **Move to Trash:** Clicking this link sends the entire post into the Trash bin. Your post isn't deleted permanently, which is a relief if you happen to click that link by accident; instead, it's saved in the Trash where you can retrieve it later, if you want to. You can find the items in Trash by clicking the All Posts link under the Posts menu in the Dashboard; then click the Trash link.

✔ **Publish:** This button wastes no time! It bypasses all the previous draft, pending review, and sticky settings and publishes the post directly to your site immediately.

After you choose an option from the drop-down menu, click the Save button. The Add New Post page saves your publishing-status option.

If you want to publish your post right away, skip all the other options in the Publish module and just click the Publish button. This method eliminates the fuss with the Publish Status options and sends your new post to your site in all its glory.

If you click Publish and for some reason don't see the post you just published on your live site, you probably left the Publish Status drop-down menu set to Unpublished. Your new post is in the draft posts, which you'll find by clicking the All Posts on the Posts menu.

Editing your post

While I write this book, I have editors looking over my shoulder, making recommendations, correcting my typos and grammatical errors, and helping me by telling me when I get too long-winded.

You, on the other hand, are not so lucky! You are your own editor and have full control of what you write, when you write it, and how you write it. You can always go back and edit previous posts to correct typos, grammatical errors, and other mistakes by following these steps:

1. **Find the post that you want to edit by clicking the All Posts link in the Posts menu.**

   The Posts page opens and lists the 20 most recent posts you've made to your blog.

   You can filter that listing of posts by date from the Show All Dates drop-down menu at the top of the Posts page. For example, if you choose February 2015, the Posts page reloads, displaying only those posts that were published in the month of February 2015.

   You can also filter the post listing by category. Select your desired category from the View All Categories drop-down menu.

2. **When you find the post you need, click its title.**

   The Edit Post window opens. In this window, you can edit the post and/or any of its options.

   You can also click the Edit link that appears beneath the post title on the Posts page.

   If you need to edit only the post options, click the Quick Edit link. The post options open, and you can configure post options such as the title, status, password, categories, tags, comments, and time stamp. Click the Save button to save your changes without ever leaving the Post page in your Dashboard.

3. **Edit your post; then click the Update button.**

   The Edit Post window refreshes with all your changes saved.

Look Who's Talking on Your Site

The feature that really catapulted blogging into the limelight is the comments feature, which lets visitors interact with the authors of sites. I cover the concept of comments and trackbacks in Chapter 2. They provide a great way for readers to interact with site owners, and vice versa.

Managing comments and trackbacks

To find your comments, click the Comments link in the Dashboard navigation menu; the Comments page opens. See Figure 5-8.

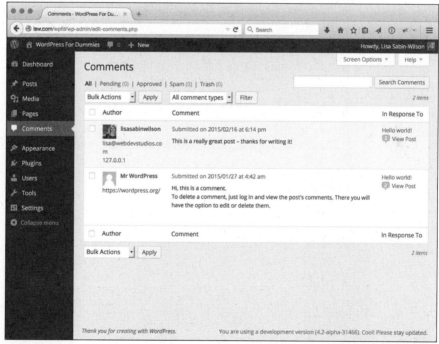

Figure 5-8: Clicking the Comments menu shows you the Comments page, with all the comments and trackbacks on your site.

When you hover your mouse pointer over your comments, several links appear that give you the opportunity to manage those comments:

✔ **Unapprove:** This link appears only if you have comment moderation turned on and with only approved comments. The comment is placed in the moderation queue, which you get to by clicking the Awaiting

Moderation link that appears below the Manage Comments header. The moderation queue is kind of a holding area for comments that haven't yet been published to your blog. (See the following section for more on the moderation queue.)

- ✔ **Reply:** Click this link and a text box drops down, into which you can type and submit your reply to the person who commented. This feature eliminates the need to have to load your live site to reply to a comment.

- ✔ **Quick Edit:** Click this link and, without ever leaving the Comments page, the comment options open, and you can configure the post options such as name, email, URL, and comment content. Click the Save button to save your changes.

- ✔ **Edit:** Click this link to open the Edit Comment page, where you can edit the different fields such as name, email, URL, and comment content. See Figure 5-9.

- ✔ **Spam:** Click this link to mark the comment as spam and toss it into the spam bin, where it will never be heard from again!

- ✔ **Trash:** This link does exactly what it says; it sends the comment to the trash can and deletes it from your blog.

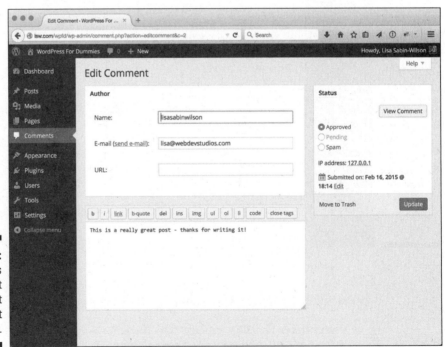

Figure 5-9: Edit a user's comment in the Edit Comment page.

If you have a lot of comments listed in the Comments page and want to bulk-manage them, select the boxes to the left of all the comments you want to manage, then select one of the following from the Actions drop-down menu at the top left of the Comments page: Approve, Mark As Spam, Unapprove, or Delete.

Moderating comments and trackbacks

If you have your options set so that comments aren't published to your site until you approve them, you can approve comments from the Comments page as well. Just click the Pending link on the Comments page and you go to the Edit Comments page. If you have comments and/or trackbacks awaiting moderation, you see them on this page and you can approve them, mark them as spam, or delete them.

A nice feature of WordPress is that it immediately notifies you of any comments sitting in the moderation queue, awaiting your action. This notification appears as a small circle to the right of the Comments menu in the left navigation menu on every single page. Figure 5-10 shows my Dashboard page with an indicator in the Comments menu that I have 1 comment awaiting moderation (there is also an indicator in the top toolbar).

Tackling spam with Akismet

I touch on Akismet a few times throughout this book because it's my humble opinion that Akismet is the mother of all plugins and that no WordPress blog is complete without a fully activated version of Akismet running in it.

Apparently WordPress agrees, because the plugin is packaged in every WordPress software release beginning with version 2.0. Akismet was created by the folks at Automattic — the same folks who brought you the WordPress.com-hosted version (discussed in Chapter 1). Automattic also works with some of the original developers of the WordPress software platform.

Akismet is the answer to combatting comment and trackback spam. Matt Mullenweg of Automattic says that Akismet is a "collaborative effort to make comment and trackback spam a non-issue and restore innocence to blogging, so you never have to worry about spam again" (from the Akismet website at http://akismet.com).

Indicators show how many comments are waiting.

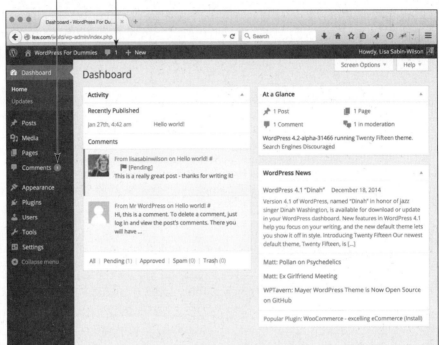

Figure 5-10: These indicators tell me I have comments awaiting moderation.

I've been blogging since 2002. I started blogging with the Movable Type blogging platform and moved to WordPress in 2003. As blogging became more and more popular, comment and trackback spam became more and more of a nuisance. One morning in 2004, I found that 2,300 pieces of disgusting comment spam had been published to my blog. Something had to be done! The folks at Automattic did a fine thing with Akismet. Since the emergence of Akismet, I've barely had to think about comment or trackback spam except for the few times a month I check my Akismet spam queue.

I talk in greater detail about plugin use in WordPress in Chapter 7, where you find out how to activate Akismet and make sure that it's protecting your blog from trackback and comment spam.

Part III

Flexing and Extending WordPress

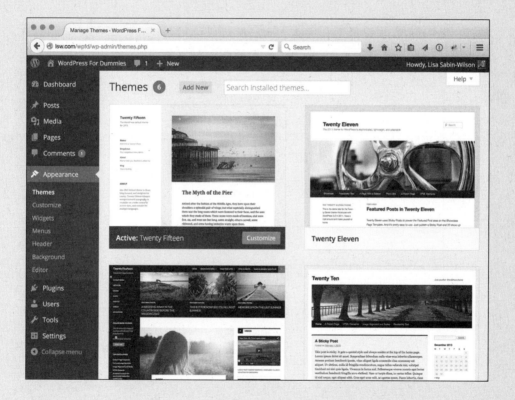

Learn how to change the layout of your WordPress Dashboard at
www.dummies.com/extras/wordpress.

In this part. . .

- ✔ Learn how to use the WordPress Media Library to manage images and media.

- ✔ Embed videos in your content to provide media for your readers to interact with.

- ✔ Discover, download, and install plugins for WordPress to extend the features available on your website.

- ✔ Find and install WordPress themes that give your website a great visual look.

Chapter 6

Media Management: Images, Audio, and Video

In This Chapter

▶ Adding images, photo galleries, and videos to your posts

▶ Uploading audio files

▶ Exploring the WordPress Media Library

*A*dding images and photos to your posts and pages can really dress up the content. By using images and photos, you give your content a dimension that you can't express in plain text. Through visual imagery, you can call attention to your content and improve the delivery of the message by adding depth to it.

The same goes for adding video and audio files to your posts and pages. Video lets you provide entertainment through moving, talking (or singing!), and streaming video. Audio files let you talk to your visitors and add a personal touch. Many website owners use video and audio to report news and to broadcast Internet radio and television shows. The possibilities are endless!

In this chapter, you discover how to enhance your website by adding images, video, and audio to your content. And you even find out how to run a full-fledged photo gallery on your site, all through the WordPress.org software and its integrated Media Library.

You add these extras to your site in the Upload/Insert area of the Add New Post page. You can add them as you're writing your post or come back and add them later. The choice is yours!

Inserting Images into Your Content

Adding images to a post is easy with the WordPress image uploader. Jump right in and give it a go by clicking the Add Media button on the Add New Post page. The Insert Media window opens and lets you choose images from your hard drive or from a location on the web. See Figure 6-1.

To add a link to an external image from the web after you click the Add Media button, follow these steps:

1. **Click the Insert from URL link in the Insert Media window.**

   The Insert from URL window opens.

2. **Type the URL (Internet address) of the image in the URL text box.**

   Type the full URL, including the `http` and www portions of the address. You can easily find the URL of any image on the web by right-clicking (PC) or Control-clicking (Mac) and selecting Properties from the menu.

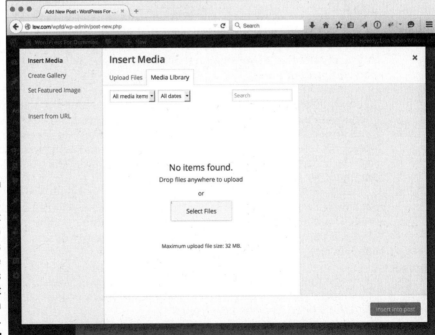

Figure 6-1:
Insert images into your posts with the WordPress Insert Media window.

3. **Type in the text you want displayed for the image link in the Link Text box.**

4. **Click the Insert into Post button.**

To add an image from your own computer's hard drive after you click the Add Media button, follow these steps:

1. **Click the Add Media link and then click the Select Files button.**

   A dialog box opens from which you can select an image (or multiple images) from your hard drive.

2. **Select your image(s); then click Open.**

   The image is uploaded from your computer to your web server. WordPress displays a progress bar on the upload and displays an image options box when the upload is finished.

3. **Edit the details for the image(s) by configuring the options that display to the right of the Insert Media window.**

   After an image is uploaded, the right side of the Insert Media window (see Figure 6-2) contains several image options:

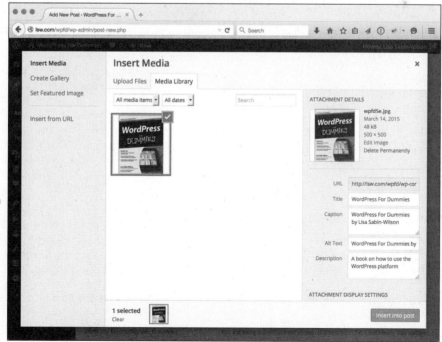

Figure 6-2:
You can set several options for your images after you upload them.

- *URL:* The direct web address to the image file (note that this is not editable by you).

- *Title:* Type a title for the image.

- *Caption:* Type a caption for the image (such as **My beautiful grand-daughter enjoying the beautiful Spring weather**).

- *Alt Text:* Type the alternate text for the image.

- *Description:* Type a description of the image.

- *Alignment:* Choose None, Left, Center, or Right. (See Table 6-1 for styling information regarding image alignment.)

Table 6-1	Styling Techniques for Image Alignment
Image Alignment	*Add This to Your Stylesheet (style.css)*
None	`img.alignnone {margin: 5px 0 5px 0;}`
Left	`img.alignleft {float:left; margin: 5px 10px 5px 0px;}`
Center	`img.aligncenter {display:block margin: 5px auto;}`
Right	`img.alignright {float:right; margin: 5px 0 5px 10px;}`

- *Link To:* Choose what you want the image linked to. Whatever option you choose determines where your readers go when they click the image you've uploaded. Type in your own URL or select one of four available presets: None (if you don't want the image to be clickable); Media File (readers can click through to the direct image); Attachment Page (readers can click through to the post the image appears in); or Custom URL (readers can click through to the URL that you type in).

- *Size:* Choose Thumbnail, Medium, Large, or Full Size.

WordPress automatically creates small and medium-size versions of the images you upload through the built-in image uploader. A *thumbnail* is a smaller version of the original file. You can edit the size of the thumbnail by clicking the Settings link and then clicking Media. In the Image Sizes section, designate your desired height and width of the small and medium thumbnail images generated by WordPress.

If you're uploading more than one image, skip to the "Inserting a photo gallery" section later in this chapter.

4. **Click the Edit Image link to the right of the thumbnail image (refer to Figure 6-2) to edit the appearance of the image. Be sure to click Save after you've edited the image.**

   The image editor (shown in Figure 6-3) options include the following tools:

   - *Crop:* Cut the image down to a smaller size.
   - *Rotate counterclockwise:* Rotate the image to the left.
   - *Rotate clockwise:* Rotate the image to the right.
   - *Flip vertically:* Flip the image upside down and back again.
   - *Flip horizontally:* Flip the image from right to left and back again.
   - *Undo:* Undo any changes you've made.
   - *Redo:* Redo image edits that you've undone.
   - *Scale Image:* Allows you to set a specific width and height for the image.

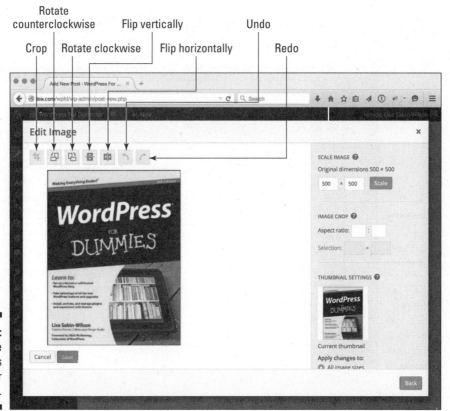

Figure 6-3: The WordPress image editor options.

5. Click the Insert into Post button.

You can find the Insert into Post button at the bottom of the Insert Media window (refer to Figure 6-1). The image uploader window closes, and you return to the Add New Post page (or the Add New Page page, if you're writing a page). WordPress has inserted the HTML to display the image in your post, as shown in Figure 6-4; you can continue editing your post, save it, or publish it.

To see the actual image and not the code, click the Visual tab that's just above the post text box.

Aligning your images

When you upload your image, you can set the alignment for your image as None, Left, Center, or Right. The WordPress theme you're using, however, may not have these alignment styles in its stylesheet. If you set the alignment to Left, for example, but the image on your site doesn't appear to be aligned at all, you may need to add a few styles to your theme's stylesheet.

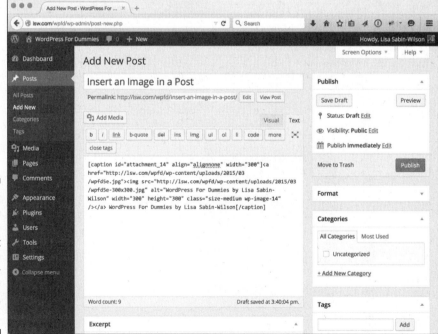

Figure 6-4:
WordPress inserts the correct HTML code for your uploaded image into your post.

I discuss themes and templates in detail in Part IV, but for the purpose of making sure that you have the correct image alignment for your newly uploaded images, here is a quick-and-dirty method:

1. **Click the Editor link in the Appearance menu.**

   The Edit Themes page opens. All the template files for your active theme are listed on the right side of the page.

2. **Click the Stylesheet template.**

   The Stylesheet (`style.css`) template opens in the text box on the left side of the page.

3. **Add your desired styles to the stylesheet.**

Refer to Table 6-1 for the styles you can add to your stylesheet to make sure that image-alignment styling is in your theme.

These styles are just examples of what you can do. Get creative with your own styling. See Chapter 10 for more information about using CSS (Cascading Style Sheets) to add style to your theme(s).

Inserting a photo gallery

You can also use the WordPress media uploader to insert a full photo gallery into your posts. Upload multiple images once you are in the Insert Media window; then, instead of clicking the Insert into Post button, click the Create Gallery link on the left side of the Insert Media window, as shown in Figure 6-5.

This link opens the Create Gallery window, along with the multiple images you uploaded. All of the images are selected, as indicated by the check mark shown at the upper right side of the image (you can deselect any image to exclude it from the gallery by clicking the check mark).

Follow these steps to insert a photo gallery into a blog post:

1. **Click the Create a New Gallery button.**

   The button is located at the bottom right of the Create Gallery window. This opens the Edit Gallery window.

2. **(Optional) Edit the gallery images.**

   If you would like to re-arrange the images, you can drag and drop the images to appear in the order you would like them to be displayed on your website. You can also include a short caption for each image by clicking the text box beneath each image and typing in your desired text.

Create Gallery link

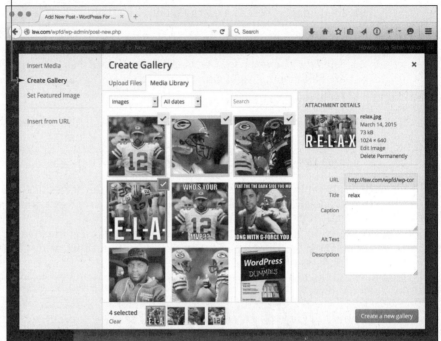

Figure 6-5:
Insert
a photo
gallery
into a post
by using
the Create
Gallery link.

3. Configure the Gallery Settings.

Located on the right side of the Edit Gallery window, these options include:

Link To: Use the drop-down menu to select the Attachment Page, Media File, or None.

Columns: Select the number of columns you would like the gallery thumbnails to be displayed in. Options in the drop-down menu include 1 to 9 columns.

Random Order: This box is deselected, by default. Selecting this box tells WordPress to ignore the defined order of images and orders them randomly on the page instead.

Size: This drop-down menu allows you to select the desired size of the images: Thumbnail, Medium, Large, or Full Size.

4. Click the Insert Gallery button.

WordPress inserts into your post a piece of shortcode that looks like this: `[gallery]`.

Table 6-2 shows some gallery shortcodes that you can use to manually set the display settings for your photo gallery.

Table 6-2	Gallery Shortcode Examples
Gallery Shortcode	*Output*
`[gallery columns="4" size="medium"]`	A four-column gallery containing medium-size images
`[gallery columns="10" id="215" size="thumbnail"]`	A ten-column gallery containing thumbnail images pulled from the blog post with the ID 215
`[gallery captiontag="p" icontag="span"]`	A three-column (default) gallery in which each image is surrounded by `<span></span>` tags and the image caption is surrounded by `<p></p>` tags

5. **(Optional) Change the order of appearance of the images in the gallery, as well as the markup (HTML tags or CSS selectors):**

   • `captiontag`: Change the markup that surrounds the image caption by altering the gallery shortcode. For example: `[gallery captiontag="div"]` places `<div></div>` tags around the image caption (the `<div>` tag is considered a block-level element and creates a separate container for the content); to have the gallery appear on a line of its own, the `[gallery captiontag="p"]` code places `<p class="gallery-caption"></p>` tags around the image caption. The default markup for the `captiontag` option is `dd`.

   • `icontag`: Defines the HTML markup around each individual thumbnail image in your gallery. Change the markup around the `icontag` (thumbnail icon) of the image by altering the gallery shortcode to something like `[gallery icontag="p"]`, which places `<p class="gallery-icon"></p>` tags around each thumbnail icon. The default markup for `icontag` is `dt`.

   • `itemtag`: Defines the HTML markup around each item in your gallery. Change the markup around the `itemtag` (each item) in the gallery by altering the gallery shortcode to something like `[gallery itemtag="span"]`, which places `<span class="gallery-item"></span>` tags around each item in the gallery. The default markup for the `itemtag` is `dl`.

   • `orderby`: Defines the order that the images are displayed within your gallery. Change the order used to display the thumbnails in the gallery by altering the gallery shortcode to something like `[gallery orderby="menu_order ASC"]`, which displays the thumbnails in ascending menu order. Another parameter you can use is `ID_order ASC`, which displays the thumbnails in ascending order according to their IDs.

6. Define the style of the `<span>` tags in your CSS stylesheet.

The `<span>` tags create an inline element; an element contained within a `<span>` tag stays on the same line as the element before it; there is no line break. You need a little knowledge of CSS to alter the `<span>` tags. Click the Editor link in the Appearance menu in your WordPress Dashboard to edit the stylesheet for your theme. Here's an example of what you can add to the stylesheet (`style.css`) for your current theme:

```
span.gallery-icon img {
    padding: 3px;
    background: white;
    border: 1px solid black;
    margin: 0 5px;
}
```

Placing this bit of CSS in the stylesheet (`style.css`) of your active theme automatically places a one-pixel black border around each thumbnail, with three pixels of padding and a white background. The left and right margins are five pixels wide, creating nice spacing between images in the gallery.

7. Click the Update File button to save changes to your stylesheet (`style.css`) template.

Figure 6-6 shows my post with my photo gallery displayed, using the default gallery styling.

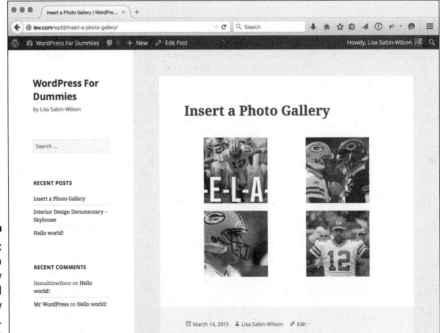

Figure 6-6:
A photo gallery inserted into my post.

WordPress gallery plugins

Here is a handful of great plugins:

- **NextGEN Gallery by Alex Rabe** (https://wordpress.org/plugins/nextgen-gallery): Create sortable photo galleries and more.

- **Gallery by BestWebSoft** (https://wordpress.org/plugins/gallery-plugin): Implement as many galleries as you want with multiple photos and a description for each gallery; show them all at once or as individual galleries.

- **Slideshow Gallery by Antonie Potgieter** (https://wordpress.org/plugins/slideshow-gallery): Use this JavaScript-powered slideshow gallery to display multiple galleries inside a dynamic slideshow.

- **WP Easy Gallery by Tyson Hahn** (https://wordpress.org/plugins/wp-easy-gallery): Create and manage multiple galleries using WordPress shortcodes for easy integration.

Matt Mullenweg, co-founder of the WordPress platform, created an extensive photo gallery by using the built-in gallery options in WordPress. Check out the fabulous photo gallery at http://ma.tt/category/gallery/.

Some great WordPress plugins work in tandem with the WordPress gallery feature. Check out Chapter 7 for information on how to install and use WordPress plugins in your website.

Inserting Video Files into Your Posts

Whether you're producing your own videos for publication or want to embed other people's videos that you find interesting, placing a video file in a post or page has never been easier with WordPress.

Check out a good example of a video blog at www.thedogfiles.com. The Dog Files is a website about dogs and the people who love them; the site serves up videos for information and entertainment.

Several video galleries on the web today allow you to add videos to blog posts; Google's YouTube (https://www.youtube.com) is a good example of a third-party video service that allows you to share videos. To add a video from the web, click the Add Media icon and then click the Insert from URL link and follow these steps:

1. Type the URL (Internet address) of the video in the URL text box.

Type the full URL, including the http and www portions of the address. Video providers, such as YouTube, usually list the direct link for the video file on their sites; you can copy and paste it into the URL text box.

2. **(Optional) Type the title of the video in the Title text box.**

Giving a title to the video allows you to provide a bit of a description of the video. It's a good idea to provide a title if you can so that your readers know what the video is about.

3. **Click the Insert into Post button.**

A link to the video is inserted into your post. WordPress doesn't embed the actual video in the post; it inserts only a link to the video. Your blog visitors click the link to load another page where the video can be played.

The previous steps give you the ability to insert a hyperlink that your readers can click and view the video on another website (such as YouTube.com). WordPress also has a nifty feature called Auto-Embed that automatically embeds videos within your posts and pages when you simply type the URL for the video into the body of your post or page.

WordPress automatically detects that a URL you typed in your post is a video from YouTube (for example) and automatically wraps the correct HTML embed code around that URL to make sure that the video player displays in your post (in a standards- and XHTML-compliant way).

You do not need to do anything to enable the Auto-Embed feature — this is built into WordPress and it does it for you automatically.

Currently, WordPress automatically detects and then embeds videos from several video providers, such as blip.tv, DailyMotion, Flickr, FunnyOrDie. com, Hulu, Instagram, Photobucket, PollDaddy, Rdio, Revision3, Scribd, SlideShare, SmugMug, SoundCloud, Spotify, Twitter, Vimeo, YouTube, and WordPress.tv. Find out more about these services, including the full list of videos sites you can embed from, in the WordPress Codex: `http://codex. wordpress.org/Embeds`.

To upload and publish a video from your computer, click the Add Media icon on the Edit Post or Add New Post page. Then follow these steps:

1. **Click the Select Files button.**

An Open dialog box opens.

2. **Select the video file you want to upload and click Open (or double-click the file).**

You return to the file uploader window in WordPress, which shows a progress bar while your video uploads. When the upload is complete, a box containing several options drops down.

3. **Type a title for the file in the Title text box.**

4. **Type a caption for the file in the Caption text box.**

5. **Type a description of the file in the Description text box.**

6. **Select the Attachment Display Settings.**

   In the Attachment Display Settings drop-down menu, you can select Embed Media Player (embeds the video file in a video player on your site); Link to Media File (inserts the title of the video file, linked to the file itself); or Link to Attachment Page (inserts the title of the video file, linked to a page containing the file).

7. **Click the Insert into Post button.**

Inserting Audio Files into Your Posts

Audio files can be music files or a recording of you speaking to your readers. Audio adds a nice personal touch to your blog, and you can easily share audio files on your blog through the use of the Upload Audio feature in WordPress. After you've inserted an audio file in your blog posts, your readers can listen to it on their computers or download it onto an MP3 player and listen to it while they drive to work.

Click the Add Media icon on the Edit Post or Add New Post page and follow these steps to upload an audio file to your blog post:

1. **Click the Select Files button.**

   An Open dialog box opens.

2. **Choose the file you want to upload and click Open (or double-click the file).**

   You return to the file uploader window in WordPress, which shows a progress bar while your audio file uploads. When the upload is complete, a box containing several options drops down.

3. **Type a title for the file in the Title text box.**

4. **Type a caption for the file in the Caption text box.**

5. **Type a description of the file in the Description text box.**

6. **Configure the Attachment Display Settings.**

   In the Attachment Display Settings drop-down menu, you can select Embed Media Player (embeds the audio file in an audio player on your site); Link to Media File (inserts the title of the audio file, linked to the file itself); or Link to Attachment Page (inserts the title of the audio file, linked to a post containing the file).

7. Click the Insert into Post button.

The audio file is inserted into your post using the method you selected in Step 6.

Some great WordPress plugins for audio handling can enhance the functionality of the file uploader and help you manage audio files in your blog posts. Check out Chapter 7 for information on how to install and use WordPress plugins in your blog.

Keeping Media Files Organized

If you've been running your blog for any length of time, you can easily forget what files you've uploaded with the WordPress uploader. I used to have to log in to my web server via FTP and view the Uploads folder to see what I had in there. Now, the WordPress Media Library makes it very convenient and easy to discover which files are in your Uploads folder.

To find an image, video, or audio file that you've already uploaded using the file uploader and use that file in a new post, follow these steps on the Add New Post page:

1. Click the Add Media button to open the Insert Media window.

2. Click the Media Library link at the top.

You see all the files you've ever uploaded to your blog with the file uploader feature; see Figure 6-7. Files you've uploaded through other methods, such as FTP, are not displayed in the Media Library.

3. Select the file you want to reuse by clicking on the image.

The Attachment Details panel displays on the right side of the Insert Media window.

4. Set the options for that image: Title, Caption, Description, Link URL, Order, Alignment, and Size.

5. Click the Insert into Post button.

The correct HTML code is inserted into the post text box.

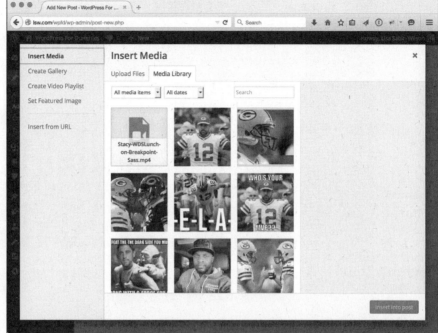

Figure 6-7:
The Media
Library
shows all
the files
you've ever
uploaded to
your blog.

If you want to view only the files you've uploaded and don't need a particular image or file for a new post, click the Library link in the Media menu, which opens the Media Library page. The Media Library page lists all the files you've ever uploaded to your WordPress blog. By default, the page displays all types of files, but you can click the Images, Audio, or Video links to specify which file type you want to see; see Figure 6-8.

You can do the following tasks on the Media Library page:

- ✔ **Filter media files by date.** If you want to view all media files that were uploaded in December 2015, choose that date from the drop-down menu. The page reloads and displays only the media files uploaded in the month of December 2015.

- ✔ **Search media files using a specific keyword.** If you want to search your Media Library for all files that reference kittens, type the word **kittens** in the Search box in the upper-right side of the Media Library page. The page reloads and displays only media files that contain the keyword or tag of `kittens`.

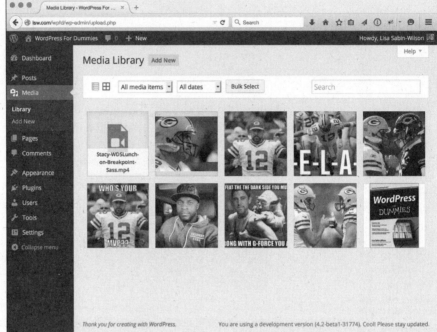

Figure 6-8:
Manage
your media
files with the
WordPress
Media
Library
page.

✔ **Delete media files.** Click the image you want to delete, and the Attachment Detail window opens. Click the Delete Permanently link, and WordPress pops up an alert that says "You are about to permanently delete this item. 'Cancel' to stop. 'OK' to delete — click OK to permanently delete the file."

✔ **View media files.** On the Media Library page, click the thumbnail of the file you'd like to view, and the Attachment Details page opens with the image displayed.

WordPress video and audio plugins

There are some great WordPress plugins for audio and video handling. Check out Chapter 7 for information on how to install and use WordPress plugins.

Here is a handful of great plugins for audio:

- **CP Media Player** (`https://wordpress.org/plugins/audio-and-video-player/`): Associate a playlist to your media player and change its looks to match the design of your blog as closely as possible.

- **Compact WP Audio Player** (`https://wordpress.org/plugins/compact-wp-audio-player/`): Used to embed an mp3 audio file on your WordPress post or page using a shortcode. The audio player is cute and compact and will play on all major browsers.

- **PowerPress by Angelo Mandato** (`https://wordpress.org/plugins/powerpress/`): This plugin supports several media formats and automatically creates a podcast RSS feed. It is up to date with the latest iTunes podcasting specifications.

Here is a handful of great plugins for video:

- **VideoPress by Automattic** (`https://wordpress.org/plugins/video`): The VideoPress plugin allows site administrators to upload new videos to their WordPress.com video account and manage existing videos from the convenience of their self-hosted WordPress.org blog's administrative interface. A VideoPress account is required: `http://videopress.com`, as well as an account on WordPress.com: `https://wordpress.com`.

- **Smart YouTube PRO by Vladimir Prelovac** (`https://wordpress.org/plugins/smart-youtube`): With this plugin, insert videos into blog posts, comments, and RSS feeds. It currently supports videos from YouTube, Vimeo, Metacafe, LiveLeak, and Facebook.

Chapter 7

Making the Most of WordPress Plugins

*H*alf the fun of running a WordPress-powered website is playing with the hundreds of plugins that you can install to extend your site's functions and options. WordPress plugins are like those really cool custom rims you put on your car: Although they don't come with the car, they're awesome accessories that make your car better than all the rest.

By itself, WordPress is a very powerful program for web publishing, but by customizing WordPress with *plugins* — add-on programs that give WordPress almost limitless ways to handle web content — you can make it even more powerful. You can choose any plugins you need to expand your online possibilities. Plugins can turn your WordPress installation into a full-featured gallery for posting images on the web, an online store to sell your products, a user forum, or a social networking site. WordPress plugins can be simple, adding, say, a few minor features, or they can be complex enough to change your entire WordPress site's functionality.

In this chapter, you find out what plugins are, how to find and install them, and how they enhance your site to make it unique. Using plugins can also greatly improve your readers' experiences by providing them various tools to interact and participate — just the way you want them to!

Developing plugins — a community activity

Although plugins are written and developed by people who have the skills required to do so, the WordPress user community is also largely responsible for the ongoing development of plugins. Ultimately, the end users are the ones who put those plugins to the true test in their own sites. Those same users are also the first to speak up and let the developers know when something isn't working right, helping the developers troubleshoot and fine-tune their plugins.

The most popular plugins are created by developers who encourage open communication with the user base. Overall, WordPress is one of those great open source projects in which the relationship between developers and users fosters a creative environment that keeps the project fresh and exciting every step of the way.

In this chapter, I assume that you already have WordPress installed on your web server. If you're skipping around in the book and haven't yet installed WordPress on your web server, you can find instructions in Chapter 3.

WordPress.com users can't install or configure plugins on their hosted blogs. I don't make the rules, so please don't kill the messenger.

Finding Out What Plugins Are

A *plugin* is a small program that, when added to WordPress, interacts with the software to provide some extensibility to the software. Plugins aren't part of the core software, nor are they software programs themselves. They typically don't function as standalone software. They do require the host program (WordPress, in this case) to function.

Plugin developers are the people who write these gems and share them with the rest of us — usually for free. As is WordPress, many plugins are free to anyone who wants to further tailor and customize a site to meet specific needs.

Literally thousands of plugins are available for WordPress — certainly way too many for me to list in this chapter alone. I could, but then you'd need heavy machinery to lift this book off the shelf! So here are just a few examples of things that plugins let you add to your WordPress blog:

✔ **Email notification:** Your biggest fans can sign up to have an email notification sent to them every time you update your website.

✔ **Submit your website to social networking services:** Allow your readers to submit your content to some of the most popular social networking services such as Digg, Twitter, Facebook, and Reddit.

✔ **Stats program:** Keep track of where your traffic is coming from; which posts on your site are the most popular; and how much traffic is coming through your website on a daily, monthly, and yearly basis.

Chapter 15 gives you a peek at some of the most popular plugins on the scene today. In the meantime, this chapter takes you through the process of finding plugins, installing them in your WordPress blog, and managing and troubleshooting them.

Exploring the Plugins page

Before you start installing plugins on your site, it's important for you to explore the Plugins page on your WordPress Dashboard and understand how to manage the plugins after you install them. Click the Installed Plugins link in the Plugins menu on your WordPress Dashboard to view the Plugins page shown in Figure 7-1.

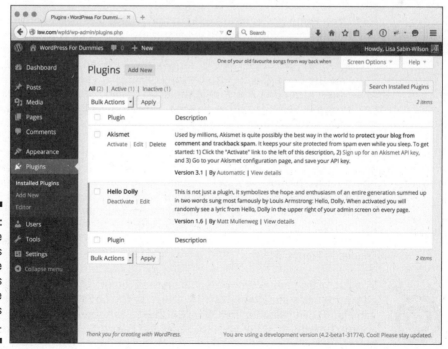

Figure 7-1: Manage your plugins with the Plugins page on the WordPress Dashboard.

The Plugins page is where you manage all the plugins you install on your WordPress site. By default, the Plugins page displays a full listing of all the WordPress plugins you currently have installed. You can filter the listing of plugins using the links shown directly below the Plugins page title:

- ✔ **All:** This is the default view for the Plugins page and shows a listing of all plugins currently installed on your WordPress website, whether they are active or not.

- ✔ **Active:** Clicking this link shows a list of the plugins that are currently activated and in use on your WordPress website.

- ✔ **Inactive:** Clicking this link changes the display and shows the list of plugins that are installed but not currently active. (*Note:* This link displays on the Plugins page only if you have inactive plugins.)

- ✔ **Recently Active:** This link appears only if you have deactivated a plugin recently. It's helpful if you know that you've deactivated a plugin, but cannot remember which one.

- ✔ **Must Use:** This link appears only if you have plugins installed in the /wp-content/mu-plugins folder. Must-Use plugins are standard WordPress plugins that need to be manually installed (usually by a developer) and do not give the site administrators the ability to remove or deactivate them from the Dashboard.

- ✔ **Drop-Ins:** A few select plugins actually have files that change the behavior of WordPress so substantially that it lets you know about it, just in case there's a question later. These plugins drop files into the wp-content directory that modify the core settings of WordPress (mostly having to do with caching or other server-specific settings). These files don't show up in the main plugin listing because they typically belong to other plugins. The Drop-Ins link appears only if you have drop-in plugins installed.

With a quick glance at the Plugins page, you can easily tell which plugins are active — and which aren't — by the background color of each plugin listed. A blue background means that the plugin is active. A white background means that the plugin *is not* active. In Figure 7-1, the background of the Akismet plugin is white and the background of the Hello Dolly plugin is blue. Akismet isn't active, but Hello Dolly is (the figures in this book are black and white, so you cannot see the blue color — but you can see the different darker/lighter shades in Figure 7-1).

You can mass-manage your plugins on the Plugins page. You can deactivate all your plugins simultaneously by selecting the box to the left of each plugin name and then selecting Deactivate in the Bulk Actions drop-down menu at the top or bottom of the page (as shown in Figure 7-1). Then click the Apply button. Likewise, you can activate, upgrade, or delete the plugins listed by selecting Activate, Update, or Delete in the Bulk Actions drop-down menu. To quickly select all your plugins with one click, select the box to the left of the Plugin heading on the Plugins page.

The Plugins page displays plugins in two columns, which give details for each plugin:

✔ **Plugin:** This column lists the plugin name so that you can find it easily when browsing the Plugins page. Directly beneath the plugin name, you see a few links for easy plugin management:

  • *Activate:* This link appears below the title of only inactive plugins. Click the link to activate a plugin.

  • *Deactivate:* This link appears below the title of only active plugins. Click the link to deactivate a plugin.

  • *Delete:* This link appears below the title of only inactive plugins. Click the link to delete the plugin from your site. (See more about this topic in the "Uninstalling Plugins" section later in this chapter.)

  • *Edit:* This link appears below all listed plugins, whether they are active or not. Click the link to visit the Edit Plugins page. If you feel comfortable doing so, you can edit the individual plugin files.

Sometimes, a plugin will have a separate settings page; in that case, an additional link labeled Settings is displayed underneath the plugin name. Clicking that link takes you to the settings page for that plugin.

✔ **Description:** This column lists a description for the plugin. Depending on the plugin, you may also see brief instructions on using the plugin. Directly below the description are the version number of the plugin, the plugin author's name, and a link to the website where you can read more information about the plugin.

Discovering the one-click plugin update

For a lot of reasons, mainly security reasons and feature updates, always use the most up-to-date versions of the plugins in your blog. With everything you have to do every day, how can you possibly keep up with knowing whether the plugins you're using have been updated?

You don't have to. WordPress does it for you.

Figure 7-2 shows an out-of-date version (2.5.9) of Akismet installed. WordPress notifies you when a new update is available for a plugin in four different ways, as shown in Figure 7-2:

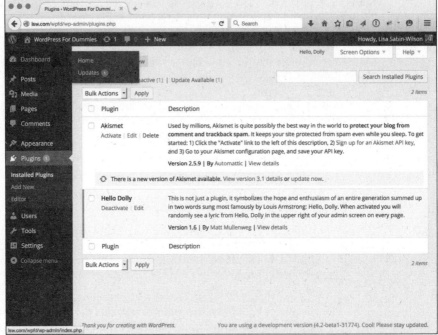

Figure 7-2:
WordPress
tells you
when a
new plugin
version is
available.

✔ **Dashboard Updates link:** The Updates link below the Dashboard menu displays a circle with a white number. The number indicates how many plugins have updates available. In Figure 7-2, you see that there is one plugin with an update available on my site. Click the Updates link to see which plugins have updates available.

✔ **Toolbar:** When there is a new update available, a small icon appears in the toolbar at the top of your Dashboard to the right of your site title, as shown in Figure 7-2.

✔ **Plugins menu title:** The Plugins menu title also displays a circle with a number. As with the Updates link, the number indicates how many plugins have updates available, as shown in Figure 7-2.

✔ **Plugins page:** Figure 7-2 shows the Plugins page. Below the Akismet plugin you see a message that says `There is a new version of Akismet available. View version 3.1 details or update now.`

WordPress gives you not only a message that a new version of the plugin is available, but also a link to a page where you can download the new version, or a link that you can click to update the plugin right there and then — WordPress's one-click plugin update.

Click the Update Now link, and WordPress grabs the new files off the WordPress.org server, uploads them to your plugins directory, deletes the old plugin, and activates the new one. (If a plugin is deactivated at the time it's updated, WordPress gives you the option to activate the plugin after your update process is completed.) Figure 7-3 shows the *Updated* message on the Plugins page that you see after the plugin has been upgraded.

WordPress notifies you of an out-of-date plugin and provides you with the one-click upgrade function *only* for plugins that are in the official WordPress Plugin Directory (`https://wordpress.org/plugins`). If a plugin you are using is not listed in the directory, the notification and one-click upgrade function won't be present for that plugin.

Whatever you do, do *not* ignore the plugin update messages that WordPress gives you. Plugin developers usually release new versions because of security problems or vulnerabilities that require an upgrade. If you notice that an upgrade is available for a plugin you're using, stop what you're doing and upgrade it — it takes only a few seconds.

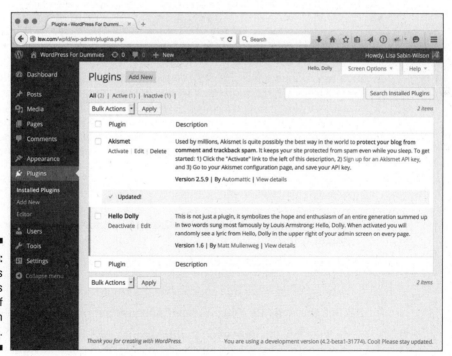

Figure 7-3:
The Plugins page shows the status of your plugin update.

For the automatic plugin upgrade to work, your plugin directory (/wp-content/plugins) must be writable on your web server, which means that you should have set permissions of 755 or 777 (depending on your web server configuration). See Chapter 3 for information about changing file permissions on your web server, or contact your web-hosting provider for assistance.

Exploring the Plugins Included with WordPress

At this writing, WordPress packages two plugins with the installation files:

- ✔ **Akismet:** This plugin is essential.
- ✔ **Hello Dolly:** This plugin isn't necessary to make your site run smoothly, but it adds some fun.

Incorporating Akismet

I touch on Akismet a few times throughout this book. It's my humble opinion that Akismet is the mother of all plugins and that no WordPress blog is complete without a fully activated version. Apparently WordPress agrees, because the plugin has been packaged in every WordPress software release since version 2.0. Akismet was created by the folks at Automattic — the same folks who bring you the JetPack plugin. Akismet is the answer to comment and trackback spam.

To use the plugin, follow these steps:

1. **On the Plugins page, click the Activate link under the Akismet plugin name.**

   A box appears at the top of the page, saying `Activate your Akismet account. Almost done — activate your account and say goodbye to comment spam.` (See Figure 7-4.)

2. **Click the Activate Your Akismet Account button.**

   Clicking this link takes you to the Akismet page in your WordPress Dashboard, where you can create an API key, required in order to use the Akismet plugin.

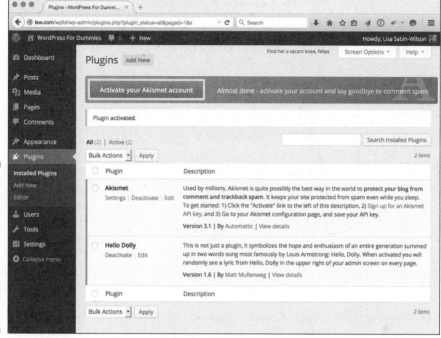

Figure 7-4:
After you
activate
Akismet,
WordPress
tells you
that the
plugin isn't
quite ready
to use yet.

3. Click the Get Your API Key button.

This opens the Akismet website in your browser window at `http://akismet.com/wordpress`.

4. Click the Get an Akismet API Key button.

This opens the signup page on the Akismet website. Because Akismet is hooked into the WordPress.com service, if you already have a WordPress.com account, click the I Already Have a WordPress.com Account! link; otherwise, fill in the text fields and provide your email address, desired username, and password to create one.

After you have done this, Akismet requests that you authorize your account with Akismet — click OK.

5. Enter the URL of the site where you'll use Akismet and select a plan:

- *Enterprise:* $50/month for people who own multiple WordPress-powered websites and want to use Akismet on all of them.

- *Business:* $5/month for people who own one small, nonpersonal (or business) WordPress-powered site.

- *Personal:* $0–$48/year for people who own one small, personal, WordPress-powered blog. You can choose to pay nothing ($0), or if you'd like to contribute a little cash toward the cause of combating spam, you can opt to spend up to $48 per year for your Akismet key subscription.

6. **Select and pay for (if needed) your Akismet key.**

   After you've gone through the signup process, Akismet provides you with an API key. Copy that key by selecting it with your mouse pointer, right-clicking, and selecting Copy.

7. **When you have your API key, go to the Akismet page by clicking the Akismet link in the Settings menu on your WordPress Dashboard.**

8. **Enter your Akismet API key in the text box labeled Manually Enter an API Key, and then click the Use This Key button to fully activate the Akismet plugin.**

On the Akismet configuration page, after you've entered and saved your key (see Figure 7-5), you also have two options that you can select to further manage your spam protection:

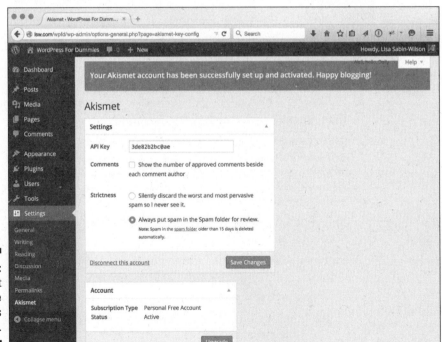

Figure 7-5:
The Akismet page on the WordPress Dashboard.

- ✔ **Comments:** Select the Show the Number of Approved Comments Beside Each Comment Author check box to tell Akismet to display the number of approved comments each comment author has on your blog.

- ✔ **Strictness:** By default, Akismet always puts detected spam email in the spam folder for your review. You can, however, select the Silently Discard the Worst and Most Pervasive Spam So I Never See It radio button.

Akismet catches spam and throws it into a queue, holding the spam for 15 days and then deleting it from your database. It's probably worth your while to check the Akismet Spam page once a week to make sure that the plugin hasn't captured any legitimate comments or trackbacks.

You can rescue those nonspam-captured comments and trackbacks by doing the following (after you've logged on to your WordPress Dashboard):

1. **Click the Comments menu.**

   The Comments page appears, displaying a list of the most recent comments on your blog.

2. **Click the Spam link.**

   The Comments page now displays all spam comments that the plugin caught.

3. **Browse through the list of spam comments, looking for any legitimate comments or trackbacks.**

4. **If you locate one that's legitimate, click the Not Spam link that appears directly below the entry when you hover your mouse pointer over it.**

   The comment is marked as legitimate. In other words, you don't consider this comment to be spam. The comment is then approved and published on your blog.

Check your spam filter often. I just found four legitimate comments caught in my spam filter and was able to de-spam them, releasing them from the binds of Akismet and unleashing them upon the world. Check out Chapter 5 for more information on managing comments in WordPress.

The folks at Automattic did a fine thing with Akismet. Since the emergence of Akismet, I've barely had to think about comment or trackback spam, except for the few times a month I check my Akismet spam queue.

Saying Hello Dolly

Matt Mullenweg, co-founder of WordPress, developed the Hello Dolly plugin. Anyone who follows the development of WordPress knows that Matt is a huge jazz fan. How do we know this? Every single release of WordPress is named after some jazz great. One of the most recent releases of the software, for example, is named Parker, after jazz great Charles Parker; another release was named Coltrane, after the late American jazz saxophonist and composer John Coltrane.

So, knowing this, it isn't surprising that Mullenweg developed a plugin named Hello Dolly. Here's the description of it that you see in the Plugins page on your Dashboard:

> This is not just a plugin, it symbolizes the hope and enthusiasm of an entire generation summed up in two words sung most famously by Louis Armstrong: "Hello, Dolly." When activated, you will randomly see a lyric from "Hello, Dolly" in the upper right of your admin screen on every page.

Is it necessary? No. Is it fun? Sure!

Activate the Hello Dolly plugin on the Plugins page on your WordPress Dashboard. When you've activated it, your WordPress blog greets you with a different lyric from the song "Hello, Dolly!" each time.

If you want to change the lyrics in this plugin, you can edit them by clicking the Edit link to the right of the Hello Dolly plugin on the Plugins page. The Plugin Editor opens and lets you edit the file in a text editor. Make sure that each line of the lyric has its own line in the plugin file. This plugin may not seem very useful to you and, in fact, it may not be useful to the majority of WordPress users, but the real purpose behind the plugin is to provide WordPress plugin developers with a simple example of how to write a plugin.

This book does not cover topics on how to create your own plugin, but if you are interested in that, you may want to check out my other book, *WordPress All-in-One For Dummies* (John Wiley & Sons, Inc.), which covers that topic in detail.

Using Plugins: Just the Basics

In this section, I show you how to install a plugin in your WordPress blog using the built-in plugins feature. The auto-installation of plugins from within your WordPress Dashboard works only for plugins that are included in the official WordPress Plugin Directory (https://wordpress.org/plugins). You can manually install plugins on your WordPress blog, a process that I cover in the next section.

WordPress makes it super easy to find, install, and then activate plugins for use on your blog. Just follow these simple steps:

1. **Click the Add New link in the Plugins menu.**

   The Install Plugins page opens, and you can browse the official WordPress Plugins Directory from your WordPress Dashboard.

2. **Search for a plugin to install on your blog:**

   Enter a keyword for a plugin you'd like to search for. For example, if you want to search for plugins that allow you to add features for integration with Twitter on your site, enter the word **Twitter** in the Search Plugins text box to return a list of plugins that deal specifically with the social network called Twitter.

   You can also discover new plugins by clicking any of the provided methods at the top of the Add Plugins page: Featured, Popular, Recommended, or Favorites.

   Figure 7-6 shows the results page for the Twitter search phrase. The first plugin listed is simply called "Twitter," which is a plugin developed by the developers at Twitter — this is the one I want to install.

3. **Click the More Details link below the plugin name.**

   A Description window opens, giving you information about the Twitter plugin, including a description of the plugin, version number, author name, and an Install Now button.

4. **Click the Install Now button.**

   You go to the Installing Plugins page within your WordPress Dashboard, where you find a confirmation message that the plugin has been downloaded, unpacked, and successfully installed.

5. **Specify whether to activate the plugin or proceed to the Plugins page.**

   Two links are shown below the confirmation message:

   - *Activate Plugin:* Click this link to activate the plugin you just installed on your blog.

   - *Return to Plugin Installer:* Click this link to go to the Install Plugins page without activating the plugin.

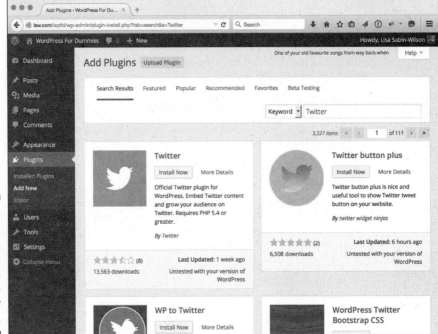

Figure 7-6:
Finding a
plugin to
install using
the built-in
Plugin
Directory
search.

The auto-installation of plugins from your WordPress Dashboard works on most web-hosting configurations. However, some web-hosting services don't allow the kind of access that WordPress needs to complete the auto-installation. If you get any errors or find that you are unable to use the plugin auto-installation feature, get in touch with your web-hosting provider to find out whether it can assist you.

Installing Plugins Manually

In the following sections, I show you how to find, upload, and install the very popular Twitter plugin, developed by Twitter. I'm using the Twitter plugin as a real-world example to take you through the mechanics involved in downloading, unpacking, uploading, activating, and using a plugin in WordPress.

The Twitter plugin gives your readers the opportunity to share your content on the Twitter social networking site.

Installing the Twitter plugin takes you through the process, but keep in mind every plugin is different. Reading the description and installation instructions for each plugin you want to install is very important.

Finding and downloading the files

The first step in using plugins is locating the one you want to install. The absolute best place to find WordPress plugins is the official WordPress Plugins Directory found at `https://wordpress.org/plugins` where, at the time of this writing, you will find over 36,700 plugins available for download.

To find the Twitter plugin, follow these steps:

1. **Go to the official WordPress Plugin Directory, located at** `https:// wordpress.org/plugins`.

2. **In the search box at the top of the Plugin Directory home page, enter the keyword** Twitter **and then click the Search Plugins button.**

3. **Locate the Twitter plugin on the search results page (see Figure 7-7) and click the plugin name.**

   The Twitter plugin page opens in the WordPress Plugin Directory, where you find a description of the plugin as well as other information about the plugin (see Figure 7-8). For example, in Figure 7-8, take note of the important information on the right side of the page:

Figure 7-7: Use the search feature of the WordPress Plugin Directory page to find the plugin you need.

- *Download Version:* This is the download link that you click to download the plugin, and the number shown in this area is the most recent version number of the plugin.

- *Requires:* This tells you what version of WordPress you need to successfully use this plugin. For example, Figure 7-8 shows that the Twitter plugin requires WordPress version 3.9 or higher; this means that this plugin doesn't work with WordPress versions lower than 3.9. Helpful!

- *Compatible Up To:* This tells you what version of WordPress this plugin is compatible up to. For example, if this section tells you that the plugin is compatible up to version 4.2, this means that you usually can't use the plugin with versions higher than 4.2. I say *usually* because the plugin developer may not update the information in this section — especially if the plugin files themselves haven't changed. The best way to check is to download the plugin, install it, and see whether it works! (Figure 7-8 shows that the Twitter plugin is compatible up to WordPress version 4.1.1.)

- *Last Updated:* This displays the date that the plugin was last updated by the author.

- *Active Installs:* This number tells you how many times this plugin has been downloaded and used by other WordPress users.

- *Ratings:* With a rating system of 1–5 stars (1 being the lowest, 5 being the highest), you can see how other WordPress users have rated this plugin.

4. **Click the Download button for the plugin version you want to download.**

   If you're using Internet Explorer, click the Download button and a dialog box opens, asking whether you want to open or save the file. Click Save to save the zip file to your hard drive, and *remember where you saved it.*

   If you're using Mozilla Firefox, click the Download button and a dialog box opens, asking what Firefox should do with the file. Select the Save File radio button and then click OK to save it to your hard drive. Again, *remember where you saved it.*

   For other browsers, follow the download instructions in the corresponding dialog box.

5. **Locate the file on your hard drive and open it with your favorite decompression program.**

   If you're unsure how to use your decompression program, refer to the documentation available with the program.

6. **Unpack (decompress) the plugin files you downloaded for the Twitter plugin.**

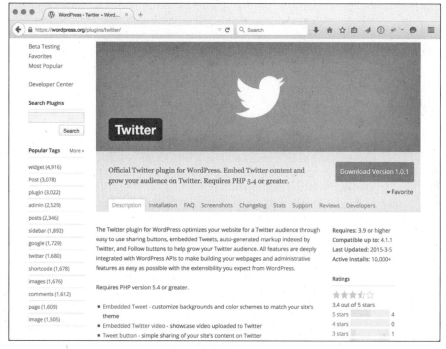

Figure 7-8:
The
download
page for
the Twitter
plugin.

Reading the instructions

Frequently, the plugin developer includes a `readme` file inside the zip file. Do what the title of the file says: Read it. Often, it contains the exact documentation and instructions that you will find on the plugin developer's page.

Make sure that you read the instructions carefully and follow them correctly. Ninety-nine percent of WordPress plugins have great documentation and instructions from the plugin developer. If you don't follow the instructions correctly, the best scenario is that the plugin just doesn't work on your blog. At worst, the plugin creates all sorts of ugly errors, requiring you to start the plugin installation over from step one.

You can open `readme.txt` files in any text-editor program, such as Notepad or WordPad on a PC or TextEdit on a Mac.

In the case of the Twitter plugin, the `readme.txt` file contains information regarding the requirements of the plugin and useful information on how to use the plugin once you have it installed and activated on your site.

Every plugin is different in terms of where the plugin files are uploaded and what configurations and setup are necessary to make the plugin work on your site. Read the installation instructions very carefully and follow those instructions to the letter to install the plugin correctly on your site.

Uploading and Activating Plugins

Now you're ready to upload the plugin files to your web server. In earlier versions of WordPress, you needed to upload the unpacked plugin files to your web server via FTP (see Chapter 3). Now, all you need to do is upload the zip file you just downloaded from the WordPress Plugin Directory. Be sure you are logged on to your WordPress Dashboard.

Unpacking the zip file you've downloaded is helpful because it can contain files that give you insight into the use of the plugin itself. Locate the plugin files you just unpacked on your hard drive. In the event that the plugin developer didn't include a `readme.txt` file with instructions, check the plugin developer's page for specific instructions on how to install the plugin in your WordPress blog. Specifically, the documentation in the `readme.txt` file and/or on the plugin's website should address the following points:

✔ What directory on your web server you upload the plugin files to.

✔ What to do if you need to change permissions for any of the plugin files after you upload them to your web server. (See Chapter 3 if you need information on changing file permissions.)

✔ What to do if you need to set specific configurations in the plugin file to make it work.

✔ What to do if you need to modify your theme template files to include the plugin's functions in your blog.

Uploading a new plugin

To install the Twitter plugin via the WordPress Dashboard, follow these easy steps:

1. **Click the Add New link in the Plugins menu.**

   This opens the Install Plugins page on your Dashboard.

2. **Click the Upload Plugin link at the top of the Install Plugins page.**

   The resulting page gives you an interface for uploading a plugin in zip format.

3. Click the Choose File button.

In the resulting File Upload dialog box, you can locate the zip file for the plugin you'd like to install. In this case, the file is `twitter.1.0.1.zip` (see Figure 7-9). Click the file to select it and then click the Open button to return to the Install Plugins page.

4. Click the Install Now button.

WordPress uploads the plugin's zip file into the `/wp-content/plugins/` folder on your web server, unpacks it, and installs it. Figure 7-10 shows the Installing Plugin page with messages for you during and after the (hopefully successful) installation.

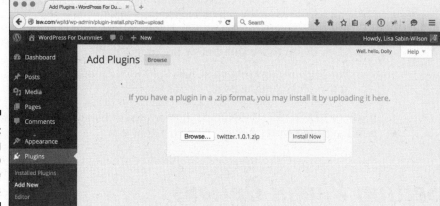

Figure 7-9: Uploading a plugin zip file via the Dashboard.

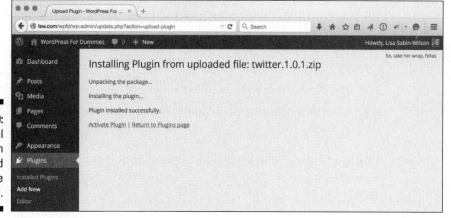

Figure 7-10: Successful plugin upload via the Dashboard.

Activating the plugin

All plugins listed on the Plugins page are either active or inactive (except the Drop-In plugins, which are active by default). When you want to activate an inactive plugin, follow these easy steps (in this case, you are activating the Twitter plugin that you installed in the previous section):

1. **Click the Installed Plugins link on the Plugins menu.**

   The Plugins page opens, listing all the plugins installed in your WordPress site.

2. **Locate the Twitter plugin.**

   If you have a lot of plugins installed on your WordPress website, you can narrow your search by clicking the Inactive link, which lists the currently inactive plugins.

3. **Click the Activate link below the plugin name.**

   The Plugins page refreshes, and the Twitter plugin now appears as an active plugin on the page.

If you've followed all these steps in your own website, congratulations — you now have the Twitter plugin installed. Great job!

Setting Plugin Options

Some, but not all, WordPress plugins provide an administration page where you can set options that are specific to that particular plugin. You may find the plugin administration page in any of these places:

- The Settings page (click the Settings menu)
- The Tools menu (located in the navigation menu)
- The Plugins menu (located in the navigation menu)
- A Dashboard menu (some plugins even create their own menus!)
- The Admin Toolbar (at the top of any Dashboard page)

You can find the Twitter Settings page by clicking the Twitter link in the main Dashboard navigation menu. The Twitter Settings page opens (see Figure 7-11).

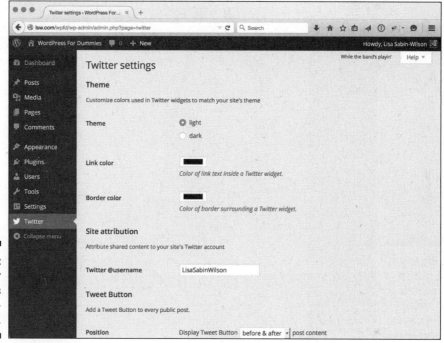

Figure 7-11:
The Twitter
Settings
administra-
tion page.

Uninstalling Plugins

After all this talk about installing and activating plugins, what happens if you install and activate a plugin and then at some point decide that it just isn't what you want? Don't worry — you aren't stuck forever with a plugin that you don't want. WordPress lets you be fickle and finicky in your plugin choices!

To uninstall a plugin from your WordPress blog, follow these steps:

1. **Click the Installed Plugins link on the Plugins menu.**

   The Plugins page opens.

2. **Locate the plugin you want to uninstall.**

3. **Click the Deactivate link below the plugin title.**

   The Plugins page refreshes, and the plugin now appears as deactivated (or inactive).

4. **Click the Delete link that now appears below the plugin title.**

   The Delete Plugin page opens, and a confirmation message displays asking you whether you're sure you want to delete this plugin. (See Figure 7-12.)

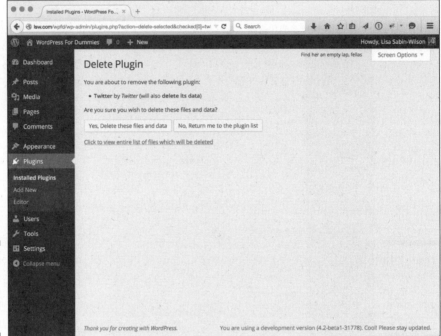

Figure 7-12:
Confirmation
question on
the Delete
Plugin page.

5. **Click the Yes, Delete These Files and Data button.**

   The Plugins page refreshes, and the plugin you just deleted is gone from the lists of plugins, with a message displayed at the top confirming the deletion of the plugin.

Bang! You're done. That's all it takes.

Don't forget to remove any bits of code that you may have added to your theme templates for that particular plugin; otherwise, it may cause ugly error messages to appear in your blog.

Understanding the Open Source Environment

The WordPress software was built on an existing platform called b2. Matt Mullenweg, co-founder of WordPress, was using b2 as a blogging platform at the time the developer of that program abandoned it. What did this mean for its users? It meant no more development unless someone somewhere picked up the ball and continued with the platform. Enter Mullenweg and WordPress.

Apply this same concept to plugin development, and you'll understand that plugins sometimes fall by the wayside and drop off the face of the earth. Unless someone takes over when the original developer loses interest, future development of that plugin ceases. It's important to understand that most plugins are developed in an open source environment, which means a few things for you, the end user:

- ✔ **The developers who created your favorite plugin aren't obligated to continue development.** If they find a new hobby or simply tire of the work, they can give it up completely. If no one picks up where they left off, you can kiss that plugin goodbye if it doesn't work with the latest WordPress release.

- ✔ **Developers of popular plugins don't hold to a specific timetable.** Generally, developers are extremely good about updating their plugins when new versions of WordPress are released, or when a security bug or flaw is discovered. Keep in mind, however, that no timetable exists for these developers to follow. Many of these folks have day jobs, classes, or families that can keep them from devoting as much time to the project as you want them to.

- ✔ **In the world of plugin development, it's easy come, easy go.** Beware of the pitfalls of falling in love with any particular WordPress plugin. For example, don't let your website become dependent on a plugin, and don't be surprised if a plugin you love doesn't exist tomorrow. You can use the plugin for as long as it continues to work for you, but when it stops working (such as with a new WordPress release or a

Getting commercial plugins

Not all plugins were created equally. In 2010, the WordPress community saw the emergence of premium, or paid, plugins. These plugins are slightly different from the plugins you find in the official WordPress Plugin Directory, mainly because they have a nominal fee associated with them. Most of the premium plugins also provide great value and support.

One example of premium plugin directories available today is Plugin Buddy (`https://ithemes.com/find/plugins/`). Run by WordPress experts and veterans from the team at iThemes (`https://ithemes.com`), Plugin Buddy is a repository of quality premium plugins like BackupBuddy and Billboard.

security exploit that makes it unusable), you have a tough decision to make. You can

- Stop using the plugin and try to find a suitable alternative.

- Hope that another developer takes over the project when the original developer discontinues his involvement.

- Try to find someone to provide a fix for you (in which case, you'll more than likely have to pay that someone for her time).

I don't want to make the world of WordPress plugins sound like gloom and doom, but I do think it's very important for you to understand the dynamics in play. Consider this section to be food for thought.

Chapter 8

Finding and Installing WordPress Themes

. . . .

In This Chapter

▶ Finding free WordPress themes

▶ Distinguishing between safe and unsafe WordPress themes

▶ Downloading, installing, and activating themes

▶ Browsing and installing themes from your Dashboard

▶ Going with commercial themes

. . . .

*I*n previous chapters, I cover how to use the WordPress platform to publish your posts and pages. In those chapters, you discover how to categorize your posts, build your link lists, and set the publishing and profile options in the WordPress Dashboard. In this chapter, I focus on the visual look and format of your blog — in other words, how other people see your blog after you start publishing your content.

In Chapter 7, I introduce WordPress plugins and discuss some of the thousands of free plugins you can use to add functionality to your blog. Similarly, thousands of free themes are available for you to download and use. This chapter shows you where to find them and takes you through the processes of downloading, installing, and using them.

Getting Started with Free Themes

WordPress comes packaged with one very useful default theme called Twenty Fifteen (named after the year 2015, it was released in version 4.0 of WordPress). Most bloggers who use WordPress usually don't waste any time at all in finding a theme that they like better than the default theme. The Twenty Fifteen theme is meant to get you started. Although you're not limited to the default theme, it's a very functional theme for a basic website. Feel free to use it to get you started on your way.

Are all WordPress themes free?

Not all WordPress themes are created equal, and it's important for you, the user, to know the difference between free and commercial themes:

✔ **Free:** These themes are free, period. You can download and use them on your website at absolutely no cost. It's a courtesy to include a link to the designer in the footer of your blog — but you can even remove that link if you want.

✔ **Commercial:** These themes cost money. You usually find commercial themes available for download only after you've paid anywhere from $10 to $500 or more. The designer feels that these themes are a cut above the rest and, therefore, worth the money you spend for them. I provide information on where to find commercial themes at the end of this chapter.

Free WordPress themes, such as those I discuss in Chapter 16, are popular because of their appealing designs and their ease of installation and use. They're great tools to use when you launch your new blog, and if you dabble a bit in graphic design and CSS (Cascading Style Sheets), you can customize one of the free WordPress themes to fit your own needs. (See Chapter 9 for some resources and tools for templates and template tags, as well as a few great CSS references.) Also see the previous "Are all WordPress themes free?" sidebar for information about free versus premium themes.

By using free themes, you can have your blog up and running with a new design — without the help of a professional — pretty fast. And with thousands of themes available, you can change your theme as often as you want.

Finding free themes

Finding the theme that fits you best may take some time, but with thousands available, you'll eventually find one that suits you. Trying out several free themes is like trying on different "outfits" for your blog. You can change outfits as needed until you find just the right theme.

In July 2008, WordPress launched the official WordPress Themes Directory at https://wordpress.org/themes (see Figure 8-1).

The WordPress Themes Directory isn't the only place on the web to find free WordPress themes, but it's the place to find the most functional and *safe* themes available. Safe themes contain clean code and basic, fundamental WordPress functions to ensure that your WordPress blog functions with the minimum requirements.

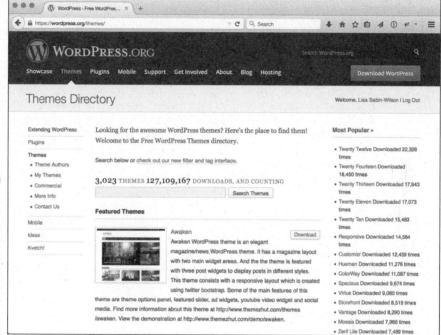

Figure 8-1:
Find the right theme for your website in the WordPress Themes Directory.

The WordPress.org website lists the basic requirements that theme designers have to meet before their theme is accepted into the themes directory; you can find that listing of requirements at `https://wordpress.org/themes/about`.

Avoiding unsafe themes

Unsafe themes, on the other hand, are developed by people who are looking to take advantage of the blog owners who use them. These particular themes are not allowed in the official WordPress Themes Directory. They contain elements such as the following:

- **Spam links:** These links usually appear in the footer of the theme and can link to some pretty unsavory places. The designers of these themes hope to benefit from traffic from your site. They count on the idea that most blog owners won't notice the links or know how to remove them.

- **Malicious code:** Unscrupulous theme designers can, and do, place code in theme files that inserts hidden malware and/or virus links and spam.

> Sometimes you see a line or two of encrypted code that looks as though it's just part of the theme code, and unless you have a great deal of knowledge of PHP, you may not know that the theme is infected with dangerous code.

The results of these unsafe theme elements can range from simply annoying to downright dangerous, affecting the integrity and security of your computer, hosting account, or both. For this reason, the official WordPress Themes Directory is intended and set up to be a safe place from which to download free themes. WordPress designers develop these themes and upload them to the theme directory, and each theme gets vetted by the folks behind the WordPress platform. In the official directory, themes that contain unsafe elements are simply not allowed to play.

If you suspect or worry that you have malicious code on your site — either through a theme you're using or a plugin you've activated — the absolute best place to get your site checked is the Sucuri website (`http://sitecheck.sucuri.net`), which offers a free website malware scanner. Sucuri provides expertise in the field of web security, for WordPress users in particular, and even has a free plugin you can install to periodically check your WordPress site for malware and/or malicious code: `https://wordpress.org/plugins/sucuri-scanner/`.

My strong recommendation for finding free themes is to stick with the official WordPress Themes Directory. That way, you know you're getting a clean, quality theme for your blog. You can rest assured that themes from the official directory are safe and free of spam and malicious code.

Previewing themes

While you're visiting the WordPress Themes Directory, you can easily browse the various themes by using the following features:

- ✔ **Search:** Type a keyword in the box in the center of the page (refer to Figure 8-1) and then click the Search Themes button. A new page opens, displaying themes related to the keyword you searched for.
- ✔ **Featured Themes:** These themes are listed in the center of the themes directory, randomly. WordPress changes the featured themes listing regularly.
- ✔ **Most Popular:** These themes have been downloaded most often.
- ✔ **Newest Themes:** These themes are the latest to be added to the directory.
- ✔ **Recently Updated:** These themes have been updated most recently by their designers.

When you find a theme in the directory that you want to take a closer look at, click its name to open a page that describes that theme (see Figure 8-2):

✔ **Download:** Click this button to download the theme to your computer.

✔ **Preview:** Click this button to open a new window that shows what the theme looks like in a live blog.

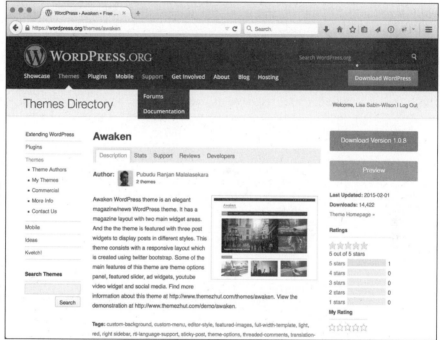

Figure 8-2: Download or preview a particular theme from the WordPress Themes Directory.

Downloading themes

To download the theme you want, follow these steps:

1. **Click the Download button on the theme page (refer to Figure 8-2).**

   The theme files show up on your computer as a compressed `.zip` file.

2. **Use your favorite decompression program to unpack the files to your own computer.**

3. **Connect to your web server via FTP and upload the entire theme folder to the `/wp-content/themes/` directory of your web server.**

(You can also upload the theme zip file in the Dashboard via Themes ⇨ Install Themes ⇨ Upload.)

You find the `/wp-content/themes/` folder in the WordPress installation directory on your web server.

Activating a New Theme

When you have uploaded the theme to your web server, you can activate it by logging on to your WordPress Dashboard and following these simple steps:

1. Click the Themes link in the Appearance menu.

The Themes page opens, listing all the themes currently installed in your `/themes` directory. The active theme is shown as the first theme listed at the top of the page. All available themes you may have uploaded to your web server are shown after the first, active theme (see Figure 8-3).

Available themes appear on the Themes page in alphabetical order. If you have a lot of themes in your `/themes` directory, you'll see ten to a page, with Next and Previous links to help you navigate all the themes available for your blog.

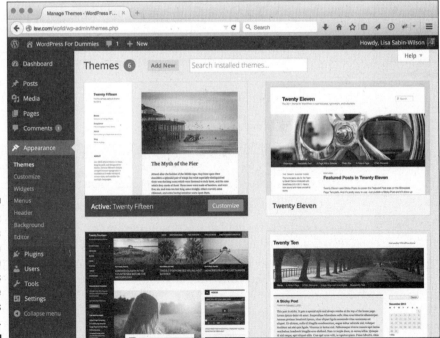

Figure 8-3:
Themes displayed on the Manage Themes page in the WordPress Dashboard.

2. **Hover your mouse over the thumbnail image of the theme you want to use.**

   A Theme Details button appears — click that button and the window pops up and displays information about the theme, such as a small thumbnail and text description about its features.

3. **Click the Live Preview button.**

   A preview window opens, showing you what your blog will look like with this new theme applied (see Figure 8-4). The preview window also has basic theme configuration settings so you can customize your theme before you activate it. You can customize items such as site title and tagline, theme colors, header and background images, and the static front page so that your theme is ready to go when you activate it. If you skip the customization step, you can return to the Manage Themes page and click the Customize link in the theme description to revisit the customization page.

   Click the X in the top-left corner of the preview window to close the theme without customizing or activating it.

4. **Click the Save & Activate button.**

   This button resides in the top-left corner of the preview window.

   WordPress applies the theme you chose to your blog.

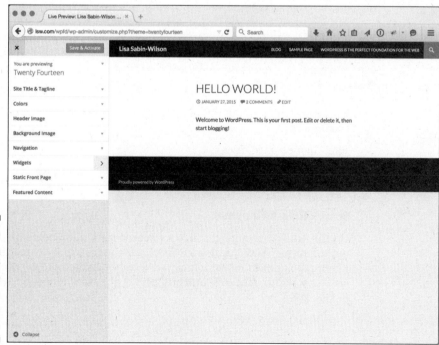

Figure 8-4: Theme preview window in the WordPress Dashboard.

Using sidebar widgets

Most free WordPress themes come with built-in code that lets you take advantage of sidebar widgets for your blog. WordPress widgets are wonderful! (Say *that* ten times fast, why don't you?) Widgets are so wonderful because they let you arrange the content in your blog sidebar, such as your blogroll(s), recent posts, and monthly and category archive listings. With widgets, you can accomplish this arranging without needing to know a single bit of code.

WordPress.org users have the use of plugins (see Chapter 7). Some plugins have a built-in feature that enables you to include that plugin's functions in your sidebar through the use of a widget. (WordPress.com doesn't have this feature because it doesn't allow uploading and activating various plugins.)

Browsing and Installing Themes from the Dashboard

Earlier in this chapter, I cover how to find and install a new theme on your WordPress blog by downloading it from the WordPress Themes Directory, uploading it to your web server via FTP, and activating the theme within your WordPress Dashboard.

The WordPress platform does give you a much easier way to browse the Themes Directory to find, preview, and install themes on your site without ever leaving the comfort of the WordPress Dashboard. The following steps show you how to do it:

1. **Click the Themes link in the Appearance menu of your WordPress Dashboard.**

   The Themes page opens.

2. **Click the Add New button at the top of the Themes page.**

   This opens the Add Themes page.

3. **Search for a new theme.**

   On the Add Themes page, you can search for a new theme by keyword, author, or tag. You can also further filter the results by using the Feature Filter check boxes, which allow you to filter theme results by color, columns, width, features, and subjects. The Add Themes page is shown in Figure 8-5.

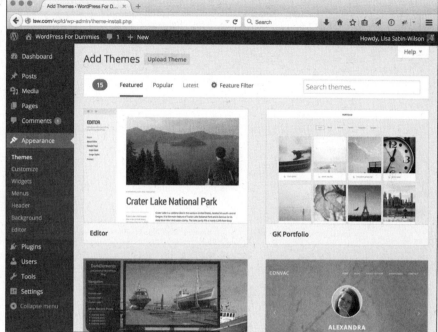

Figure 8-5:
Find new
themes on
the Add
Themes
page in your
WordPress
Dashboard.

4. Preview a new theme.

After you search for a new theme, the search results page displays a list of themes for you to choose from. Click the Preview link underneath the theme of your choice to view a sample of how the theme looks. Figure 8-6 shows a preview window of a theme called *WinterDream*, which I found by searching for the keyword *Minimalistic* on the Add Themes page.

5. Install a new theme on your blog.

After you find a theme you like, click the Install button located at the top left of the theme preview window to install the theme on your blog. This installs the theme and loads the Installing Theme page on your Dashboard with a message telling you that the theme installation was successful.

6. Activate the new theme.

Click the Activate link shown on the Installing Theme page to activate, display, and use the new theme on your site.

Figure 8-6:
A preview of
the Winter
Dream
theme on
the Add
Themes
page.

At the beginning of this chapter, I mention that the only themes found in the official WordPress Themes Directory are free and vetted by the WordPress folks; you can trust that these themes are not only free of charge, but also free of any virus or malicious code. The same holds true for the themes you find by using the Add New Themes feature in your WordPress Dashboard. This feature hooks into the official WordPress Themes Directory, so you are sure to find only those themes that are free and safe.

Deciding to Use Commercial Themes

As WordPress becomes more and more popular, I keep seeing many different business models crop up around the web that focus on providing WordPress users with commercial services and support, such as custom design, consulting, and development.

Commercial WordPress themes have become a very popular way for talented designers to provide a service they are very passionate about (designing themes) while making a little money for their efforts. Commercial themes are also known as premium themes. There are many schools of thought as to what makes a theme *premium* as opposed to free. Actually, the topic of what is considered premium and what is not, with regard to WordPress themes, is guaranteed to spark passionate debate among designers and theme users alike. However, almost everyone agrees there are indicators of premium themes, for example:

- ✔ **High quality:** Very high-quality graphic design and CSS development.

- ✔ **Flexibility and ease of use:** A theme structure with functions that make it very easy for users to customize and adjust the theme to suit their own needs. This includes, but is not limited to, altering the header graphic/logo and color scheme and changing images and icons.

- ✔ **Comprehensive documentation:** Provides the user with extensive instructions on how to use the theme, especially if the theme has multiple features and customization options.

- ✔ **Supported:** Premium themes are fully supported by the designer who created them. Typically, when you buy a premium theme, you should expect full support on the use of that theme for as long as you're using it.

- ✔ **Expensive:** Premium themes are not free. I've seen pricing on premium themes in the range of $10 to $500 or more.

This is not to say that some free themes don't have some, or all, of the features I just listed — it's just that, for the most part, they don't. Keep in mind that just because a designer calls a theme *premium* doesn't mean that the theme has passed through any kind of official quality review. One designer's view of what constitutes a premium theme can, and will, differ from the next.

Fully investigate any theme before you put money down on it. Some things to check out before you pay:

- ✔ Email the designer who is selling the premium theme and ask about a support policy.

- ✔ Find people who have purchased the theme and contact them to find out their experiences with the theme and the designer.

- ✔ Carefully read any terms that the designer has published on his site to find out any restrictions that exist with licensing.

- ✔ If the premium theme designer has a support forum, ask whether you can browse through the forum to find out how actively the designer answers questions and provides support. Are users waiting weeks to get their questions answered? Or does the designer seem to be on top of support requests?

- ✔ Do a search in Google for the theme and the designer. Often, users of premium themes post about their experiences with the theme and the designer. You can find out a lot of positive and, potentially, negative information about the theme and the designer before you buy it.

Although premium themes are cropping up all over the web, a handful really stand out with quality products and services. The following two commercial theme providers are tried and true, with a very stable and successful following of clients who use them:

- ✔ **iThemes:** Cory Miller and his team of designers and code wranglers provide a total of 30 premium themes available for purchase, with prices ranging from $80 to $200 each. You can also purchase an all-in-one package that includes all themes for $150/year. All theme purchases at iThemes include full support on the use of the theme(s) for the lifetime of your membership at iThemes. The iThemes premium themes can be found at `https://ithemes.com`.

- ✔ **StudioPress:** Created by long-time WordPress user, expert, and veteran Brian Gardner, StudioPress offers a variety of high-quality premium WordPress themes that you can purchase with a starting price of $99.95. You may also purchase an all-inclusive themes package starting at $299.95. Theme purchases at StudioPress include a complete support package with access to a support forum staffed by people who are ready to assist you with your most burning questions. You can find StudioPress and browse through its premium theme offerings at `www.studiopress.com`.

You can't find, preview, or install commercial themes using the Add New Themes feature in your WordPress Dashboard (covered in the previous section of this chapter). You can find, purchase, and download premium themes only at an official third-party website. After you find a premium theme you like, you need to install it via the FTP method that I cover in the "Downloading themes" section in this chapter. You can find a very nice selection of premium themes on the WordPress website: `https://wordpress.org/themes/commercial`.

Part IV
Customizing WordPress

Learn how to avoid unsafe WordPress themes at www.dummies.com/extras/wordpress.

In this part. . .

- ✔ Learn all about the basic templates used to make up a WordPress theme, including basic template tags.

- ✔ Utilize basic HTML markup and CSS to tweak the look and feel of your existing theme.

- ✔ Understand the basic concept behind Parent/Child themes in WordPress and learn how to create your own custom theme based on an existing theme.

- ✔ Discover how to use WordPress as a content management system and add support for features such as custom post types, featured images, and post formats.

- ✔ Find out what it takes to migrate your existing website to WordPress (if it's currently using a different publishing platform) or move it to a new hosting provider.

Chapter 9

Understanding Themes and Templates

*I*f, like me, you like to get your hands dirty, you need to read this chapter. WordPress users who create their own themes do so in the interest of

✔ **Individuality:** You can have a theme that no one else has. (If you use one of the free themes, you can pretty much count on the fact that at *least* a dozen other WordPress websites will have the same look as yours.)

✔ **Creativity:** You can display your own personal flair and style.

✔ **Control:** You can have full control of how the site looks, acts, and delivers your content.

Many of you aren't at all interested in creating your own theme for your WordPress blog, however. Sometimes, it's just easier to leave matters to the professionals and hire an experienced WordPress theme developer to create a custom look for your WordPress website or to use one of the thousands of free themes provided by WordPress designers (see Chapter 8). Chapter 16 also tells you where you can get ten free WordPress themes.

Creating themes requires you to step into the code of the templates, which can be a scary place sometimes — especially if you don't really know what you're looking at. A good place to start is by understanding the structure of a WordPress website. Separately, the parts won't do you any good. But when you put them together, the real magic begins! This chapter covers the basics of doing just that, and near the end of the chapter, you find specific steps to put your own theme together.

You don't need to know HTML to use WordPress. If you plan to create and design WordPress themes, however, you need some basic knowledge of HTML and Cascading Style Sheets (CSS). For assistance with HTML, check out *HTML 4 For Dummies,* 5th Edition, by Ed Tittel and Mary Burmeister, or *HTML, XHTML, and CSS Bible,* 5th Edition, by Steven M. Schafer (both published by John Wiley & Sons, Inc.).

Using WordPress Themes: The Basics

A WordPress theme is a collection of WordPress templates made up of WordPress template tags. When I refer to a WordPress *theme,* I'm talking about the group of templates that makes up the theme. When I talk about a WordPress *template,* I'm referring to only one of the template files that contain WordPress template tags. WordPress template tags make all the templates work together as a theme (more about this topic in the "Examining the Anatomy of a Template Tag" section, later in this chapter).

Understanding theme structure

The rest of this chapter provides important information about the steps to building a WordPress theme, but here is an overview of the templates that make up a WordPress theme and where you find them, both on your server and within your WordPress Dashboard. Follow these steps:

1. **Connect to your web server via FTP and have a look at the existing WordPress themes on your server.**

   The correct location is `/wp-content/themes/` (see the right side of Figure 9-1). When you open this folder, you find the `/twentyfifteen` theme folder.

   If a theme is uploaded to any folder other than `/wp-content/themes`, it won't work.

2. **Open the folder for the Twenty Fifteen theme (`/wp-content/themes/twentyfifteen`) and look at the template files inside.**

   When you open the Twenty Fifteen theme folder, you see several files. At minimum, you find these five templates in the default theme:

   - *Stylesheet* (`style.css`)

   - *Header template* (`header.php`)

   - *Main Index* (`index.php`)

   - *Sidebar template* (`sidebar.php`)

   - *Footer template* (`footer.php`)

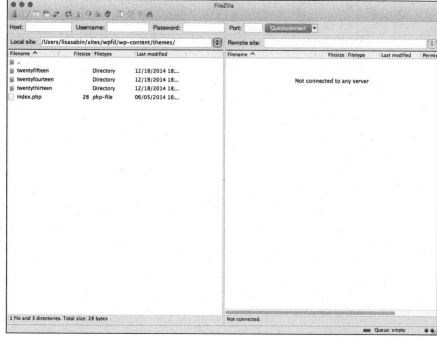

Figure 9-1:
WordPress
themes in
the /wp-
content/
themes
folder in
FTP.

These files are the main WordPress template files, and I discuss them in more detail in this chapter. There are several other template files, however, and you should try to explore them all if you can. Take a peek inside and see the different template functions they contain. These filenames are the same in every WordPress theme. See the "Contemplating the Structure of a WordPress Website" section later in this chapter for more information about these template files.

3. **Click the Editor link on the Appearance menu to look at the template files within a theme.**

   This Edit Themes page lists the various templates available within the active theme. (Figure 9-2 shows the templates in the default Twenty Fifteen theme.) A text box on the left side of the screen displays the contents of each template, and this box is also where you can edit the template file(s). To view and edit a template file, click the template name in the list on the right side of the page.

The Edit Themes page also shows the HTML markup (see Chapter 10) and template tags within the template file. These tags make all the magic happen in your website; they connect all the templates to form a theme. The next section of this chapter discusses these template tags in detail, showing you what they mean and how they function. The "Putting a Theme Together" section later in this chapter provides steps for putting them all together to create your own theme (or edit an existing theme).

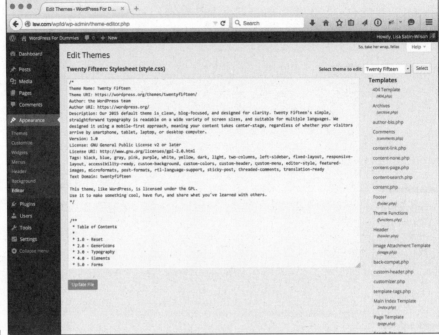

Figure 9-2:
A list of templates available in the default Twenty Fifteen WordPress theme.

Below the text box on the Edit Themes page is a drop-down menu labeled Documentation. Click the arrow on the right side of the menu, and a list drops down that contains all of the template tags used in the template you're currently viewing. This list is helpful when you edit templates and it gives you some insight into some of the different template tags used to create functions and features within your WordPress theme. (*Note:* The Documentation menu does not appear when you view the Stylesheet because no template tags are used in the `style.css` template — only CSS, which I cover in Chapter 10.)

Connecting templates

The template files don't work alone; for the theme to function, the files need one another. To tie these files together as one working entity, you use template tags to pull the information from each template — Header, Sidebar, and Footer — into the Main Index. I refer to this procedure as *calling* one template into another. (You can find more information in the "Getting Familiar with the Four Main Templates" section later in this chapter.)

Contemplating the Structure of a WordPress Website

A WordPress blog, in its very basic form, has four main areas (labeled in Figure 9-3).

Header

Body   Footer   Sidebar

Figure 9-3: The four main sections of a WordPress blog.

These four main areas appear in the default theme that comes in every version of WordPress:

- ✔ **Header:** This area usually contains the name of the site along with the site tagline or slogan. Sometimes the header also contains a graphic or image.

- ✔ **Body:** This area is where the main content of your website appears; for example, blog posts displayed in chronological order.

- ✔ **Sidebar:** This area is where you find lists of blog-related elements, such as the blogroll, the archives, and a list of recent posts.

✔ **Footer:** This area, at the bottom of the page, often contains links to further information about the website, such as who designed it, which company provides hosting for the site, and copyright information.

These four areas are the absolute bare bones of a *basic* WordPress blog template. You can extend these areas and create new sections that carry more information, of course, but for the purpose of this chapter, I'm focusing on the basics.

The default WordPress theme is called Twenty Fifteen, and in my opinion, it's a pretty doggone wonderful starting point for you, especially if you're just getting your feet wet in web publishing. I don't cover all the tags and templates that the Twenty Fifteen theme includes; rather, I touch on the basics to get you on your way to understanding templates and template tags for WordPress.

Many themes developed for WordPress are free for public use, and I strongly recommend finding one that you like and downloading it. Use the free themes as a jumping-off place to get started in theme development. Really, why reinvent the wheel? With the free themes available today, most of the work has already been completed for you, and you may find it easier to use one of these themes than to start a theme from scratch.

Each free theme available for download is different, depending on what the developer included (such as CSS styling, display options, format, and layout). So experimenting with a few themes is a fun and great way to learn more about the development of WordPress themes. A great place to find free WordPress themes is the official WordPress Themes Directory at `https://wordpress.org/themes`.

To build a *basic* WordPress theme that covers the four basic areas of a website, you need these five templates:

✔ `header.php`

✔ `index.php`

✔ `sidebar.php`

✔ `footer.php`

✔ `style.css`

Each WordPress theme comes with a stylesheet (`style.css`), which drives the formatting and layout of your blog template in terms of where the elements are positioned on the page, what the font looks like, what colors your hyperlinks will be, and so on. As you may have already figured out, you don't use CSS to put content on your site; rather, you use CSS to style the content that's already there.

Chapter 10 provides information on tweaking the design of your theme by combining the template tags presented in this chapter with some CSS adjustments in your theme files.

Right now, I'm covering only the very basics; at the end of this chapter, however, I provide some ideas on how you can use various templates to further extend your website functionality — using templates for categories, archives, static pages, multiple sidebars, and so on. After you build the basics, you can spread your wings and step into more advanced themes.

Examining the Anatomy of a Template Tag

Before starting to play around with template tags in your WordPress templates, it's important to understand what makes up a template tag, and why.

WordPress is based in PHP (a scripting language for creating web pages) and uses PHP commands to pull information from the MySQL database. Every tag begins with the function to start PHP and ends with the function to stop PHP. In the middle of those two commands lives the request to the database that tells WordPress to grab the data and display it.

A typical template tag looks like this:

```
<?php get_info(); ?>
```

This entire example tells WordPress to do three things:

- ✔ Start PHP (`<?php`).
- ✔ Use PHP to get information from the MySQL database and deliver it to your blog (`get_info();`).
- ✔ Stop PHP (`?>`).

In this case, `get_info` represents the tag function, which grabs information from the database to deliver it to your site. What information is retrieved depends on what tag function appears between the two PHP commands. As you may notice, a lot of starting and stopping of PHP happens throughout the WordPress templates. The process seems as though it would be resource intensive, if not exhaustive — but it really isn't.

For every PHP command you start, you need a stop command. Every time a command begins with `<?php`, somewhere later in the code is the closing `?>` command. PHP commands that aren't structured properly cause really ugly errors on your site, and they've been known to send programmers, developers, and hosting providers into loud screaming fits.

Getting Familiar with the Four Main Templates

In the following sections, I cover some of the template tags that pull in the information you want to include in your website. To keep this chapter shorter than 1,000 pages, I focus on the four main templates that get you going with creating your own theme or with editing the template tags in the theme you're currently using. Here are those four main templates:

- ✔ Header
- ✔ Main Index
- ✔ Sidebar
- ✔ Footer

The difference between a template and a theme can cause confusion. *Templates* are individual files. Each template file provides the structure in which your content appears. A *theme* is a set of templates. The theme uses the templates to make the whole site.

The Header template

The Header template is the starting point for every WordPress theme because it tells web browsers the following:

- ✔ The title of your blog
- ✔ The location of the CSS
- ✔ The RSS feed URL
- ✔ The blog URL
- ✔ The tagline (or description) of the website

Every page on the web has to start with a few pieces of code. In every `header.php` file in any WordPress theme, you find these bits of code at the top:

✔ The DOCTYPE (which stands for *document type declaration*) tells the browser which type of XHTML standards you're using. The Twenty Fifteen theme uses `<!DOCTYPE html>`, which is a declaration for W3C standards compliance mode and covers all major browser systems.

✔ The `<html>` tag (*HTML* stands for *Hypertext Markup Language*) tells the browser which language you're using to write your web pages.

✔ The `<head>` tag tells the browser that the information contained within the tag shouldn't be displayed on the site; rather, that information is *about* the document.

In the Header template of the Twenty Fifteen theme, these bits of code look like the following example, and you should leave them intact:

```
<!DOCTYPE html>
<html <?php language_attributes(); ?> class="no-js">
<head>
```

On the Edit Themes page, click the Header template link to display the template code in the text box. Look closely and you see that the `<!DOCTYPE html>` declaration, `<html>` tag, and `<head>` tag show up in the template.

The `<head>` tag needs to be closed at the end of the Header template, and the closing tag looks like this: `</head>`. You also need to include a fourth tag, the `<body>` tag, which tells the browser where the information you want to display begins. Both the `<body>` and `<html>` tags need to be closed at the end of the template files (in the `footer.php`), like this: `</body></html>`.

Using bloginfo parameters

The Header template makes much use of one WordPress template tag in particular: `bloginfo();`.

A *parameter* differentiates the type of information that a tag pulls in. Parameters are placed inside the parentheses of the tag, enclosed in single quotes. For the most part, these parameters pull information from the settings in your WordPress Dashboard. The template tag to get your site title, for example, looks like this:

```
<?php bloginfo( 'name' ); ?>
```

Table 9-1 lists the various parameters you need for the `bloginfo();` tag and shows you what the template tag looks like. The parameters in Table 9-1 are commonly used in the `header.php` template file in many WordPress themes and pertain to the `bloginfo();` template tag only.

Parameter	Information	Tag
Table 9-1	**Tag Values for bloginfo(); Commonly Used in WordPress Themes**	
`charset`	Character settings, set in Settings/General	`<?php bloginfo ( 'charset' ); ?>`
`name`	Site title, set in Settings/General	`<?php bloginfo ( 'name' ); ?>`
`description`	Tagline for your site, set in Settings/General	`<?php bloginfo ( 'description' ); ?>`
`url`	Your site's web address, set in Settings/General	`<?php bloginfo ( 'url' ); ?>`
`stylesheet_url`	URL of primary CSS file	`<?php bloginfo ( 'stylesheet url' ); ?>`
`pingback_url`	Displays the trackback URL for your site on single post pages	`<?php bloginfo ( 'pingback_url' ); ?>`

Creating title tags

Here's a useful tip about your site's `<title>` tag: Search engines pick up the words used in the `<title>` tag as keywords to categorize your site in their search engine directories.

The `<title></title>` tags are HTML tags that tell the browser to display the title of your website in the title bar of a visitor's browser. Figure 9-4 shows how the title of my personal blog sits in the title bar of the browser window. The *title bar* is the top bar in your browser. In Figure 9-4, it says Lisa Sabin-Wilson — Designer, Author: WordPress For Dummies.

Search engines love the title bar. The more you can tweak that title to provide detailed descriptions of your site (otherwise known as *search engine optimization*, or SEO), the more the search engines love your blog site. Browsers show that love by giving your site higher rankings in their results.

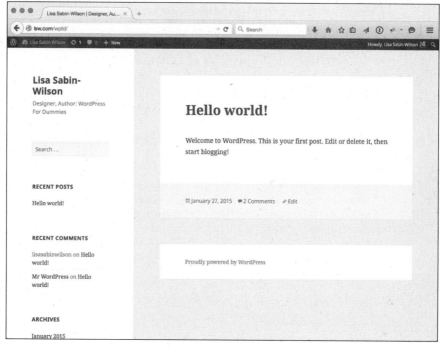

Figure 9-4:
The title
bar of a
browser.

The blog `<title>` tag is the code that lives in the Header template between these two tag markers: `<title></title>`. In the default Twenty Fifteen theme, this bit of code looks like this, and is found in the `functions.php` template file of the theme:

```
add_theme_support( 'title-tag' );
```

The `add_theme_support( 'title-tag' );` in the `functions.php` template tells WordPress to place the title tag in the `<head>` section of the website.

It may help for me to put this example into plain English. The way the `add_theme_support( 'title-tag' );` function displays the title is based on the type of page that's being displayed — and it shrewdly uses SEO to help you with the browser powers that be.

The title bar of the browser window always displays your site name unless you're on a single post page. In that case, it shows your site title plus the title of the post on that page.

Displaying your site name and tagline

Most WordPress themes show your site name and tagline in the header of the site, which means it is displayed in easy, readable text for all visitors (not just search engines) to see. My site name and tagline are

- **Site name:** Lisa Sabin-Wilson
- **Site tagline:** Designer, Author: WordPress For Dummies

Refer to Figure 9-4 to see these two elements in the header of the site.

You can use the `bloginfo();` tag plus a little HTML code to display your site name and tagline. Most sites have a clickable title, which is a site title that takes you back to the main page when clicked. No matter where your visitors are on your site, they can always go back home by clicking the title of your site in the header.

To create a clickable title, use the following HTML markup and WordPress template tags:

```
<a href="<?php bloginfo( 'url' ); ?>"><?php bloginfo
        ( 'name' ); ?></a>
```

The `bloginfo( 'url' );` tag is your main site Internet address, and the `bloginfo( 'name' );` tag is the name of your site (refer to Table 9-1). So the code creates a link that looks something like this:

```
<a href="http://yourdomain.com">Your Site Name</a>
```

The tagline generally isn't linked back home. You can display it by using the following tag:

```
<?php bloginfo( 'description' ); ?>
```

This tag pulls the tagline directly from the one that you've set up on the General Settings page in your WordPress Dashboard.

This example shows how WordPress is intuitive and user-friendly; you can do things such as change the blog name and tagline with a few keystrokes in the Dashboard. Changing your options in the Dashboard creates the change on every page of your site — no coding experience required. Beautiful, isn't it?

In the default Twenty Fifteen templates, these tags are surrounded by tags that look like these: `<h1></h1>` or `<p></p>`. These tags are HTML markup tags, which define the look and layout of the blog name and tagline in the CSS of your theme. I cover CSS further in Chapter 10.

The `header.php` template file also includes the `sidebar.php` template file, which means it tells WordPress to execute and display all of the template functions included in the Sidebar template (`sidebar.php`). The line of code from the Header template that does this looks like this:

```
get_sidebar();
```

I cover more about including other templates by calling them in through the use of template functions in the next sections of this chapter.

The Main Index template

The Main Index template drags your blog posts out of the MySQL database and inserts them into your site. This template is to your blog what the dance floor is to a nightclub — where all the action happens.

The filename of the Main Index template is `index.php`. In the default Twenty Fifteen theme, you can find it in the `/wp-content/themes/twentyfifteen/` folder.

The first template tag in the Main Index template calls in the Header template, meaning that it pulls the information from the Header template into the Main Index template, as follows:

```
<?php get_header(); ?>
```

Your theme can work without calling in the Header template, but it'll be missing several essential pieces — the CSS and the blog name and tagline, for starters. Without the call to the Header template, your blog resembles the image shown in Figure 9-5.

The Main Index template in the default theme, Twenty Fifteen, calls in two other files in a similar fashion:

- ✔ `get_template_part( 'content', 'get_post_format' );`: This function calls in the template file named `content.php` as well as prepares the theme to accept special templates for a feature called Post Formats, which I cover in Chapter 12.

- ✔ `get_footer();`: This function calls in the template file named `footer.php`.

Each of these two functions and template files is covered in upcoming sections of this chapter.

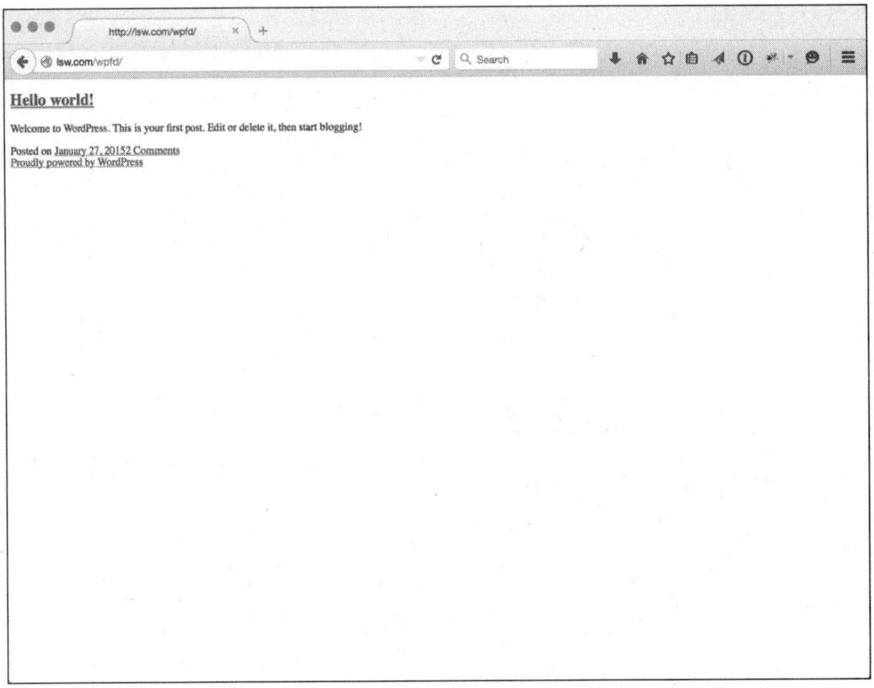

Figure 9-5:
A Word-
Press blog
missing the
call to the
header. It's
naked!

Earlier in this chapter, in the "Connecting templates" section, I explain the concept of *calling in* a template file using a function or template tag. That is exactly what the Main Index template does with the four functions for the Header, Loop, Sidebar, and Footer templates explained in this section.

The Loop

I'm not talking about America's second-largest downtown business district, originating at the corner of State and Madison streets in Chicago. I could write about some interesting experiences I've had there . . . but that would be a different book.

The Loop in this case is a function that WordPress uses to display content on your site such as blog posts and page content. The Loop has a starting point and an ending point; anything placed in between is used to display each post, including any HTML, PHP, or CSS tags and codes.

Quite a few variations of the WordPress Loop are available, but I cover the most common use in this section. When you understand the common use, you can begin to push the envelope a bit further and use variations to suit your needs. This common use displays your posts in chronological order, starting with your most recent post and followed by less recent posts, ordered by date.

The basic and most common use of The Loop in WordPress is to pull blog posts from the database and display them on your website. In the default Twenty Fifteen theme, you find The Loop in the Main Index template (index.php) and it contains these four lines of code:

```
<?php if ( have_posts() ) : ?>

<?php
// Start the Loop.
while ( have_posts() ) : the_post();
```

At the bottom of the template, The Loop ends with these lines of code:

```
endwhile;
endif;
```

Here's a look at what the WordPress Codex calls "The World's Simplest Index":

```
<?php
get_header();
if (have_posts()) :
   while (have_posts()) :
     the_post();
     the_content();
   endwhile;
endif;
get_sidebar();
get_footer();
?>
```

First, the template starts by opening the php tag. Next, it includes the header, meaning that it retrieves anything contained in the header.php file and displays it. Now the good stuff starts happening. The Loop begins with the while (have_posts()) : bit. Anything between the while and the endwhile repeats for each post that displays. The number of posts displayed is determined in the settings section of the WordPress Dashboard.

Misplacement of the while or endwhile statements causes The Loop to break. If you're having trouble with The Loop in an existing template, check your version against the original and see whether the while statements are misplaced.

In your travels as a WordPress user, you may run across plugins or scripts with instructions that say something like this: "This must be placed within The Loop." That's The Loop that we discuss in this section, so pay particular attention. Understanding The Loop arms you with the knowledge you need for tackling and understanding your WordPress themes.

The Loop is no different from any other template tag; it must begin with a function to start PHP, and it must end with a function to stop PHP. The Loop begins with PHP and then makes a request: "While there are posts in my blog, display them on this page." This PHP function tells WordPress to grab the blog post information from the database and return it to the blog page. The end of The Loop is like a traffic cop with a big red stop sign telling WordPress to stop the function completely.

You can set the number of posts displayed per page in the Reading Settings page in the WordPress Dashboard. The Loop abides by this rule and displays only the number of posts per page that you've set.

The big if

PHP functions in a pretty simple, logical manner. It functions by doing what you and I do on a daily basis — making decisions based on questions and answers. PHP deals with three basic variables:

- if
- then
- else

The basic idea is this: IF this, THEN that, or ELSE this.

If your blog has posts (and most do, even when you first install it), WordPress proceeds with The Loop, starting with the piece of code that looks like this:

```
<?php while (have_posts()) : the_post(); ?>
```

This code tells WordPress to grab the posts from the MySQL database and display them on your blog page. Then The Loop closes with this tag:

```
<?php endwhile; ?>
```

If, then, and else

We deal with if, then, else situations every day, as in these examples:

- **IF** I have a dollar, **THEN** I'll buy coffee, or **ELSE** I won't drink coffee.

- **IF** it's warm outside, **THEN** I'll take a walk, or **ELSE** I won't take a walk.

- **IF** I understand this code, **THEN** I'll be happy, or **ELSE** I won't be happy.

In some themes, near the beginning of The Loop template you may see a template tag that looks like this:

```
<?php if ( ! have_posts() ) : ?>
```

The exclamation point (!) preceding the function: `have_posts()` means "does not." So a translation of that template tag into plain English reads: `If [this blog] does not have posts.`

In the Twenty Fifteen theme, your blog meets that condition (that is, if it doesn't have any posts), WordPress skips The Loop and displays a message that no posts exist by calling in the `content-none.php` template part:

```
<section class="no-results not-found">
<header class="page-header">
<h1 class="page-title"><?php _e( 'Nothing Found', 'twentyfifteen' ); ?></h1>
</header><!-- .page-header -->

<div class="page-content">

<?php if ( is_home() && current_user_can( 'publish_posts' ) ) : ?>

<p><?php printf( __( 'Ready to publish your first post? <a href="%1$s">Get
           started here</a>.', 'twentyfifteen' ), esc_url( admin_url( 'post-
           new.php' ) ) ); ?></p>

<?php elseif ( is_search() ) : ?>

<p><?php _e( 'Sorry, but nothing matched your search terms. Please try again
           with some different keywords.', 'twentyfifteen' ); ?></p>
<?php get_search_form(); ?>

<?php else : ?>

<p><?php _e( 'It seems we can't find what you're looking for. Perhaps searching
           can help.', 'twentyfifteen' ); ?></p>
<?php get_search_form(); ?>

<?php endif; ?>

</div><!-- .page-content -->
</section><!-- .no-results -->
```

WordPress displays the title `Nothing Found`, followed by a text statement for the visitor, depending on some factors that are seen in the `if` or `else` statements in the code snippet above:

- `<?php if ( is_home() && current_user_can( 'publish_posts' ) ) : ?>`: This statement says that if you are viewing the home page and you are currently logged in as a user who has the capability to publish posts on the site, then display the following text: `Ready to publish your first post? Get started here.`

✔ `<?php elseif ( is_search() ) : ?>`: This statement says that if the visitor is on a search page, then display the following statement: `Sorry, but nothing matched your search terms, please try again with some different keywords`. This statement is followed by the template tag to include a searchbox that allows users to search the site for more information: `<?php get_search_form(); ?>`.

✔ `<?php else : ?>`: This statement says that if the visitor is visiting a page that does not meet any of the above two conditions, then display the following statement: `It seems we can't find what you're looking for. Perhaps searching can help`. The template tag to include the search form, as in the previous example, follows this statement.

Mixed within the template tags and functions explained in these sections of this chapter, you find basic HTML markup. For example:

```
<section class="">
```

and

```
<header class="">
```

HTML and CSS (Cascading Style Sheets) are explained in Chapter 10. HTML and CSS drive the formatting and style of your overall theme, from a visual standpoint (fonts, colors, images, and so on).

WordPress uses other template files besides the Main Index, such as the Header, Sidebar, and Footer templates. The next section gives you a closer look at a few of them.

The Sidebar template

The filename of the default Sidebar template is `sidebar.php`. Typically, the sidebar is displayed on the right or left side of your WordPress template. In the default Twenty Fifteen theme, the sidebar is displayed on the right side of the template, by default (refer to Figure 9-3).

The Sidebar template is called into the Header template, which, as mentioned previously, is called into the Main Index template. The Sidebar template gets called in using this template tag (as seen in `header.php` in the Twenty Fifteen theme):

```
<?php get_sidebar(): ?>
```

This code calls the Sidebar template and all the information it contains into your blog page. Chapter 12 addresses some additional ways you can call in the Sidebar template, including having multiple Sidebar templates and using an `include` statement to pull them into the Main Index template.

In the "Using Tags with Parameters for Sidebars" section later in this chapter, you find information on template tags to use in the sidebar to display the usual sidebar elements, such as a list of the most recent posts or a list of categories.

The Footer template

The filename of the Footer template is `footer.php`. Usually, the footer sits at the bottom of the page (refer to Figure 9-3) and contains brief information about the site, such as copyright statements, credits to the theme designer or hosting company, or even a list of links to other pages within the site.

The default Twenty Fifteen theme shows a statement that says "Proudly powered by WordPress." You can use the footer to include all sorts of information about your site, however; you don't have to restrict it to small bits of information. In this chapter, I cover the typical footer that you see in the default Twenty Fifteen theme.

Similarly to the Header and Sidebar templates, the Footer template is called into the Main Index template through this bit of code:

```
<?php get_footer(); ?>
```

You can write calls for the Sidebar and Footer templates that are written as part of a larger call:

```
<?php
get_sidebar();
get_footer();
?>
```

It is possible, and common, to wrap two template tags in one PHP function like that, if they appear directly after one another. The examples I have given in this chapter separate them out into single functions to make sure you're clear on what the actual function is.

This code calls the Footer and all the information it contains into your website page.

Other templates

Other templates are in the default Twenty Fifteen theme, and I don't cover all of them in depth in this chapter, but having at least a basic understanding of them is a good idea. The ones I list in this section give you that good, solid kick in the pants you need to get started with understanding WordPress templates. When you have that task licked, you can move on to learning the rest.

These other (optional) templates include

- **Comments template** (`comments.php`): The Comments template is required if you plan to host comments on your blog; it provides all the template tags you need to display those comments. The template tag used to call the comments into the template is `<?php comments_ template(); ?>`.

- **Single Post template** (`single.php`): When your visitors click the title or permalink of a post you've published to your blog, they're taken to that post's individual page. There, they can read the entire post, and if you have comments enabled, they see the comments form and can leave comments.

- **Page template** (`page.php`): You can use a Page template for static pages in your WordPress site.

- **Search Results** (`search.php`): You can use this template to create a custom display of search results on your site. When someone uses the search feature to search your site for specific keywords, this template formats the return of those results.

- **404 template** (`404.php`): Use this template to create a custom 404 page, which is the page visitors get when the browser can't find the page requested and returns that ugly 404 Page Cannot Be Found error.

The templates in the preceding list are optional. If these templates don't exist in your WordPress `themes` folder, nothing breaks. The Main Index template handles the default display of these items (the single post page, the search results page, and so on). The only exception is the Comments template. If you want to display comments on your site, you must have that template included in your theme.

Putting a Theme Together

In this section, you put together a basic theme by using the information on templates and tags I've provided so far in this chapter. Template files can't do a whole lot by themselves. The real power comes when they're put together.

Connecting the templates

WordPress has built-in functions to include the main template files, such as `header.php`, `sidebar.php`, and `footer.php`, in other templates. An `include` function is a custom PHP function built in to WordPress, allowing you to retrieve the content of another template file and display it along with the content of another template file. Table 9-2 shows the templates and the functions to include them.

Table 9-2	Template Files and Include Functions
Template Name	*include Function*
`header.php`	`<?php get_header(); ?>`
`sidebar.php`	`<?php get_sidebar(); ?>`
`footer.php`	`<?php get_footer(); ?>`
`search.php`	`<?php get_search_form(); ?>`
`comments.php`	`<?php comments_template(); ?>`

If you want to include a file that doesn't have a built-in `include` function, you need a different piece of code. For example, if you want to add a unique sidebar (different from the default `sidebar.php` file within your existing theme) to a certain page template, name the sidebar file `sidebar-page.php`. To include that in another template, use the following code:

```
<?php get_template_part('sidebar', 'page'); ?>
```

In this statement, the `get_template_part('sidebar', 'page');` function looks through the main theme folder for the `sidebar-page.php` file and displays the sidebar. The beautiful part about the `get template part()` template tag is that WordPress looks for the `sidebar-page.php` template first, but if it doesn't find it, it defaults to using the `sidebar.php` template.

In this section, you put together the guts of a basic Main Index template by using the information on templates and tags provided so far in this chapter. There seem to be endless lines of code when you view the `index.php` template file in the Twenty Fifteen theme, so I've simplified it for you with the following steps. These steps should give you a basic understanding of the WordPress Loop and common template tags and functions that you can use to create your own.

You create a new WordPress theme using some of the basic WordPress templates. The first steps in pulling everything together are as follows:

1. **Connect to your web server via FTP, click the** `wp-content` **folder, and then click the** `themes` **folder.**

   This folder contains the themes that are currently installed in your WordPress blog. (See Chapter 3 for more information on FTP.)

2. **Create a new folder and call it** `mytheme`.

   In most FTP programs, you can right-click and choose New Folder. (If you aren't sure how to create a folder, refer to your FTP program's help files.)

3. **In your favored text editor (such as Notepad for the PC or TextEdit for the Mac), create and save the following files with the lines of code I've provided for each:**

   • **Header template:** Create the file with the following lines of code and then save with the filename `header.php`:

```
<!DOCTYPE html>
<html <?php language_attributes(); ?> class="no-js">
<head>
<meta charset="<?php bloginfo( 'charset' ); ?>">
<link rel="stylesheet" type="text/css" media="all" href="<?php bloginfo
        ( 'stylesheet_url' ); ?>" />
<?php wp_head(); ?>
</head>
<body <?php body_class() ?>>
<header class="masthead">
<h1><a href="<?php bloginfo( 'url' ); ?>"><?php bloginfo(  'name' ); ?></
        a></h1>
<h2><?php bloginfo( 'description' ); ?></h2>
</header>
<div id="main">
```

   • **Theme Functions:** Create the file with the following lines of code and then save it using the filename `functions.php`:

```
<?php
add_theme_support( 'title-tag' );
if ( function_exists( 'register_sidebar' ) ) register_sidebar( array
        ( 'name'=>'Sidebar',
));
?>
```

   The Theme Functions file registers the widget area for your site so that you're able to add widgets to your sidebar using the WordPress widgets available on the Widget page in the Dashboard.

- **Sidebar template:** Create the file with the following lines of code and then save it using the filename `sidebar.php`:

```
<aside class="sidebar">
<ul>
<?php if ( !function_exists( 'dynamic_sidebar ') || !dynamic_sidebar(
        'Sidebar' ) ) : ?>
<?php endif; ?>
</ul>
</aside>
```

The code here tells WordPress where you would like the WordPress widgets to display in your theme; in this case, widgets are displayed in the sidebar of your site.

- **Footer template:** Create the file with the following lines of code and then save with the filename `footer.php`:

```
<footer>
<p>&copy; Copyright <a href="<?php bloginfo( 'url' ); ?>"><?php bloginfo
        ( 'name' ); ?></a>. All Rights Reserved</p>
</footer>
<?php wp_footer(); ?>
</body>
</html>
```

- **Stylesheet:** Create the file with the following lines of code and then save it with the filename `style.css` (more CSS is covered in Chapter 10 — this example gives you just some *very* basic styling to create your sample theme):

```
/*
Theme Name: My Theme
Description: Basic Theme from WordPress For Dummies example
Author: Lisa Sabin-Wilson
Author URI: http://lisasabin-wilson.com
*/

body {
font-family: verdana, arial, helvetica, sans-serif;
font-size: 16px;
color: #555;
background: #ffffff;
}

header.masthead {
width: 950px;
margin: 0 auto;
background: black;
color: white;
padding: 5px;
text-align:center;
}
```

```
header.masthead h1 a {
color: white;
font-size: 28px;
font-family: Georgia;
text-decoration: none;
}

header.masthead h2 {
font-size: 16px;
font-family: Georgia;
color: #eee;
}

header.masthead nav {
background: #ffffff;
text-align: left;
height: 25px;
padding: 4px;
}

header.masthead nav ul {
list-style:none;
margin:0;
}

#main {
width: 950px;
margin: 0 auto;
padding: 20px ;
}

#main section {
width: 500px;
float:left;
}

#main .hentry {
margin: 10px 0;
}

aside.sidebar {
width: 290px;
margin: 0 15px;
float:right;
}

aside.sidebar ul {
list-style:none;
}
```

```
footer {
clear:both;
width: 960px;
height: 50px;
background: black;
color: white;
margin: 0 auto;
}

footer p {
text-align:center;
padding: 15px 0;
}

footer a {
color:white;
}
```

Using the tags provided in Table 9-3, along with the information on The Loop and the calls to the Header, Sidebar, and Footer templates provided in earlier sections, you can follow the next steps for a bare-bones example of what the Main Index template looks like when you put the tags together.

Table 9-3	Template Tags for Blog Posts
Tag	*Function*
`get_the_date();`	Displays the date of the post.
`get_the_time();`	Displays the time of the post.
`the_title();`	Displays the title of the post.
`get_permalink();`	Displays the permalink (URL) of the post.
`get_the_author();`	Displays the post author's name.
`the_author_posts_url();`	Displays the URL of the post author's site.
`the_content('Read More...');`	Displays the content of the post. (If you use an excerpt [next item], the words *Read More* appear and are linked to the individual post page.)
`the_excerpt();`	Displays an excerpt (snippet) of the post.
`the_category();`	Displays the category (or categories) assigned to the post. If the post is assigned to multiple categories, they are separated by commas.

(continued)

Table 9-3 *(continued)*

Tag	Function
`comments_popup_link('No Comments', 'Comment (1)', 'Comments(%)');`	Displays a link to the comments, along with the comment count for the post in parentheses. (If no comments exist, it displays a *No Comments* message.)
`next_posts_link('&laquo; Previous Entries')`	Displays the words *Previous Entries* linked to the previous page of blog entries.*
`previous_posts_link('Next Entries &raquo;')`	Displays the words *Next Entries* linked to the next page of blog entries.*

*These two tags aren't like the others. You don't place these tags in The Loop; instead, you insert them after The Loop but before the `if statement ends.` Here's an example:

```
<?php endwhile; ?>
<?php next_posts_link('&laquo; Previous Entries') ?>
<?php previous_posts_link('Next Entries &raquo;') ?>
<?php endif; ?>
```

When typing templates, use a text editor such as Notepad or TextEdit. Using a word-processing program such as Microsoft Word opens a whole slew of problems in your code. Word-processing programs insert hidden characters and format quotation marks in a way that WordPress can't read.

Now that you have the basic theme foundation, the last template file you need to create is the Main Index template. To create a Main Index template to work with the other templates in your WordPress theme, open a new window in a text editor and then go through the following steps. (Type the text in each of these steps on its own line. Press the Enter key after typing each line so that each tag starts on a new line.)

1. **Type** `<?php get_header(); ?>`.

   This template tag pulls the information in the Header template of your WordPress theme.

2. **Type** `<section>`.

   This is HTML5 markup that tells the browser that this is a grouping of content (in this case, blog posts).

3. **Type** `<?php if (have_posts()) : ?>`.

   This template tag is an `if` statement that asks, "Does this blog have posts?" If the answer is yes, it grabs the post content information from your MySQL database and displays the posts in your blog.

4. Type `<?php while (have_posts()) : the_post(); ?>`.

This template tag starts The Loop.

5. Type `<article <?php post_class() ?> id="post-<?php the_ID(); ?>">`.

This is HTML5 markup that tells the browser that this is the start of a new, single article, along with the `post_class` CSS designation (covered in Chapter 12).

6. Type `<h1><a href="<?php the_permalink(); ?>"><?php the_title(); ?></a></h1>`.

This tag tells your blog to display the title of a post that's clickable (linked) to the URL of the post, surrounded by HTML Header tags.

7. Type `Posted on <?php the_date(); ?> at <?php the_time(); ?>`.

This template tag displays the date and time when the post was made. With these template tags, the date and time format are determined by the format you set in the Dashboard.

8. Type `Posted in <?php the_category( ',' ); ?>`.

This template tag displays a comma-separated list of the categories to which you've assigned the post — *Posted in: category 1, category 2,* for example.

9. Type `<?php the_content( 'Read More..' ); ?>`.

This template tag displays the actual content of the blog post. The `'Read More..'` portion of this tag tells WordPress to display the words *Read More,* which are clickable (hyperlinked) to the post's permalink, where the reader can read the rest of the post in its entirety. This tag applies when you're displaying a post excerpt, as determined by the actual post configuration in the Dashboard.

10. Type `Posted by: <?php the_author(); ?>`.

This template tag displays the author of the post in this manner: *Posted by: Lisa Sabin-Wilson.*

11. Type `</article>`.

This is HTML5 markup that tells the browser that the article has ended.

12. Type `<?php endwhile; ?>`.

This template tag ends The Loop and tells WordPress to stop displaying blog posts here. WordPress knows exactly how many times The Loop needs to work, based on the setting in the WordPress Dashboard. That's exactly how many times WordPress will execute The Loop.

13. **Type** `<?php next_posts_link('&laquo; Previous Entries'); ?>`.

    This template tag displays a clickable link to the previous page of blog entries, if any.

14. **Type** `<?php previous posts link('&raquo; Next Entries'); ?>`.

    This template tag displays a clickable link to the next page of blog entries, if any.

15. **Type** `<?php else : ?>`.

    This template tag refers to the `if` question asked in Step 3. If the answer to that question is no, this step provides the `else` statement — IF this blog has posts, THEN list them here (Steps 3 and 4), or ELSE display the following message.

16. **Type** `Not Found. Sorry, but you are looking for something that isn't here.`

    This is the message followed by the template tag displayed after the `else` statement from Step 15. You can reword this statement to have it say whatever you want.

17. **Type** `<?php endif; ?>`.

    This template tag ends the `if` statement from Step 3.

18. **Type** `</section>`.

    This is HTML5 markup that closes the `<section>` tag opened in Step 2, and tells the browser that this grouping of content has ended.

19. **Type** `<?php get_sidebar(); ?>`.

    This template tag calls in the Sidebar template and pulls that information into the Main Index template.

20. **Type** `</div>`.

    This is HTML markup closing the `<div id="main">` that was opened in the `header.php` file.

21. **Type** `<?php get_footer(); ?>`.

    This template tag calls in the Footer template and pulls that information into the Main Index template. *Note:* The code in the `footer.php` template ends the `<body>` and `<html>` tags that were started in the Header template (`header.php`).

    When you're done, the display of the Main Index template code looks like this:

```
<?php get_header(); ?>
<section>
<?php if (have_posts()) : ?>

<?php while (have_posts()) : the_post(); ?>
<article <?php post_class() ?> id="post-<?php the_ID(); ?>">
        <h1><a href="<?php the_permalink(); ?>"><?php the_title(); ?></
         a></h1>
        Posted on: <?php the_date(); ?> at <?php the_time(); ?>
        Posted in: <?php the_category(','); ?>
        <?php the_content('Read More..'); ?>
        Posted by: <?php the_author(); ?>
</article>

<?php endwhile; ?>
<?php next_posts_link( '&laquo; Previous Entries' ) ?>
<?php previous_posts_link( 'Next Entries &raquo;' ) ?>
<?php else : ?>
<p>Not Found
Sorry, but you are looking for something that isn't here.</p>
<?php endif; ?>
</section>
<?php get_sidebar(); ?>
</div>
<?php get_footer(); ?>
```

22. **Save this file as** index.php **and upload it to the** mythemes **folder.**

In Notepad or TextEdit, you can save it by choosing File➪Save As. Type the name of the file in the File Name text box and click Save.

23. **Activate the theme in the WordPress Dashboard and view your blog to see your handiwork in action!**

My Main Index template code has one template tag that I explain in Chapter 12; that template tag is `<article <?php post_class() ?> id="post-<?php the_ID(); ?>">`. This tag helps you create some interesting styles in your template using CSS, so check out Chapter 12 to find out all about it!

This very simple and basic Main Index template that you just built does not have the standard HTML markup in it, so you will find that the visual display of your blog differs from the default Twenty Fifteen theme. This example was used to give you the bare-bones basics of the Main Index template and The Loop in action. Chapter 10 goes into details about using HTML and CSS to create nice styling and formatting for your posts and pages.

If you're having a hard time typing out the code provided, I have made this sample theme available for download on my website. The zip file contains the files discussed in this chapter so you can compare your efforts with mine, electronically. You can download the theme zip file here: `http://lisasabin-wilson.com/wpfd/my-theme.zip`.

Using additional stylesheets

Often a theme uses multiple stylesheets for browser compatibility or consistent organization. If you use multiple stylesheets, the process for including them in the template is the same as with any other stylesheet.

To add a new stylesheet, create a directory in the root theme folder called `css`. Next, create a new file called `mystyle.css` within the `css` folder. To include the file, you must edit the `header.php` file. The following example shows the code you need to include in the new CSS file:

```
<link rel="stylesheet" href="<?php bloginfo('stylesheet_directory');
?>/css/mystyle.css" type="text/css" media="screen" />
```

Additional stylesheets come in handy when working with a concept called Parent/Child themes, which is the practice of creating a child theme that depends upon a separate parent theme for features and functions. I write more about Parent/Child themes, as well as provide you with additional information on HTML and CSS, in Chapter 11.

Customizing Your Blog Posts with Template Tags

This section covers the template tags that you use to display the body of each blog post you publish. The body of a blog post includes information such as the post date and time, title, author name, category, and content. Table 9-3 lists the common template tags you can use for posts, available for you to use in any WordPress theme template. The tags in Table 9-3 work only if you place them within The Loop (covered earlier in this chapter and found in the `index.php` template file in the Twenty Fifteen default theme).

Using Tags with Parameters for Sidebars

If you've been following along in this chapter as I've covered the Header and Main Index templates and tags, you have a functional WordPress site with blog posts and various metadata displayed in each post.

In this section, I give you the template tags for the items commonly placed in the sidebar of a site. I say "commonly placed," because it's possible to get creative with these template tags and place them in other locations (the Footer template, for example). To keep this introduction to Sidebar template tags simple, I stick with the most common use, leaving the creative and uncommon uses for you to try when you're comfortable with building the basics.

This section also introduces *tag parameters,* which are additional options you can include in the tag to control some of its display properties. Not all template tags have parameters. You place tag parameters inside the parentheses of the tag. Many of the parameters discussed in this section were obtained from the WordPress software documentation in the WordPress Codex at `http://codex.wordpress.org`.

Table 9-4 helps you understand the three variations of parameters used by WordPress.

Table 9-4	Three Variations of Template Parameters	
Variation	*Description*	*Example*
Tags without parameters	These tags have no additional options available. Tags without parameters have nothing within the parentheses.	`the_tag();`
Tags with PHP function-style parameters	These tags have a comma-separated list of values placed within the tag parentheses.	`the_tag( '1,2,3' );`
Tags with query-string parameters	These tags generally have several available parameters. This tag style enables you to change the value for each parameter without being required to provide values for all available parameters for the tag.	`the_tag ( 'parameter=true ');`

Identifying some post metadata

Metadata is simply data about data. In WordPress, *metadata* refers to the data about each post or page, including:

✔ The author name

✔ The category or categories to which the post is assigned

✔ The date and time of the post

✔ The comments link and number of comments

You need to know these three types of parameters:

✔ **String:** A line of text that can be anything from a single letter to a long list of words. A string is placed between single quotation marks and sets an option for the parameter or is displayed as text.

✔ **Integer:** A positive or negative number. Integers are placed within the parentheses and either inside or outside single quotation marks. Either way, they'll be processed correctly.

✔ **Boolean:** Sets the parameter options to true or false. This parameter can be numeric (0=false and 1=true) or textual. Boolean parameters aren't placed within quotation marks.

The WordPress Codex, located at http://codex.wordpress.org, has every conceivable template tag and possible parameter known to the WordPress software. The tags and parameters that I share with you in this chapter are the ones used most often.

The calendar

The calendar tag displays a calendar that highlights each day of the week on which you've posted a blog. Those days are also hyperlinked to the original blog post. Here's the tag to use to display the calendar:

```php
<?php get_calendar(); ?>
```

The calendar tag has only one parameter, and it's Boolean. Set this parameter to true and it displays the day of the week with one letter (Friday = F, for example). Set this parameter to false and it displays the day of the week as a three-letter abbreviation (Friday = Fri., for example). Here are examples of the template tag used to display the calendar on your WordPress blog:

```
<?php get_calendar( true ); ?>
<?php get_calendar( false ); ?>
```

List pages

The `<?php wp_list_pages(); ?>` tag displays a list of the static pages you can create on your WordPress site (such as About Me or Contact pages). Displaying a link to the static pages makes them available so that readers can click the links and read the content you've provided.

WordPress has a handy navigation menu–building tool that I cover in Chapter 10. It allows you to build different custom navigation menus. If you like the navigation tool, you may never need to use the `wp_list_pages();` template tag. Still, I'm including it here because you may want to use it if you want to have complete control over how the list of pages appears on your website.

The `<list>` tag parameters use the string style. (Table 9-5 lists the most common parameters used for the `wp_list_pages` template tag.)

Table 9-5	Most Common Parameters (Query-String) for wp_list_pages();	
Parameter	**Type**	**Description and Values**
`child_of`	integer	Displays only the subpages of the page; uses the numeric ID for a page as the value. Defaults to `0` (display all pages).
`sort_column`	string	Sorts pages with one of the following options:
		`'post_title'` — Sorts alphabetically by page title (default).
		`'menu_order'` — Sorts by page order (the order in which they appear in the Manage tab and Pages subtab in the Dashboard).
		`'post_date'` — Sorts by the date on which pages were created.
		`'post_modified'` — Sorts by the time when the page was last modified.
		`'post_author'` — Sorts by author, according to the author ID.
		`#.'post_name'` — Sorts alphabetically by the post slug.
		`'ID'` — Sorts by numeric Page ID.

(continued)

Table 9-5 *(continued)*

Parameter	Type	Description and Values
Exclude	string	Lists the numeric page ID numbers, separated by commas, that you want to exclude from the page list display (for example, `'exclude=10, 20, 30'`). There is no default value.
Depth	integer	Uses a numeric value for how many levels of pages are displayed in the list of pages. Possible options: `0` — Displays all pages, including main and subpages (default). `-1` — Shows subpages but doesn't indent them in the list display. `1` — Shows only main pages (no subpages). `2, 3 ...` — Displays pages to the given depth.
show_date	string	Displays the date when the page was created or last modified. Possible options: `' '` — Displays no date (default). `'modified'` — Displays the date when the page was last modified. `'created'` — Displays the date when the page was created.
date_format	string	Sets the format of the date to be displayed. Defaults to the date format configured in the Options tab and General subtab in the Dashboard.
title_li	string	Types text for the heading of the page list. Defaults to display the text: `"Pages"`. If value is empty ("), no heading is displayed; for example, `'title_li=My Pages"` displays the heading `My Pages` above the page list.

An alternative to using the `wp_list_pages()` template tag to create a navigation system is to use the built-in feature in WordPress called Menus, which enables you to build custom menus that aren't completely dependent upon your WordPress pages but that can include links to posts, categories, and custom links that you define. Chapter 10 contains information about the

Menus feature, along with the `wp_nav_menu()` template tag that you use to display menus.

Page lists are displayed in an *unordered list* (you may know it by the term *bulleted list*). Whichever term you use, it's a list with a bullet point in front of every page link.

The following tag and query string displays a list of pages without the text heading `"Pages"`. In other words, it displays no title at the top of the page's link list:

```
<?php wp_list_pages( 'title_li=' ); ?>
```

The next tag and query string displays the list of pages sorted by the date when they were created; the date is also displayed along with the page name:

```
<?php wp_list_pages( 'sort_column=post_date&show_date='created' ); ?>
```

Take a look at the way query-string parameters are written:

```
'parameter1=value&parameter2=value&parameter3=value'
```

The entire string is surrounded by single quotation marks, and no white space is within the query string. Each parameter is joined to its value by the = character. When you use multiple parameters/values, you separate them with the & character. You can think of the string like this: parameter1= value**AND**parameter2=value**AND**parameter3=value. Keep this convention in mind for the remaining template tags and parameters in this chapter.

Post archives

The `<?php wp_get_archives(); ?>` template tag displays the blog post archives in a number of ways, using the parameters and values shown in Table 9-6. Values that appear in bold are the default values set by WordPress. Here are just a few examples of what you can produce with this template tag:

- ✔ Display the titles of the last 15 posts you've made to your site.
- ✔ Display the titles of the posts you've made in the past ten days.
- ✔ Display a monthly list of archives.

Table 9-6	Most Common Parameters (Query-String) for wp_get_archives();	
Parameter and Type	*Possible Values*	*Example*
`type` (string) Determines the type of archive to display.	`monthlydailyweekly-postbypost`	`<?php wp_get_ archives( 'type= postbypost' ); ?>` Displays the titles of the most recent blog posts.
`format` (string) Formats the display of the links in the archive list.	`html` — Surrounds the links with `<li>` `</li>` tags. `option` — Places archive list in drop-down menu format. `link` — Surrounds the links with `<link>` `</link>` tags. `custom` — Use your own HTML tags, using the before and after parameters.	`<?php wp_get_ archives( 'format= html' ); ?>` Displays the list of archive links where each link is surrounded by the `<li>` `</li>` HTML tags.
`limit` (integer) Limits the number of archives to display.	If no value, all are displayed.	`<?php wp_get_ archives( 'limit= 10' ); ?>` Displays the last ten archives in a list.
`before` (string) Places text or formatting before the link in the archive list when using the custom parameter.	No default	`<?php wp_get_ archives( 'before= <strong>' ); ?>` Inserts the `<strong>` HTML tag before each link in the archive link list.
`after` (string) Inserts text or formatting after the link in the archive list when using the custom parameter.	No default	`<?php wp_get_ archives( 'after= </strong>' ); ?>` Inserts the `</strong>` HTML tag after each link in the archive link list.

Parameter and Type	Possible Values	Example

`show_post_count` (Boolean) This value displays the number of posts in the archive. You would use this if you use the `'type'` of `monthly`.	true or 1
	false or 0
		`<? wp_get_archives(`
		`'show_post_count=1'`
		`); ?>`
		Displays the number of posts in each archive after each archive link.

Here are a couple of examples of tags used to display blog-post archives.

This tag displays a linked list of monthly archives (for example, November 2015, December 2015, and so on).

```php
<?php wp_get_archives( 'type=monthly' ); ?>
```

This next tag displays a linked list of the 15 most recent blog posts:

```php
<?php wp_get_archives( 'type=postbypost&limit=15' ); ?>
```

Categories

WordPress lets you create categories and assign posts to a specific category (or multiple categories). Categories provide an organized navigation system that helps you and your readers find posts you've made on certain topics.

The `<?php wp_list_categories(); ?>` template tag lets you display a list of your categories by using the available parameters and values. (Table 9-7 shows some of the most popular parameters.) Each category is linked to the appropriate category page that lists all the posts you've assigned to it. The values that appear in bold are the default values set by WordPress.

Here are a couple of examples of tags used to display a list of your categories.

This example, with its parameters, displays a list of categories sorted by name without showing the number of posts made in each category; the example also displays the RSS feed for each category title:

```php
<?php wp_list_categories( 'orderby=name&show_count=0&feed=RSS' ); ?>
```

Table 9-7	Most Common Parameters (Query-String) for wp_list_categories();	
Parameter and Type	**Possible Values**	**Example**
`orderby` (string) Determines how the category list will be ordered.	`ID` name	`<?php wp_list_categories ( 'orderby=name' ); ?>` Displays the list of categories by name, alphabetically, as they appear in the Dashboard.
`style` (string) Determines the format of the category list display.	**List** none	`<?php wp_list_categories ( 'style=list' ); ?>` Displays the list of category links where each link is surrounded by the `<li>` `</li>` HTML tags. `<?php wp_list_categories ( 'style=none' ); ?>` Displays the list of category links with a simple line break after each link.
`show_count` (Boolean) Determines whether to display the post count for each listed category.	`true` or `1` **false** or 0	`<?php wp_list_categories ( 'show_count=1' ); ?>` Displays the post count, in parentheses, after each category list. Espresso `(10)`, for example, means that there are ten posts in the Espresso category.
`hide_empty` (Boolean) Determines whether empty categories should be displayed in the list (meaning a category with zero posts assigned to it).	**true** or **1** false or 0	`<?php wp_list_categories ( 'hide_empty=0' ); ?>` Displays only those categories that currently have posts assigned to them.
`feed` (string) Determines whether the RSS feed should be displayed for each category in the list.	Rss Default is no feeds displayed.	`<?php wp_list_categories ( 'feed=rss' ); ?>` Displays category titles with an RSS link next to each one.
`feed_image` (string) Provides the path/file-name for an image for the feed.	No default	`<?php wp_list_categories ( 'feed_image=/wp-content/ images/feed.gif' ); ?>` Displays the `feed.gif` image for each category title. This image is linked to the RSS feed for that category.

Parameter and Type	Possible Values	Example
`hierarchical` (Boolean) Determines whether the child categories should be displayed after each parent category in the category link list.	**true** or **1** `false` or 0	`<?php wp_list_categories ( 'hierarchical=0' ); ?>` Doesn't display the child categories after each parent category in the category list.

This example, with its parameters, displays a list of categories sorted by name with the post count showing and shows the subcategories of every parent category:

```
<?php wp_list_categories( 'orderby=name&show_count=1&hierarchical=1' ); '>
```

Getting widgetized

About 99.99 percent of the WordPress themes available today are coded with *widgetized sidebars* — which means you can use the widgets within WordPress to populate your sidebar area with content, navigation menus, and lists.

With widgets in place, you generally have no reason to mess around with the code in the `sidebar.php` template file because most of the content you want to add into your sidebar can be added through the use of widgets.

In a WordPress theme, the Theme Functions template (`functions.php`) and the Sidebar template (`sidebar.php`) create the functionality and the possibility for widgets to exist within your theme. You're not limited to where you place and use widgets, by and large. I am using the Sidebar template (`sidebar.php`) in this example.

First, you have to define the widgets in your theme. This means that you need to alert WordPress to the fact that this theme can handle widgets — which is known as *registering* a widget with the WordPress software. To register a widget, add the `register_sidebar` function to the Theme Functions template (`functions.php`). In the `functions.php` file in the Twenty Fifteen theme, the code for registering a widget looks like this:

```
register_sidebar( array(
'name' => __( 'Widget Area', 'twentyfifteen' ),
'id' => 'sidebar-1',
'description' => __( 'Main sidebar that appears on the left.', 'twentyfifteen'),
'before_widget' => '<aside id="%1$s" class="widget %2$s">',
'after_widget'  => '</aside>',
'before_title'  => '<h1 class="widget-title">',
'after_title'   => '</h1>',
) );
```

Within that code, you see seven different *arrays*. An array is a set of values that tells WordPress how you would like your widgets handled and displayed:

✔ `name`: This name is unique to the widget and appears on the Widgets page in the Dashboard. It is helpful if you register several different widgetized areas on your site.

✔ `id`: This is the unique ID given to the widget.

✔ `description` (`optional`): This is a text description of the widget. The text that gets placed here displays on the Widgets page in the Dashboard.

✔ `before_widget`: This is the HTML markup that gets inserted directly before the widget. It is helpful for CSS styling purposes.

✔ `after_widget`: This is the HTML markup that gets inserted directly after the widget.

✔ `before_title`: This is the HTML markup that gets inserted directly before the widget title.

✔ `after_title`: This is the HTML markup that gets inserted directly after the widget title.

With that code in your `functions.php` file, WordPress now recognizes that you've registered a widget called Widget Area for your theme and makes the widget area available for you to drag and drop widgets onto the Widgets page in the Dashboard. All that's left to do now is to call that widget into your `sidebar.php` file. By doing so, you allow the widgets to display on your site. Follow these steps to call widgets to your site (these steps assume that the widget code isn't already in the Sidebar template):

1. Click the Editor link below the Appearance menu.

The Edit Themes page opens.

2. **Click the Sidebar (**`sidebar.php`**) template.**

   The Sidebar template opens in the text box on the left side of the page.

3. **Type the following code in the Sidebar (**`sidebar.php`**) template:**

```php
<?php if ( ! dynamic_sidebar( 'Primary Widget Area' ) ) : ?>
<?php endif; ?>
```

   The parameter within the `dynamic_sidebar` template tag corresponds to the name that you provided in the widget array called *name* earlier in this section. It must be the same; otherwise, it will not display on your website.

4. **Click the Update File button.**

   The changes you've made to the Sidebar (`sidebar.php`) template file are now saved.

You can register an unlimited number of widgets for your theme. This flexibility allows you to create several different widgetized areas and widget features in different areas of your site. Chapter 12 goes into more detail about using different Sidebar templates to create different widgetized areas and features on your site.

Chapter 10

Tweaking WordPress Themes

- -

- -

Chapter 8 shows how you can use free WordPress themes in your website. Many people are quite happy to use these themes without making any adjustments to them at all. I can't tell you, however, how many times people have asked me whether they can customize a theme that they've found. The answer to their question is always, "Of course you can make changes on your own."

The practice of changing a few elements of an existing WordPress theme is known as *tweaking*. Thousands of WordPress site owners tweak their existing themes on a regular basis. This chapter provides information on some of the most common tweaks you can make to your theme, such as changing the header image, changing the color of the background or the text links, and changing font styles — and these changes are pretty easy to make, too! You'll be tweaking your own theme in no time flat.

Using a theme exactly as a theme author released it is great. If a new version is released that fixes a browser compatibility issue or adds features offered by a new version of WordPress, a quick theme upgrade is very easy to do.

However, chances are good that you'll want to tinker with the design, add new features, or modify the theme structure. If you modify the theme, you won't be able to upgrade to a newly released version without modifying the theme again.

If only you could upgrade customized versions of themes with new features when they're released. Fortunately, child themes give you this best-of-both-worlds theme solution. Chapter 11 explores what child themes are, how to create a parent theme that's child-theme ready, and how to get the most out of using child themes.

Before you go too wild with tweaking templates, make a backup of your theme so that you have the original files from which to easily restore it if necessary. You can back up your theme files by connecting to your web server via FTP (see Chapter 3) and downloading your theme folder to your computer. When you have the original theme files safe and secure on your hard drive, feel free to tweak away, comfortable in the knowledge that you have a backup.

Styling with CSS: The Basics

A *Cascading Style Sheet (CSS)* is a cascading sheet of style markup that controls the appearance of content on a website. Every single WordPress theme you use in your blog uses CSS. The CSS provides style and design flair to the template tags in your templates. (See Chapter 9 for information about WordPress template tags.) The CSS for your WordPress theme is pulled in through the Header template (`header.php`) and is named `style.css`.

In the Header template (`header.php`) of most WordPress themes, you find the following line of code, which pulls the CSS (`style.css`) into the page to provide the formatting of the elements of your blog:

```
<link rel="stylesheet" type="text/css" media="all" href="<?php bloginfo
        ( 'stylesheet_url' ); ?>" />
```

Don't tweak the line of code that pulls in the `style.css` file; otherwise, the CSS won't work for your blog.

Chapter 9 covers the commonly used parameters for the `bloginfo();` template tag used in WordPress themes.

CSS selectors

With CSS, you can provide style (such as size, color, and placement) to the display of elements on your blog (such as text links, header images, font size and colors, paragraph margins, and line spacing). *CSS selectors* contain names, properties, and values to define which HTML elements in the templates you will style with CSS. CSS selectors are used to declare (or select) which part of the markup the style applies to. Table 10-1 provides some examples of CSS selectors and their use.

Table 10-1		Basic CSS Selectors	
CSS Selector	**Description**	**HTML**	**CSS**
body	Sets the style for the overall body of the site, such as background color and default fonts.	`<body>`	`body {background-color: white}` The background color on all pages is white.
p	Defines how paragraphs are formatted.	`<p>This is a paragraph</p>`	`p {color:black}` The color of the fonts used in all paragraphs is black.
h1, h2, h3, h4, h5, h6	Provides bold headers for different sections of your site.	`<h1>This is a site title </h1>`	`h1 {font-weight: bold;}` A font surrounded by the `<h1>..</h1>` HTML tags is bold.
a	Defines how text links display in your site.	`<a href= "http://wiley. com">Wiley Publishing</a>`	`a {color: red}` All text links appear in red.

Classes and IDs

You can find the stylesheet (`style.css`) for the default Twenty Fifteen theme on the Edit Themes page in your Dashboard (see Figure 10-1). Everything in it may look foreign to you right now, but I want to bring your attention to two items you see when you scroll down that template:

✔ `#content`: One type of CSS selector. The hash mark (#) indicates that it's a CSS *ID*.

✔ `.singular`: Another type of CSS selector. The period (.) indicates that it's a CSS *class*.

IDs and classes define styling properties for different sections of your WordPress theme. Table 10-2 shows examples of IDs and classes from the `header.php` template in the Twenty Fifteen WordPress theme. Armed with this information, you'll know where to look in the stylesheet when you want to change the styling for a particular area of your theme.

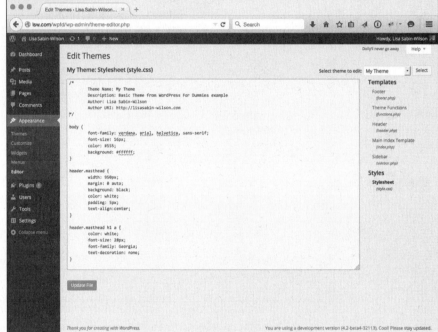

Figure 10-1:
A
WordPress
theme
stylesheet
(style.css).

Table 10-2	Connecting HTML with CSS Selectors	
HTML	*CSS Selector*	*Description*
`<div id="page">`	`#page`	Styles the elements for the `page` ID in your template(s).
`<div class=". site-header">`	`.site-header`	Styles the elements for the `site-header` class in your template(s).
`<h1 class= "site-title">`	`.site-title`	Styles the elements for your `site-title` class in your template(s), but also follows rules for the `h1` values set in the CSS.
`<div class= "search-toggle">`	`.search-toggle`	Styles the elements for your `search-toggle` class in your template(s).
`<div id= "content">`	`#content`	Styles the elements for the `content` ID in your template(s).

If you find an element in the template code that says id (such as div id= or p id=), look for the hash symbol in the stylesheet. If you find an element in the template code that says class (such as div class= or p class=), look for the period in the stylesheet followed by the selector name.

CSS properties and values

CSS properties are assigned to the CSS selector name. You also need to provide values for the CSS properties to define the style elements for the particular CSS selector you're working with.

In the default Twenty Fifteen WordPress theme, the markup on line 30 in the Header template (header.php) is <div class="site-branding">. This class, with the name site-header, provides styling for the site header.

In the default Twenty Fifteen WordPress theme stylesheet, the CSS defined for the site-header class is as follows:

```
.site-branding {
min-height: 2em;
padding-right: 60px;
position: relative;
}
```

Every CSS property needs to be followed by a colon (:), and each CSS value needs to be followed by a semicolon (;).

The CSS selector is .site-branding, which has three properties:

- ✔ The first CSS property is min-height, which has the value of 2em;.

- ✔ The second CSS property is padding-right, which has the value 60px;.

- ✔ The third CSS property is position, which has the value of relative;.

Table 10-3 provides some examples of commonly used CSS properties and values.

Table 10-3	Common CSS Properties and Values	
CSS Property	**CSS Value**	**Examples**
`background-color`	Defines the color of the background (such as red, black, or white).	**Markup:** `<div id="page">` **CSS:** `#page {background-color: white}`
`background`	Defines a background image.	**Markup:** `<header id="banner">` **CSS:** `header#banner {background: url(images/header.jpg) no-repeat;}`
`font-family`*	Defines the fonts used for the selector.	**Markup:** `<body>` **CSS:** `body { font-family: 'Lucida Grande', Verdana, Arial, Sans-Serif;}`
`color`	Defines the color of the text.	**Markup:** `<h1>Website Title </h1>` **CSS:** `h1 {color: blue}`
`font-size`**	Defines the size of the font used for the text.	**Markup:** `<h1>Website Title </h1>` **CSS:** `h1 {font-size: 18px;}`
`text-align`	Defines the alignment of the text (left, center, right, or justified).	**Markup:** `<div id="wrapper">` **CSS:** `#wrapper {text-align: left;}`

*W3Schools has a good resource on the `font-family` property here: www.w3schools.com/cssref/pr_font_font-family.asp

**W3Schools has a good resource on the `font-size` property here: www.w3schools.com/cssref/pr_font_font-size.asp

Changing the Background Color

In Chapter 9, I discuss the Header template (`header.php`) in detail. In this section, I show you how to tweak the background color in the default Twenty Fifteen theme. If you're not using the default Twenty Fifteen theme, you can also use the `<body>` tag in a Header template to change the background color of your website.

Creating a custom background

The Twenty Fifteen WordPress theme is packaged with the option to change the background to a different color or use an image for your background. To use the nifty, built-in custom background feature to change the Twenty Fifteen background for your blog, follow these steps:

1. **Click the Background link under the Appearance menu.**

   The Custom Background page loads in the Dashboard.

2. **Click the Select Color to change the background color.**

   You can enter a hex color code in the text box provided shown in Figure 10-2.

   If you don't know what hex color code you want to use, click the Select Color link and click a color within the provided color picker (see Figure 10-2). The color selected in Figure 10-2 is #f1f1f1, which is gray.

A hexadecimal (or *hex*) code represents a certain color. Hex codes always start with a hash symbol (#) and have six letters and/or numbers to represent a particular color; for example, the code #f1f1f1 represents the color gray in hexadecimal code. I talk more about hexadecimal values in the following section, "Changing the background using CSS."

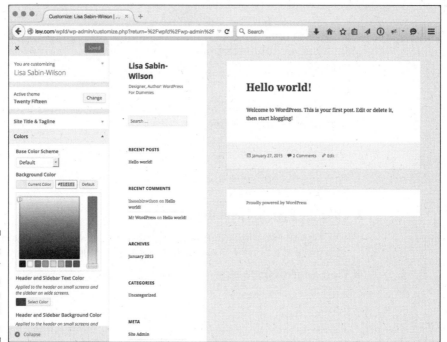

Figure 10-2:
The color picker on the Custom Background page.

3. **Click Background Image to use an image file for the background or upload an image from your computer.**

   Click the Browse button under Background Image and select a file from your the existing WordPress Media Library, or click Upload Files to upload an image from your computer. Then click the Choose Image.

4. **Change the display options for your new background image.**

   - *Background Repeat:* Select No Repeat, Tile, Tile Horizontally, or Tile Vertically in the drop-down menu to set the image repeat behavior of the background image on your website.

   - *Background Position:* Select Left, Center, or Right to set the screen position of the background image on your website.

   - *Background Attachment:* Select Scroll to set the background image to scroll down the page, or select Fixed to set the background image in a static position (so that it doesn't scroll down the page).

If you do not see the Background link under the Appearances menu in the Dashboard, that means that the theme you are using does not currently support custom backgrounds (note that the default theme, Twenty Fifteen, does). You can add support for the Custom Background feature to any theme with just a few lines of code.

Just follow these steps:

1. **Browse to the Edit Themes page and click the Theme Functions (**`functions.php`**) template.**

   The Theme Functions template opens in the text editor on the left side of the page.

2. **Add the following line of code to the Theme Functions template somewhere after the line that says** `<?php`**:**

   ```
   add_theme_support( 'custom-background' );
   ```

   This line of code tells WordPress that your theme has added the Custom Background feature.

3. **Click the Update File button.**

   The Theme Functions template is saved, along with your changes. The Background link now displays below the Appearance menu.

4. **View your website page to see your changes.**

Changing the background using CSS

The <body> tag is simple HTML markup. Every theme has this tag, which defines the overall default content for each page of your website — the site's *body*. In the Twenty Fifteen stylesheet (style.css), the background for the body is defined like this:

```
body {
background-color: #fff;
}
```

The background for the <body> tag uses a hexadecimal color code of #fff that gives the background a white color. You can use a color or an image (or both) to style the background of your website:

- ✔ **Color:** The W3Schools website has a great resource on hex codes and color names at www.w3schools.com/HTML/html_colornames.asp.

- ✔ **Image:** You can easily use an image as a background for your site by uploading the image to the images folder in your theme directory. That value looks like background: url (images/*yourimage*.jpg). (***Note:*** The url portion of this code automatically pulls in the URL of your website, so you just need to leave the url text as is.)

You can also use a combination of colors and images in your backgrounds.

In the case of some basic colors, you don't have to use the hex code. For colors such as white, black, red, blue, and silver, you can just use their names — background-color: white, for example.

If you want to change the background color of your theme, follow these steps:

1. **In the WordPress Dashboard, click the Editor link on the Appearance menu.**

   The Edit Themes page opens.

2. **From the Select Theme to Edit drop-down menu, choose the theme you want to change.**

3. **Click the Stylesheet template link.**

   The style.css template opens in the text editor on the left side of the Edit Themes page (refer to Figure 10-1).

4. **Scroll down in the text editor until you find the CSS selector body.**

   If you're tweaking the default theme, this section is what you're looking for:

   ```
   body:before {
   background-color: #fff;
   }
   ```

   If you're tweaking a different template, the CSS selector body will look similar.

5. **Edit the** `background` **property's values.**

   For example, in the default template, if you want to change the background color to black, you can use one of the following:

   ```
   background-color: #000000;
   ```

   or

   ```
   background-color: black;
   ```

6. **Click the Update File button in the bottom-left corner of the page.**

   Your changes are saved and applied to your theme.

7. **Visit your site in your web browser.**

   The background color of your theme has changed.

Using Your Own Header Image

Most themes have a header image that appears at the top of the page. This image is generated by a graphic defined either in the CSS value for the property that represents the header area, or through the use of a feature in WordPress called a custom header. In the WordPress default Twenty Fifteen theme, all the hard work's been done for you. Including a custom header image on a blog that uses the Twenty Fifteen theme is pretty darn easy.

To upload a new header image, click the Header link in the Appearances menu in your Dashboard, and follow these steps:

1. **Click the Add New Image button under the Header Image title.**

   Select the image from the WordPress Media Library, or upload an image from your computer and then click Open.

2. **Click Select and Crop.**

   The Crop Image page appears, where you can crop the image and adjust which portion of the header image you would like displayed (see Figure 10-3).

3. **Click the Crop Image button.**

   The Header Image page appears, and your new header image is now displayed.

4. **View your website.**

   Your new header image appears at the top of your website.

In themes that do not have the custom header image feature, you can easily define a background image for the header image using CSS.

For purposes of this example, the HTML markup for the header in the template is this:

```
<header id="site-header"></div>
```

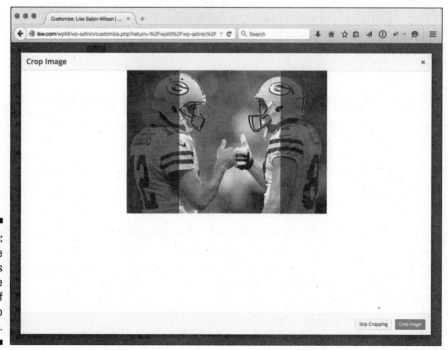

Figure 10-3:
Adjust the dotted lines to choose the area of the image to display.

In the CSS (`style.css`) file, you can use a background image by defining it in the CSS properties for `#site-header`. Use this code:

```
#site-header {
background: url(/images/header-image.jpg) no-repeat;
max-width: 100%;
height: auto;
}
```

The background value indicates an image called `header-image.jpg`. For it to display on your site, you need to create the image and upload it to your web server under `/wp-content/theme-name/images/`.

Creating Custom Navigation Menus

A *navigation menu* is a listing of links displayed on your site. These links can be to pages, posts, or categories within your site, or they can be links to other sites. Either way, you can define navigation menus on your site through the built-in Custom Menu feature in WordPress.

It's to your advantage to provide at least one navigation menu on your site so that readers can see everything your site has to offer. Providing visitors with a link — or several — to click keeps the point-and-click spirit of the web.

Adding the Custom Menu feature to your theme

The Custom Menu feature is already built in to the default Twenty Fifteen WordPress theme, so you don't have to worry about preparing your theme for it. However, if you're using a different theme, adding support for the Menu feature to your theme is easy:

1. **Click the Editor link under the Appearance menu. Then click the Theme Functions (`functions.php`) template.**

   The Theme Functions template opens in the text editor on the left side of the Edit Themes page.

2. **Type the following function on a new line in the Theme Functions template file in your theme:**

   ```
   add_theme_support( 'nav-menus' );
   ```

3. Click the Update File button to save the changes to the template.

This template tag tells WordPress that your theme can use the Custom Menu feature, and a Menus link now appears under the Appearance menu in the Dashboard.

4. Open the Header template (`header.php`).

Click the Header link on the Edit Themes page to open the Header template in the text editor on the left side of the Edit Themes page.

5. Add the following template tag by typing it on a new line in the Header template (`header.php`) **somewhere after the** `<body>` **tag:**

```
<?php wp_nav_menu(); ?>
```

This template tag is needed so that the menu you build using the Custom Menu feature will display at the top of your website. Table 10-4 details the different parameters you can use with the `wp_nav_menu();` template tag to further customize the display to suit your needs.

6. Save the changes you've made to the Header template.

Click the Update File button at the bottom of the page.

Table 10-4   Common Tag Parameters for wp_nav_menu();

Parameter	Information	Default	Tag
`id`	The unique ID of the menu (because you can create several menus, each has a unique ID number).	Blank	`wp_nav_menu ( array( 'id' => '1' ) );`
`slug`	The menu name in slug form (for example, `nav-menu`).	Blank	`wp_nav_menu ( array ( 'slug' => 'nav-menu' ) );`
`menu`	The menu name.	Blank	`wp_nav_menu ( array ( 'menu' => 'Nav Menu' ) );`
`menu_ class`	The CSS class used to style the menu list.	Menu	`wp_nav_menu ( array ( 'menu_class' => 'mymenu' ) );`
`format`	The HTML markup used to style the list — either an unordered list (`ul/li`) or `div` class.	`div`	`wp_nav_menu ( array ( 'format' => 'ul' ) );`

(continued)

Table 10-4 *(continued)*

Parameter	Information	Default	Tag
fall-back_cb	The parameter that creates a fallback if a custom menu doesn't exist.	wp_page_menu (the default list of page links)	wp_nav_menu (array(' fall-back_cb' => 'wp_page_menu'));
before	The text that displays before the link text.	None	wp_nav_menu (array ('before' => 'Click Here'));
after	The text that displays after the link text.	None	wp_nav_menu (array ('after' => '»'));

Building custom navigation menus

After you add the menu feature to your theme (or if you're already using a theme that has the menu feature), building menus is easy — just follow these steps:

1. **Click the Menus link in the Appearance menu in your Dashboard.**

   The Menus page opens in your WordPress Dashboard.

2. **Type a name in the Menu Name box and click the Create Menu button.**

   The Menus page is reloaded with a message that tells you your new menu has been created.

3. **Add links to your newly created menu.**

   WordPress gives you three ways to add links to the new menu you just created (the items in this list are shown in Figure 10-4):

   • *Pages:* Click the View All link to display a list of all the page(s) you have published on your site. Select the box next to the page names you want to add to your menu. Then click the Add to Menu button.

   • *Custom Links:* In the URL field, type the URL of the website that you want to add (https://www.google.com). Next, type the name of the link that you want displayed in your menu in the Label text field (**Google**). Then click the Add to Menu button.

   • *Categories:* Click the View All link to display a list of all the categories you've created on your site. Select the box next to the category names you want to add to the menu. Then click the Add to Menu button.

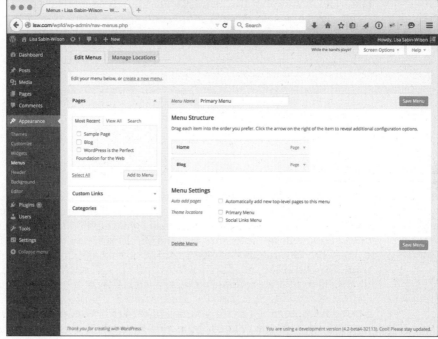

Figure 10-4:
The Custom
Menus
options on
the Menus
page in the
Dashboard.

4. Review your menu choices on the right side of the page.

When you add new menu items, the column on the right side of the
Menus page populates with your menu choices.

5. Edit your menu choices, if needed.

Click the Edit link to the right of the menu link name to edit the information of each individual link in your new menu.

6. Save your menu before leaving the Menus page.

Be sure to click the Save Menu button under Menu Settings on the right
side at the top of the Menus page. A message appears, confirming that
the new menu has been saved.

You can create as many menus as you need to for your website. Just follow
the parameters for the menu template tag to make sure you're pulling in the
correct menu in the correct spot on your theme. Pay attention to either the
menu ID or menu name in the template tag. You find more options for your
navigation menus by clicking the Screen Options tab at the top-right corner
of your Dashboard. From there, you can add things like Posts and Custom
Post Types to your menu options, as well as add descriptions for menu items.

The HTML markup for the menu is generated as an unordered list, by default, and looks like this in the sites source code:

```
<ul id="menu-main" class="menu">
<li id="menu-item-1" class="menu-item menu-item-type-custom menu-item-object-
          custom menu-item-1"><a href="/">Home</a></li>
<li id="menu-item-2" class="menu-item menu-item-type-post_type menu-item-object-
          page menu-item-2"><a href="http://localhost/wpdemo/blog/">Blog
          </a></li>
<li id="menu-item-3" class="menu-item menu-item-type-post_type menu-item-object-
          page menu-item-3"><a href="http://localhost/wpdemo/about/">About
          </a></li>
</ul>
```

Notice in the HTML markup that the first line defines CSS ID and class: `<ul id="menu-main" class="menu">`. The ID in that line reflects the name that you gave your menu. Because I gave my menu the name of "Main" when I created it in the Dashboard, the CSS ID is `menu-main`. If I had named it "Foo," the ID would instead be `menu-foo`. This assignment of menu names in the CSS and HTML markup is why WordPress allows you to use CSS to create different styles and formats for your different menus.

When developing themes for yourself or others to use, you want to make sure that the CSS you define for the menus can do things like account for subpages by creating drop-down menu effects. You can do this several different ways, and Listing 10-1 gives you just one example of a block of CSS that you can use to create a nice style for your menu (this CSS example assumes that you have a menu named "Main"; therefore, the HTML and CSS markup indicate `'menu-main'`).

The CSS you use to customize the display of your menus will differ; the example that I provide in the previous section is just that: an example. After you get the hang of using CSS, you can try different methods, colors, and styling to create a custom look of your own. (Find additional information about basic CSS later in this chapter.)

Displaying Custom Menus using widgets

You don't have to use the `wp_nav_menu()`; template tag to display the menus on your site, because WordPress also provides you with Custom Menu widgets that you can add to your theme. You can therefore use widgets instead of template tags to display the navigation menus on your site. This feature is especially helpful if you have created multiple menus in and around your site in various different places.

Listing 10-1: Sample CSS for Drop-Down Menu Navigation

```
#menu-main {
            width: 960px;
            font-family: Georgia, Times New Roman, Trebuchet MS;
            font-size: 16px;
            color: #FFFFFF;
            margin: 0 auto 0;
            clear: both;
            overflow: hidden;
            }
#menu-main ul {
            width: 100%;
            float: left;
            list-style: none;
            margin: 0;
            padding: 0;
            }
#menu-main li {
            float: left;
            list-style: none;
            }
#menu-main li a {
            color: #FFFFFF;
            display: block;
            font-size: 16px;
            margin: 0;
            padding: 12px 15px 12px 15px;
            text-decoration: none;
            position: relative;
            }
#menu-main li a:hover,
#menu-main li a:active,
#menu-main .current_page_item a,
#menu-main .current-cat a,
#menu-main .current-menu-item {
            color: #CCCCCC;
            }
#menu-main li li a,
#menu-main li li a:link,
#menu-main li li a:visited {
            background: #555555;
            color: #FFFFFF;
            width: 138px;
            font-size: 12px;
            margin: 0;
            padding: 5px 10px 5px 10px;
            border-left: 1px solid #FFFFFF;
            border-right: 1px solid #FFFFFF;
            border-bottom: 1px solid #FFFFFF;
            position: relative;
            }
```

(continued)

Listing 10-1 *(continued)*

```
#menu-main li li a:hover,
#menu-main li li a:active {
              background: #333333;
              color: #FFFFFF;
              }
#menu-main li ul {
              z-index: 9999;
              position: absolute;
              left: -999em;
              height: auto;
              width: 160px;
              }
#menu-main li ul a {
              width: 140px;
              }
#menu-main li ul ul {
              margin: -31px 0 0 159px;
              }
#menu-main li:hover ul ul,
#menu-main li:hover ul ul {
              left: -999em;
              }
#menu-main li:hover ul,
#menu-main li li:hover ul,
#menu-main li li li:hover ul, {
              left: auto;
              }
#menu-main li:hover {
              position: static;
              }
```

Your first step is to register a special widget area for your theme to handle the Custom Menu widget display. To register this widget, open your theme's functions.php file and add the following lines of code on a new line:

```
// ADD MENU WIDGET
if ( function_exists('register_sidebars') )
              register_sidebar(array('name'=>'Menu Widget',));
```

These few lines of code create a new widget area called Menu on the Widgets page in your Dashboard. At this point, you can drag the Custom Menu widget into the Menu Widget area to indicate that you want to display a Custom Menu in that area. The Available Widgets area with the Menu Widget displayed is in Figure 10-5.

To add the widget area to your theme, head over to the Theme Editor (Appearance➪Editor) and open the header.php file; then add these lines of

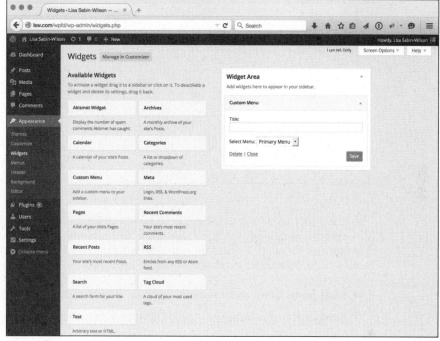

Figure 10-5:
Widget
page
displaying
the Menu
Widget
under
Available
Widgets.

code in the area you want the Menu widget displayed; for example, near the
site name:

```
<ul>
<?php if ( !function_exists('dynamic_sidebar') || !dynamic_sidebar('Menu
          Widget') ) : ?>
<?php endif; ?>
</ul>
```

These lines of code tell WordPress that you want information contained in
the Menu widget area displayed on your site.

Changing Font Family, Color, and Size

You can change the fonts in your theme for style or readability. I've seen
typographic (or font) design experts use simple font variations to achieve
amazing design results. You can use fonts to separate headlines from
body text (or widget headlines and text from the main content) to be less
distracting. Table 10-5 lists some examples of often-used font properties.

Table 10-5		Fonts
Font Properties	*Common Values*	*CSS Examples*
`font-family`	Georgia, Times, serif	`body {font-family: Georgia; serif;}`
`font-size`	px, %, em	`body {font-size: 14px;}`
`font-style`	Italic, underline	`body {font-style: italic;}`
`font-weight`	Bold, bolder, normal	`body {font-weight: normal}`

The web is actually kind of picky about how it displays fonts, as well as what sort of fonts you can use in the `font-family` property. Not all fonts appear correctly on the web. To be safe, consider sticking to some commonly used font families that appear correctly in most browsers:

- **Serif fonts:** Times New Roman, Georgia, Garamond, Bookman Old Style
- **Sans-serif fonts:** Verdana, Arial, Tahoma, Trebuchet MS

Changing font color

With more than 16 million different HTML color combinations available, you can find just the right color value for your project. After some time, you'll memorize your favorite color codes. I find that knowing codes for different shades of gray helps me quickly add an extra design touch. For example, I often use the shades of gray listed in Table 10-6 for backgrounds, borders on design elements, and widget headers.

Table 10-6	My Favorite CSS Colors
Color	*Value*
White	#FFFFFF
Black	#000000
Grays	#CCCCCC
	#DDDDDD
	#333333
	#E0E0E0

You can easily change the color of your font by changing the `color` property of the CSS selector you want to tweak. You can use hex codes to define the colors.

You can define the overall font color in your site by defining it in the body CSS selector like this:

```
body {
color: #333333;
}
```

Changing font size

To tweak the size of your font, change the `font-size` property of the CSS selector you want to change. Font sizes are generally determined by units of measurement, as in these examples:

- ✔ px: Pixel measurement. Increasing or decreasing the number of pixels increases or decreases the font size (12px is larger than 10px).

- ✔ pt: Point measurement. As with pixels, increasing or decreasing the number of points affects the font size accordingly (12pt is larger than 10pt).

- ✔ em: A scalable unit of measurement that is equal to the current font size. For example, if the font size of the body of the site is defined as 12px, then 1em is equal to 12px; likewise, 2em is equal to 24px.

- ✔ %: Percentage measurement. Increasing or decreasing the percentage number affects the font size accordingly. (If the body of the website uses 14px as the default, 50% is the equivalent to 7 pixels; 100% is the equivalent to 14 pixels.)

In the default template CSS, the font size is defined in the `<body>` tag in pixels, like this:

```
font-size: 12px;
```

When you put all three elements (font family, color, and font size) together in the `<body>` tag, they style the font for the overall body of your site. Here's how they work together in the `<body>` tag of the default template CSS:

```
body {
font-size: 12px;
font-family: Georgia, "Bitstream Charter", serif;
color: #666666;
}
```

Serif fonts have little tails, or curlicues, at the edges of letters. (This book's text is in a serif font.) *Sans-serif* fonts have straight edges and are devoid of any fancy styling. (The heading in Table 10-6 uses a sans-serif font . . . no tails!)

When you want to change a font family in your CSS, open the stylesheet (`style.css`), search for `property: font-family`, change the values for that property, and save your changes.

In the default template CSS, the font is defined in the `<body>` tag, like this:

```
font-family: Georgia, "Bitstream Charter", serif;
```

Font families, or fonts with multiple names, should appear in quotes in your stylesheet.

Adding borders

Using CSS borders can add an interesting and unique flair to elements of your theme design. Table 10-7 illustrates common properties and CSS examples for borders in your theme design.

Table 10-7	Common Border Properties	
Border Properties	*Common Values*	*CSS Examples*
`border-size`	px, em	`body {border-size: 1px;}`
`border-style`	`solid`, `dotted`, `dashed`	`body {border-style: solid}`
`border-color`	Hexadecimal values	`body {border-color: #CCCCCC}`

Finding additional CSS resources

The time may come when you want to explore customizing your theme further. Here are some recommended resources:

- ✔ **WordPress Codex** (`http://codex.wordpress.org`): Official WordPress documentation

- ✔ **W3Schools** (`www.//w3schools.com`): A free and comprehensive online HTML and CSS reference

✔ **WebDesign.com** (www.//webdesign.com): A premium library of WordPress video tutorials and training

✔ **Smashing Magazine** (www.smashingmagazine.com): Gives numerous tips and tricks for customizing a WordPress theme

Understanding Basic HTML Techniques

HTML can help you customize and organize your theme. To understand how HTML and CSS work together, think of it this way: If a website were a building, HTML would be the structure (the studs and foundation) and CSS would be the paint.

HTML contains the elements that CSS provides the styles for. All you have to do to apply a CSS style is use the right HTML element. For this example, I break down a basic block of HTML:

```
<body>
<div id="content">
<header>
<h1>Headline Goes Here</h1>
</header>
<section>
<article>
<p>This is a sample sentence of body text. <blockquote>The journey of a thousand
          miles
starts with the first step.</blockquote> I'm going to continue on this sentence
          and end it
here. </p>
<p>Click <a href="http://lisasabin-wilson.com">here</a> to visit my website.</p>
</article>
</section>
</div>
</body>
```

All HTML elements must have opening and closing tags. Opening tags are contained in less-than (<) and greater-than (>) symbols. Closing tags are the same, except that they are preceded by a forward-slash (/).

For example:

```
<h1>Headline Goes Here</h1>
```

Note that the HTML elements must be properly nested. In line eight of the preceding example, a paragraph tag is opened (`<p>`). Later in that line, a block quote is opened (`<blockquote>`) and is nesting inside the paragraph tag. When editing this line, you could not end the paragraph (`</p>`) before you end the block quote (`</blockquote>`). Nested elements must close before the elements they are nested within close.

Finally, proper *tabbing,* or indenting, is important when writing HTML, mainly for readability so that you can quickly scan through code to find what you're looking for. A good rule to follow is that if you didn't close a tag in the line above, indent one tab over. This practice allows you to see where each element begins and ends. It can also be very helpful when diagnosing problems.

You will use several very basic HTML markup practices over and over in web design and putting together websites. Earlier in this chapter, I discuss how to combine CSS styling with HTML markup to create different display styles (borders, fonts, and so on).

The following sections provide you with commonly used HTML markup samples that you will find helpful as a reference for using HTML in your website code.

Inserting images

You will probably want to insert an image into your website, whether it is within the body of a post or page, in the sidebar by using a widget, or within the template code itself. The HTML markup to insert an image looks like this:

```
<img src="/path/to/image-file.jpg" alt="Image File Name"
    />
```

I break down this code for you in easy snippets to help you understand what's at work here:

- ✔ `<img src=`: This is the HTML markup that tells the browser that the website is looking for an image file.

- ✔ `"/path/to/image-file.jpg"`: This is the actual directory path through which the web browser will find the physical image file. For example, if you uploaded an image to your web server in the `/wp-content/uploads` directory, the physical path for that image file would be `/wp-content/uploads/image-file.jpg`.

✔ `alt="Image File Name"`: The `alt` tag is part of the HTML markup and provides a description for the image that search engines will pick up and recognize as keywords. The `alt` tag description will also display as text on a browser that cannot, for some reason, load the image file; for example, if the server load time is slow, or if the user is using a screen reader with images turned off, the text description will load to at least provide visitors with a description of what the image is.

✔ `/>`: This HTML markup tag closes the initial `<img src="` tag, telling the web browser when the call to the image file is complete.

Inserting hyperlinks

You will probably want to insert a link within the body of a website — commonly referred to as a *hyperlink*, which is a line of text that is anchored to a web address (URL) so that clicking the text takes a visitor to another website or page that appears in the browser window.

The HTML markup to insert a hyperlink looks like this:

```
<a href="http://wiley.com">John Wiley & Sons, Inc. </a>
```

To break down that markup, here is a simple explanation:

✔ `<a href=`: This is the HTML markup that tells the browser that the text within this tag should be hyperlinked to the web address provided in the next point.

✔ `"http://wiley.com"`: This is the web address, or URL, that you intend the text to be anchored to. It needs to be surrounded by quotation marks, which define it as the intended anchor, or address.

✔ `>`: This markup closes the previously opened `<a href=` HTML tag.

✔ `John Wiley & Sons, Inc.`: In this example, this is the text that is linked, or anchored, by the web address, or URL. This text displays on your website and is clickable by your visitors.

✔ `</a>`: This HTML markup tag tells the web browser that the hyperlink is closed. Anything that exists between `<a href=".."> `and `</a>` will be hyperlinked, or clickable, through to the intended anchor, or web address.

Commonly, designers use URLs, or web addresses, to link words to other websites or pages; however, you can also provide hyperlinks to files such as `.pdf` (Adobe Acrobat), `.doc` (Microsoft Word), or any other file type.

Inserting lists

Say you need to provide a clean-looking format for lists of information that you publish on your website. With HTML markup, you can easily provide lists that are formatted differently, depending on your needs.

Ordered lists are numbered sequentially. An example is a step-by-step list of things to do, like this:

1. Write my book chapters.

2. Submit my book chapters to my publisher.

3. Panic a little when book is released to the public.

4. Breathe sigh of relief when public reviews are overwhelmingly positive!

Ordered lists are easy to create in a program such as Microsoft Word, or even in the WordPress post editor because you can use the WYSIWYG editor to format the list for you. However, if you want to code an ordered list using HTML, the experience is a little different. My previous step list sample looks like this when using HTML markup:

```
<ol>
<li>Write my book chapters.</li>
<li>Submit my book chapters to my publisher.</li>
<li>Panic a little when book is released to the public.</li>
<li>Breathe sigh of relief when public reviews are overwhelmingly positive!</li>
</ol>
```

The beginning `<ol>` tells your web browser to display this list as an ordered list, meaning that it will be ordered with numbers starting with the number 1. The entire list ends with the `</ol>` HTML tag, which tells your web browser that the ordered list is now complete.

Between the `<ol>` and `</ol>` are list items designated as such by the HTML markup `<li>`. Each list item starts with `<li>` and ends with `</li>`, which tells the web browser to display the line of text as one list item.

If you don't close an open HTML markup tag — for example, if you start an ordered list with `<ol>` but don't include the closing `</ol>` at the end — it messes up the display on your website because the web browser considers anything beneath the initial `<ol>` to be part of the ordered list until it recognizes the closing tag: `</ol>`.

Unordered lists are very similar to ordered lists, except that instead of using numbers, they use bullet points to display the list, like this:

- Write my book chapters.
- Submit my book chapters to my publisher.
- Panic a little when book is released to the public.
- Breathe sigh of relief when public reviews are overwhelmingly positive!

The HTML markup for an unordered list is just like the ordered list, except that instead of using the `<ol>` tag, it uses the `<ul>` tag (UL = unordered list):

```
<ul>
<li>Write my book chapters.</li>
<li>Submit my book chapters to my publisher.</li>
<li>Panic a little when book is released to the public.</li>
<li>Breathe sigh of relief when public reviews are overwhelmingly positive!</li>
</ul>
```

Note that both the ordered and unordered lists use the list item tags, `<li>` and `</li>`, and the only difference is in the first opening and last closing tags:

- **Ordered lists:** Use `<ol>` and `</ol>`
- **Unordered lists:** Use `<ul>` and `</ul>`
- **List items:** Use `<li>` and `</li>`

Chapter 11

Understanding Parent and Child Themes

*U*sing a theme exactly how the author released it is great. If a new version is released that fixes a browser compatibility issue or adds features offered by a new version of WordPress, a quick theme upgrade is very easy to do.

However, there's a good chance you'll want to tinker with the design, add new features, or modify the theme structure. If you modify the theme, you won't be able to upgrade to a newly released version without modifying the theme again.

If only you could upgrade customized versions of themes with new features when they're released. Fortunately, child themes give you this best-of-both-worlds theme solution.

This chapter explores what child themes are, how to create a child theme–ready parent theme, and how to get the most out of using child themes.

Customizing Theme Style with Child Themes

A WordPress theme consists of a collection of template files, stylesheets, images, and JavaScript files. The theme controls the layout and design that your visitors see on the site. When such a theme is properly set up as a parent theme, it allows a *child theme,* or a subset of instructions, to override its files. This ensures that a child theme can selectively modify the layout, styling, and functionality of the parent theme.

The quickest way to understand child themes is by example. In this section, you create a simple child theme that modifies the style of the parent theme.

Currently, the default WordPress theme is Twenty Fifteen. Figure 11-1 shows how the Twenty Fifteen theme appears on a sample site.

You likely have Twenty Fifteen on your WordPress site; it's a great candidate for creating a child theme.

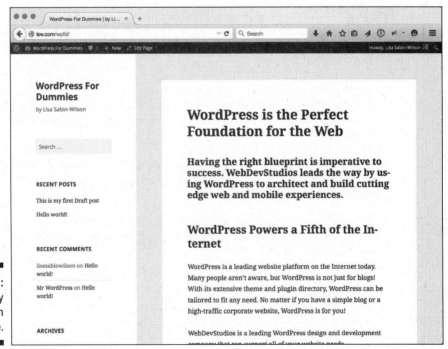

Figure 11-1:
The Twenty Fifteen theme.

Creating a child theme

Like regular themes, a child theme needs to reside in a directory inside the /wp-content/themes directory. The first step to creating a child theme is to add the directory that will hold it. For this example, connect to your hosting account via FTP and create a new directory called twentyfifteen-child inside the /wp-content/themes directory. To register the twentyfifteen-child directory as a theme and to make it a child of the Twenty Fifteen theme, create a style.css file and add the appropriate theme headers. To do this, type the following code into your favorite code or plain-text editor (such as Notepad for the PC or TextEdit for the Mac) and save the file as style.css:

```
/*
Theme Name: Twenty Fifteen Child
Description: My magnificent child theme
Author: Lisa Sabin-Wilson
Version: 1.0
Template: twentyfifteen
*/
```

Typically, you can find the following headers in a WordPress theme:

- Theme Name: The theme user sees this name in the back end of WordPress.

- Description: This header provides the user any additional information about the theme. Currently, it only appears on the Manage Themes page (accessed by clicking the Themes link on the Appearance menu).

- Author: This header lists one or more theme authors. Currently, it is shown only on the Manage Themes page (accessed by clicking the Themes link on the Appearance menu).

- Version: The version number is very useful for keeping track of outdated versions of the theme. It is always a good idea to update the version number when modifying a theme.

- Template: This header changes a theme into a child theme. The value of this header tells WordPress the directory name of the parent theme. Because your child theme uses Twenty Fifteen as the parent, your style.css needs to have a Template header with a value of Twenty Fifteen (the directory name of the Twenty Fifteen theme).

Now activate the new Twenty Fifteen Child theme as your active theme. (If you need a reminder on how to activate a theme on your site, check out Chapter 8.) You should see a site layout similar to the one shown in Figure 11-2.

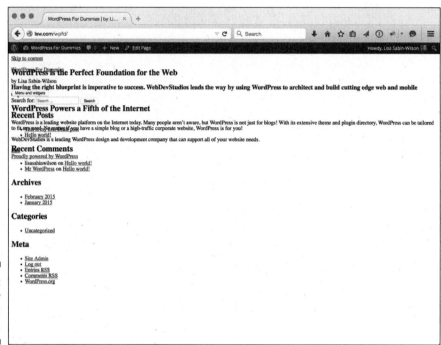

Figure 11-2:
The Twenty
Fifteen Child
theme.

Figure 11-2 shows that the new theme doesn't look quite right. The problem is that the new child theme replaced the `style.css` file of the parent theme, yet the new child theme's `style.css` file is empty.

You could just copy and paste the contents of the parent theme's `style. css` file, but that would waste some of the potential of child themes.

Loading a parent theme's style

One of the great things about CSS is how rules can override one another. If you list the same rule twice in your CSS, the rule that comes last takes precedence.

For example:

```
a {
color: blue;
}

a {
color: red;
}
```

This example is overly simple, but it nicely shows what I'm talking about. The first rule says that all links (a tags) should be blue, whereas the second rule says that links should be red. Because CSS rules state that the last instruction takes precedence, the links will be red.

Using this feature of CSS, you can inherit all the styling of the parent theme and selectively modify it by overriding the rules of the parent theme. But how can you load the parent theme's `style.css` file so that it inherits the parent theme's styling?

Fortunately, CSS has another great feature that helps you do this with ease. Just add one line to the Twenty Fifteen Child theme's `style.css` file (in bold in the following example):

```
/*
Theme Name: Twenty Fifteen Child
Description: My magnificent child theme
Author: Lisa Sabin-Wilson
Version: 1.0
Template: twentyfifteen
*/
@import url('../twentyfifteen/style.css');
```

A number of things are going on here, so let me break it down piece by piece:

- `@import`: This tells the browser to load another stylesheet. Using this allows you to pull in the parent stylesheet quickly and easily.
- `url('. . .')`: This indicates that the value is a location and not a normal value.
- `('../twentyfifteen/style.css');`: This is the location of the parent stylesheet. Notice the `/twentyfifteen` directory name. This needs to be changed to match the `Template` value in the header so that the appropriate stylesheet is loaded.

Figure 11-3 shows how the site appears after updating the child theme's `style.css` file to match the listing.

Customizing the parent theme's styling

Your Twenty Fifteen Child theme is set up to match the parent Twenty Fifteen theme. Now you can add new styling to the Twenty Fifteen Child theme's `style.css` file. A simple example of how customizing works

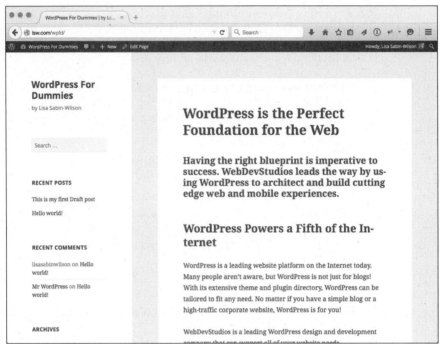

Figure 11-3:
The updated
child theme.

is to add a style that converts all h1, h2, and h3 headings to uppercase, like so:

```
/*
Theme Name: Twenty Fifteen Child
Description: My magnificent child theme
Author: Lisa Sabin-Wilson
Version: 1.0
Template: twentyfifteen
*/
@import url('../twentyfifteen/style.css');

h1, h2, h3 {
    text-transform: uppercase;
}
```

Figure 11-4 shows how the child theme looks with the code additions applied — getting better, isn't it? (*Hint:* The site title and post titles are now all uppercase, which differs from Figure 11-3.)

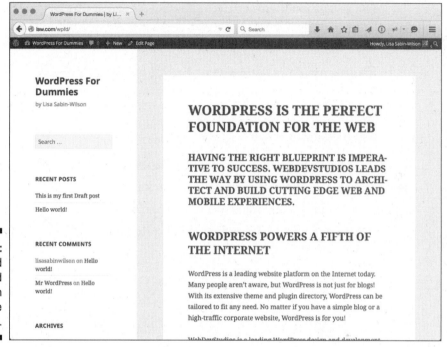

Figure 11-4:
The updated
child
theme with
uppercase
headings.

As you can see, with just a few lines in a `style.css` file, you can create a new child theme that adds specific customizations to an existing theme. Not only was it quick and easy to do, but you also didn't have to modify anything in the parent theme to make it work.

When upgrades to the parent theme are available, upgrade the parent to get the additional features without having to make your modifications again, because you have made your modifications in the child theme, not the parent theme.

Customizations that are more complex work the same way. Simply add the new rules after the import rule that adds the parent stylesheet.

Using images in child theme designs

Many themes use images to add nice touches to the design. Typically, these images are added to a directory named `images` inside the theme.

Just as a parent theme may refer to images in its `style.css` file, your child themes can have their own images directory. The following are examples of how you can use these images.

Using a child theme image in a child theme stylesheet

Including a child theme image in a child theme stylesheet is common. To do so, you simply add the new image to the child theme's `images` directory and refer to it in the child theme's `style.css` file. To get a feel for the mechanics of this process, follow these steps:

1. **Create an `images` directory inside the child theme's directory.**

2. **Add an image to use into the directory.**

   For this example, add an image called `body-bg.png`.

3. **Add the necessary styling to the child theme's `style.css` file, as follows:**

   ```
   /*
   Theme Name: Twenty Fifteen Child
   Description: My magnificent child theme
   Author: Lisa Sabin-Wilson
   Version: 1.0
   Template: twentyfifteen
   */
   @import url('../twentyfifteen/style.css');
   body {
   background: url('images/body-bg.png');
   }
   ```

With a quick refresh of the site, you see that the site now has a new background. Figure 11-5 shows the results clearly by using the browser's zoom feature to make the site smaller.

Using images in a child theme

Child theme images are acceptable for most purposes. You can add your own images to the child theme even if the image doesn't exist in the parent theme folder — and you can accomplish that without changing the parent theme at all.

In the footer of the Twenty Fifteen theme, I added a WordPress logo to the left of the phrase "Proudly powered by WordPress," as shown in Figure 11-6. The logo does not appear in the footer of the Twenty Fifteen theme by default; adding it in via the CSS in the child theme makes it happen, though!

Create a folder in your child theme called `/images` and add your selected images to that folder, then you can call those images into your child theme by using the stylesheet (`style.css`) file in your child theme folder.

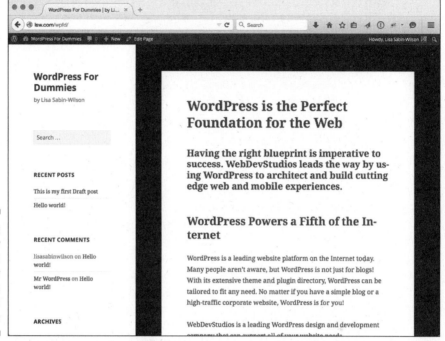

Figure 11-5:
The Twenty
Fifteen Child
theme after
editing the
background
image.

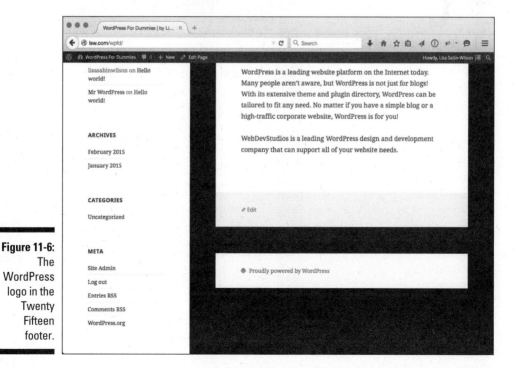

Figure 11-6:
The
WordPress
logo in the
Twenty
Fifteen
footer.

In this next example, I add the same WordPress logo in front of each widget title in the sidebar. Because the logo image already exists inside the child theme images folder (from my previous example), I can simply add a customization to the child theme's `style.css` file to make this change, as follows:

```
/*
Theme Name: Twenty Fifteen Child
Description: My magnificent child theme
Author: Lisa Sabin-Wilson
Version: 1.0
Template: twentyfifteen
*/
@import url('../twentyfifteen/style.css');
.widget-title {
background: url('images/wordpress.png') 0 50% no-repeat;
padding: 10px 15px;
}
```

Save the file and refresh the site. Now you're showing WordPress pride! (See Figure 11-7.)

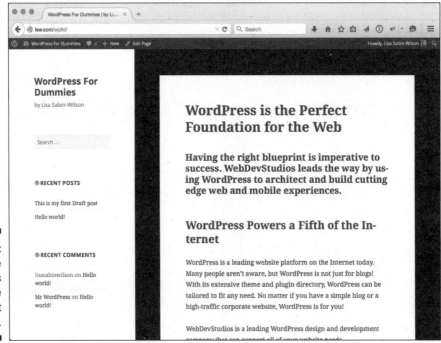

Figure 11-7: Showing the WordPress logo before each widget title.

Modifying Theme Structure with Child Themes

The preceding section showed how to use a child theme to modify the stylesheet of an existing theme. This is tremendously powerful. A talented CSS developer can use this technique to create an amazing variety of layouts and designs.

However, this is just the beginning of the power of child themes. Although every child theme overrides the parent theme's `style.css` file, the child theme can override the parent theme's template files, too. However, child themes aren't limited to just overriding template files; when needed, child themes can also supply their own template files.

Template files are PHP files that WordPress runs to render different views of your site. A site view is the type of content being looked at. Examples of different views are home, category archive, individual post, and page content.

Some examples of common template files are `index.php`, `archive.php`, `single.php`, `page.php`, `attachment.php`, and `search.php`. (You can read more about available template files, including how to use them, in Chapter 9.)

You might wonder what purpose modifying template files of a parent theme serves. Although modifying the stylesheet of a parent theme can allow for some very powerful control over the design, it can't add new content, modify the underlying site structure, or change how the theme functions. To get that level of control, you need to modify the template files.

Overriding parent template files

When both the child theme and parent theme supply the same template file, the child theme file is used. This process of replacing the original parent template file is referred to as *overriding*.

Although overriding each of the theme's template files can defeat the purpose of using a child theme — because updates to those template files won't enhance the child theme — sometimes, producing a needed result makes doing so necessary.

The easiest way to customize a specific template file in a child theme is to copy the template file from the parent theme folder to the child theme folder. After the file is copied, it can be customized as needed, and the child theme reflects the changes.

A good example of a template file that can be overridden is the `footer.php` file. Customizing the footer allows for adding site-specific branding.

Adding new template files

A child theme can override existing parent template files, but it can supply template files that don't exist in the parent, too. Although you may never need your child themes to do this, this option can open up possibilities for your designs.

For example, this technique proves most valuable with page templates. The Twenty Fifteen theme has a default page template: `page.php`. As you might expect, this page template creates a single-page layout for the content and has a sidebar on the left with the content on the right, as shown in Figure 11-8.

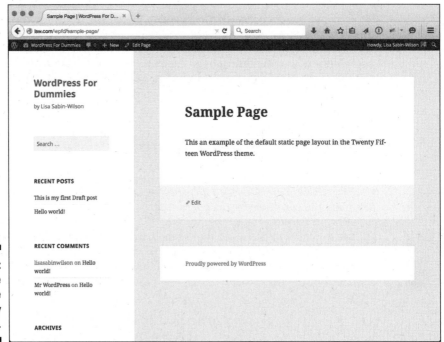

Figure 11-8:
Page
template
in Twenty
Fifteen.

The layout was intentionally set up this way to create a page template that looks just like the rest of the site, with the sidebar on the left and the content on the right. Sometimes, however, I like to have a full-width layout option, with no sidebar, so that I can embed a video, add a forum, or add other content that works well with full width. If you want to customize that template and override what the Twenty Fifteen theme currently has available, simply create a new page template with the same file name as the one you are replacing (in this case, `page.php`) and add the modifications styling to that file, and to the `style.css` file. WordPress will use the `page.php` template file in your child theme by default, completely ignoring the one that exists in the Twenty Fifteen parent theme folder.

Removing template files

You may be asking why you would want to remove a parent's template file. That's a good question. Unfortunately, the Twenty Fifteen theme doesn't provide a good example of why you would want to do this. Therefore, you must use your imagination a bit.

Imagine that you're creating a child theme built off a parent theme called Example Parent. Example Parent is well designed, and a great child theme was quickly built off it. The child theme looks and works exactly the way you want it to, but there's a problem.

The Example Parent theme has a `home.php` template file that provides a highly customized non-blog home page. This works very well, but it isn't what you want for the site. You want a standard blog home page. If the `home.php` file didn't exist in Example Parent, everything would work perfectly.

There isn't a way to remove the `home.php` file from Example Parent without modifying the theme, so you have to use a trick. Instead of removing the file, override the `home.php` file and have it emulate `index.php`.

You may think that simply copying and pasting the Example Parent `index.php` code into the child theme's `home.php` file is a good approach. Although this works, there is a better way: You can tell WordPress to run the `index.php` file so that changes to `index.php` are respected. This single line of code inside the child theme's `home.php` is all that is needed to replace `home.php` with `index.php`:

```php
<?php locate_template( array( 'index.php' ), true ); ?>
```

The `locate_template` function does a bit of magic. If the child theme supplies an `index.php` file, then it is used. If not, then the parent `index.php` file is used.

This produces the same result that removing the parent theme's `home.php` file would have. The `home.php` code is ignored, and the changes to `index.php` are respected.

Modifying the functions.php file

Like template files, child themes can provide a Theme Functions template, or `functions.php` file. Unlike template files, the `functions.php` of a child theme does not override the file of the parent theme.

When a parent theme and a child theme each have a `functions.php` file, both the parent and child `functions.php` files run. The child theme's `functions.php` file runs first and then the parent theme's `functions.php` file runs. This is intentional because it allows the child theme to replace functions defined in the parent theme. However, this works only if the functions are set up to allow this.

The Twenty Fifteen `functions.php` file defines a function called `twentyfifteen_setup`. This function handles the configuration of many theme options and activates some additional features. Child themes can replace this function to change the default configuration and features of the theme, too.

The following lines of code summarize how the `functions.php` file allows this to happen:

```
if ( ! function_exists( 'twentyfifteen_setup' ) ):
function twentyfifteen_setup() {
// removed code
}
endif;
```

Wrapping the function declaration in the `if` statement protects the site from breaking in the event of a code conflict and allows a child theme to define its own version of the function.

In the Twenty Fifteen Child theme, you can see how modifying this function affects the theme. Add a new `twentyfifteen_setup` function that adds post thumbnails support to the Twenty Fifteen Child theme's `functions.php` file:

```
<?php
function twentyfifteen_setup() {
add_theme_support( 'post-thumbnails' );
}
```

The result of this change is the child theme no longer supports other special WordPress features, such as custom editor styling, automatic feed link generation, and internationalization and location.

The take-away from this example is that a child theme can provide its own custom version of the function because the parent theme wraps the function declaration in an `if` block that checks for the function first.

Preparing a Parent Theme

WordPress makes it easy for you to make parent themes. WordPress does most of the hard work; however, you must follow some rules for a parent theme to function properly.

The words *stylesheet* and *template* have been used numerous times in many different contexts. Typically, *stylesheet* refers to a CSS file in a theme and *template* refers to a template file in the theme. However, these words also have specific meaning when working with parent and child themes. You must understand the difference between a stylesheet and a template when working with parent and child themes.

In WordPress, the active theme is the stylesheet and the active theme's parent is the template. If the theme doesn't have a parent, then the active theme is both the stylesheet and the template.

Originally, child themes could replace only the `style.css` file of a theme. The parent provided all the template files and `functions.php` code. Thus, the child theme provided style and the parent theme provided the template files. The capabilities of child themes expanded in subsequent versions of WordPress, making the use of these terms for parent and child themes somewhat confusing.

Imagine two themes: parent and child. The following code is in the parent theme's `header.php` file and loads an additional stylesheet provided by the theme:

```
<link type="text/css" rel="stylesheet" media="all" href="<?php
bloginfo('stylesheet_directory') ?>/reset.css" />
```

The `bloginfo` function prints information about the blog configuration or settings. This example uses the function to print the URL location of the stylesheet directory. The site is hosted at `http://example.com`, and the parent is the active theme. It produces the following output:

```
<link type="text/css" rel="stylesheet" media="all"
href="http://example.com/wp-content/themes/Parent/reset.css" />
```

If the child theme is activated, the output would be

```
<link type="text/css" rel="stylesheet" media="all"
href="http://example.com/wp-content/themes/Child/reset.css" />
```

The location now refers to the `reset.css` file in the child theme. This could work if every child theme copies the `reset.css` file of the parent theme, but requiring child themes to add files in order to function isn't good design. The solution is simple, however. Instead of using the `stylesheet_directory` in the `bloginfo` call, use `template_directory`. The code looks like this:

```
<link type="text/css" rel="stylesheet" media="all" href="<?php
bloginfo('template_directory') ?>/reset.css" />
```

Now, all child themes will properly load the parent `reset.css` file.

When developing, use `template_directory` in standalone parent themes and `stylesheet_directory` in child themes.

Chapter 12

WordPress as a Content Management System (CMS)

*W*ordPress isn't simply a blogging platform; it's also a solution for building your own website. WordPress is a powerful content management system that's flexible and extensible enough to run an entire website — even without a blog, if you prefer.

A *content management system* (CMS) is a system used to create and maintain your entire site; it includes tools for publishing and editing as well as for searching and retrieving information and content. A CMS lets you maintain your website with little or no HTML knowledge. You can create, modify, retrieve, and update your content and never even touch the code required to perform those tasks.

This chapter shows you a few ways that you can use WordPress to power your entire website, with or without a blog. I cover various template configurations that you can use to create separate sections of your site. I also show you how to use the front page of your site as a *static page* (a page that isn't dynamically updated, chronologically, as a blog is) or a *portal* (a page that contains snippets from other sections of your site, with links to those sections), which can include a link to an internal blog page, if you want a blog.

You can also add tools to your WordPress website that extend the basic functions of WordPress, by adding elements, such as an e-commerce store, photo galleries, and social communities. Chapter 15 recommends plugins you can add to WordPress to extend it to meet your needs, whereas this chapter shows you how to use the internal, built-in features of WordPress to get started using it as a full-blown CMS tool.

Creating the Front Page of Your Website

For the most part, when you visit a blog powered by WordPress, the blog is on the main page. My personal blog (`http://lisasabin-wilson.com`), powered by WordPress (of course), shows my latest blog posts on the front page. This setup is typical of a site run by WordPress (see Figure 12-1).

But the front page of my business site (`http://webdevstudios.com`), also powered by WordPress, contains no blog (see Figure 12-2). This site doesn't display any blog posts; rather, it displays the contents of a static page that I created in the WordPress Dashboard. This static page serves as a portal to

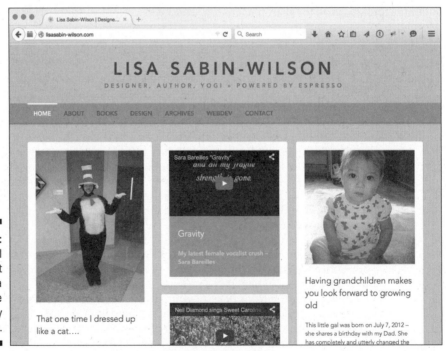

Figure 12-1: My personal blog, set up like a typical site powered by WordPress.

Figure 12-2:
My business
site, set
up as a
business
website
rather than
as a blog.

my design blog and my portfolio and to other sections of my site. The site includes a blog but also serves as a full-blown business website, with all the sections I need to provide my clients the information they want.

Both of my sites are powered by WordPress, so how can they differ significantly in what they display on their front pages? The answer lies in the template files that make up the theme (see Chapter 9).

You use static pages in WordPress to create content that you don't want to display as part of your blog but do want to display as part of your overall site (such as a bio page and a page of services).

Creating a front page is a three-step process:

1. Create a static page.

2. Designate that static page as the front page of your site.

3. Tweak the page to look like a website rather than a blog.

Using the three-step method, you can create an unlimited number of static pages to build an entire website. You don't even need to have a blog on this site unless you want to include one.

Creating a static page

To have a static page display on the front page of your site, you need to create that page. Follow these steps:

1. **From the Dashboard, select Pages⇨Add New.**

   The Edit Page screen opens, where you can write a new page to your WordPress site, as shown in Figure 12-3.

2. **Type a title for the page toward the top.**

   For example, I want to create a Welcome page as the front page of my website, so I entered **WordPress is the Perfect Foundation for the Web** as the page title.

3. **Type the content of your page in the text box.**

   The content you include here is up to you. You can simply use text or a combination of text and images (see Chapter 6 for information on including images and photo galleries), and even a featured image if your theme is using that feature in WordPress (see Chapter 15).

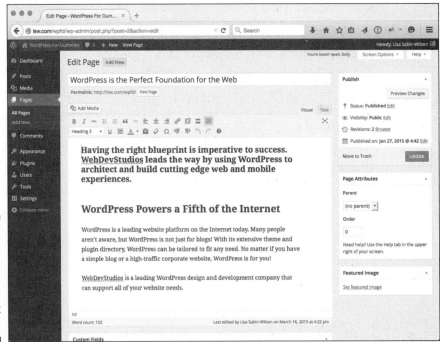

Figure 12-3: Create the static page that you want to use as your front page.

4. **In the Page Attributes section, set the options for this page, as needed:**

- *Parent:* Leave this option set to (No Parent) because this page is the one you use (in the next section) as the home page of your site. With other pages, you can set the page as a subpage, underneath a top-level (or *parent*) page to create a hierarchy of pages for your site navigation.

- *Template:* The Template option is set to Default Template. This setting tells WordPress that you want to use the default Page template (page.php in your theme template files) to format the page you're creating. The default template is the default setting for all pages you create. I discuss assigning a page to a different template in Chapter 9.

- *Order:* This is the order in which you want this page to appear in the navigation menu, if you aren't using the built-in menu feature in WordPress (see Chapter 9) and you are using the wp_list_pages() template tag (see Chapter 9).

5. **(Optional) If you want to preview your page before publishing it, click the Preview Changes button in the upper-right corner.**

6. **When you're satisfied with your page, click the Publish button.**

The page is saved to your database and published to your WordPress site with its own individual URL (or *permalink*). The URL of the static page consists of your website URL and the title of the page. For example, if you title your page About Me, the URL of the page is http://yourdomain.com/about-me.

Assigning a static page as the front page

After you create a static page, you need to tell WordPress that you want it to serve as the front page of your site. To do so, follow these steps:

1. **From the Dashboard, select Settings⇨Reading.**

The Reading Settings page appears.

2. **In the Front Page Displays section, select the A Static Page radio button.**

3. **From the Front Page drop-down list, select the static page that you want to serve as your front page.**

In Figure 12-4, I select to display the WordPress is the Perfect Foundation for the Web page (which I created in the preceding section) as the static page to use as the front page of my site. Don't worry about the rest of the options on the Reading Settings page; they don't pertain to configuring which page to use for the front page of your site.

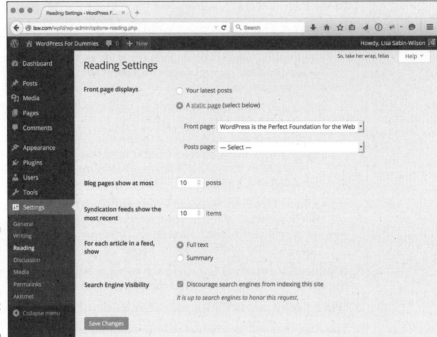

Figure 12-4:
Selecting
a page to
display as
the front
page.

4. **Click the Save Changes button at the bottom of the page.**

   WordPress displays the page you selected in Step 3 as the front page of your site. Figure 12-5 shows my site displaying the page I created as my front page.

Tweaking the page to look like a website rather than a blog

Using a static page as a home page allows you to get creative with the design and layout of your home page by assigning a page template and/or using different widgets to include several different types of content and information (see the "Creating Custom Page Templates to Achieve Different Layouts and Styles" section later in this chapter, where I cover the use of page templates), such as the following:

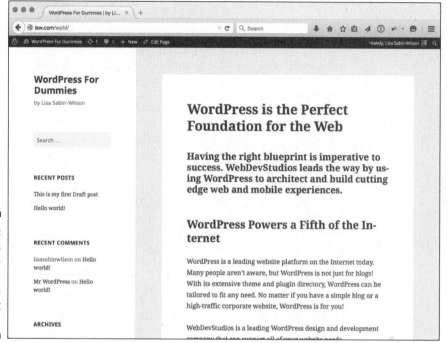

Figure 12-5:
WordPress displays the page you selected as your front page.

> ✔ **Featured Images:** Later in this chapter, I cover how to add the built-in feature in WordPress called Featured Images (or post thumbnails). You can create a page template that includes the titles and excerpts of your most recent blog posts (if you're using a blog) and display them in the body, or sidebar, with a featured image thumbnail. You use the WP_Query() class tag shown in the following code sample, which displays the four most recent posts from your blog:

```php
<?php
    $the_query = new WP_Query ( 'posts_per_page=4' );
    while ( $the_query->have_posts() ) :
    $the_query->the_post();
?>
<a href="<?php the_permalink() ?>" rel="bookmark" title="Permanent Link to
<?php the_title_attribute(); ?>"><?php the_title(); ?></a>

<?php
    if ( has_post_thumbnail() ) { the_post_thumbnail( 'thumbnail' ); }
    the_excerpt();
    endwhile;
?>
```

✔ **Featured Content Slider:** Using the nifty plugin for WordPress named Easing Slider (`https://wordpress.org/plugins/easing-slider`), you can include a slideshow of your most recent posts that contains featured images, text excerpts, and the titles of your posts on the front page, which is a nice way to invite readers into your site to read the posts you have written. The Easing Slider plugin provides you with an easy options page and widget that you can use on your front page (see Chapter 9 for more about getting widgetized by adding widget areas to your theme templates).

✔ **Testimonials:** Many business sites like to include client testimonials on their websites, and one of the best places to display them is on your front page so that your visitors can immediately see quotes from your happy clients. You can accomplish this task easily with a plugin for WordPress called Easy Testimonials (`https://wordpress.org/plugins/easy-testimonials/`). After this plugin is installed, you can create testimonials and include them on your front page using a widget that the plugin provides. (The plugin also allows you to create a full testimonials page to display all testimonials — be sure to read the plugin documentation to find out how!)

✔ **Portfolio:** Designers like to show off a portfolio page of web design projects they have completed, and photographers use a portfolio-style display for their photographs. You can accomplish a portfolio display by using WordPress categories, featured images, and the `WP_Query()` class.

Create a category in your WordPress Dashboard (select Posts ➪ Categories) called Portfolio (or whatever you want to call your body of work), and then create posts within the category. Be sure to assign featured images to the posts. The images could be screen shots that represent the design work you've done, or photography you've taken, or any images that reflect a body of work you have completed. Add a specific size for the images in the Theme Functions template called portfolio, and then using the `WP_query()` template class, insert these lines of code in your home page template to display just the images (linked to the individual posts) in a portfolio:

```php
<?php
    $the_query = new WP_Query ( 'posts_per_page=3&category_
            name=portfolio' );
    while ( $the_query->have_posts()  ) :
    $the_query->the_post();
?>
<a href="<?php the_permalink() ?>" rel="bookmark" title="Permanent Link to
<?php the_title_attribute(); ?>"><?php the_title(); ?><?php if
        ( has_post_thumbnail() ) { the_post_thumbnail( 'portfolio' ); }
        ?></a>
<?php endwhile; ?>
```

Adding a Blog to Your Website

If you want a blog on your site but you don't want to display the blog on the front page, you can add one in your WordPress Dashboard.

Creating a blank page for the blog

To create a blog for your site, first you need to create a blank page:

1. **From the Dashboard, select Pages ➪ Add New.**

   The Edit Page screen appears (refer to Figure 12-3). On this page, you can write a new post on your WordPress blog.

2. **Type a name for the page in the text box toward the top of the page.**

   For example, because this page will be the main page of your blog, enter **Blog** for the name to automatically set the page slug to `/blog`. (See Chapter 5 for information on permalinks and slugs.)

3. **Leave the text box blank.**

   The text box remains blank here because you don't want to display page content on your blog; rather, WordPress displays your blog posts using this page after you assign it as your blog (see the steps in the next section).

4. **Click the Publish button.**

   The blank Blog page is saved to your database and published to your WordPress site.

   You have a blank page that redirects to `http://yourdomain.com/blog`.

Next, you need to assign the page you just created as your Blog page.

Assigning the new page as a blog

To designate your new blank Blog page as a page for your blog posts, follow these steps:

1. **Select Settings ➪ Reading.**

   The Reading Settings page opens (refer to Figure 12-4).

2. **From the Posts Page drop-down list, select the page you just created.**

   For example, select the Blog page as a posts page.

3. **In the Blog Pages Show at Most section, type the number of posts you want to display in the Posts text box.**

   This setting specifies the number of posts you want to display on that page at any time. If you enter **5**, for example, the Blog page shows the last five posts you've made to your blog. Enter the number of posts you want to display based on your preference.

4. **Click the Save Changes button.**

   The options you just set are saved, and your blog is now located at `http://yourdomain.com/blog` (where *yourdomain*.com is the actual domain name). Figure 12-6 shows my Blog page with my latest post.

You can add a link to your blog by adding it to your custom menu. To find out how to build your own custom menu, check out Chapter 10.

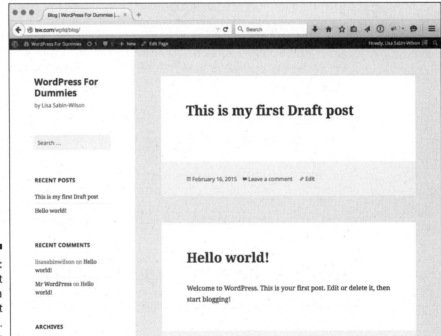

Figure 12-6:
My blog at /blog with a single post displayed.

Creating Custom Page Templates to Achieve Different Layouts and Styles

In Chapter 9, I introduce you to using content-specific WordPress templates to apply different display views for content on your website. Using Page and Category templates, you can provide a different type of reader experience by defining the style with CSS and the features and functions with template tags.

You often see this concept in play on websites that offer more than simply blogs. Websites that sell products or services — or news websites that focus on articles, content, and advertising — use different page, or content, templates to achieve various layouts and styles all within the same website, using the tools WordPress gives them to accomplish it.

Viewing the default Page template (page.php)

Using my own business website as an example, you can see that the standard Page template (page.php) file displays regular static pages on my site in a two-column format. The content is on the left, and a sidebar is on the right of the Jobs page at http://webdevstudios.com/jobs (see Figure 12-7).

The default Page template that creates the display in Figure 12-7 uses basic WordPress template tags to call in the header, content, sidebar, and footer files. The code within the template looks like Listing 12-1 in the page.php template file for my theme.

Creating a new category Page template

You can use the Page template (page.php) in Listing 12-1 to define the layout and style for all internal pages on your website, providing a standard and consistent style for your site visitors. However, if your website also publishes a portfolio of completed work for clients, you probably want that page to have a different style from the rest of the pages, mainly because it presents images that represent your past work.

To accomplish this, create a Design Portfolio category on your site, and for every entry you want to display on the Portfolio page, create a post and assign it to the Design Portfolio category. Figure 12-8 shows how my Portfolio page at http://webdevstudios.com/portfolio displays in a web browser. You can see that the page is made up mainly of thumbnail images that are clickable through to a full article that provides a case study on the design project itself.

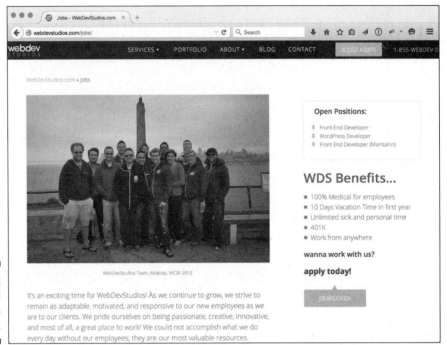

Figure 12-7:
A standard
two-column
page layout.

Listing 12-1:   Default Page Template (page.php)

```php
<?php
/**
 * The template for displaying all pages.
 *
 * This is the template that displays all pages by default.
 * Please note that this is the WordPress construct of pages
 * and that other 'pages' on your WordPress site will use a
 * different template.
 */
get_header(); ?>

<div class="site-content-wrap">
<div id="content" class="site-content">
<div id="primary" class="content-area col">
<main id="main" class="site-main" role="main">
    <?php while ( have_posts() ) : the_post(); ?>
    <article id="post-<?php the_ID(); ?>" <?php post_class(); ?>>
    <div class="entry-content">
    <?php the_content(); ?>
    <?php
    wp_link_pages( array(
```

```
        'before' => '<div class="page-links">' . __( 'Pages:', 'wds7' ),
        'after'  => '</div>',
        ) );
        ?>
        </div><!-- .entry-content -->
        </article>
        <?php endwhile; // end of the loop. ?>
</main><!-- #main -->
</div><!-- #primary -->
        <?php get_sidebar(); ?>
</div><!-- #content -->
</div><!-- .site-content-wrap -->
<?php get_footer(); ?>
```

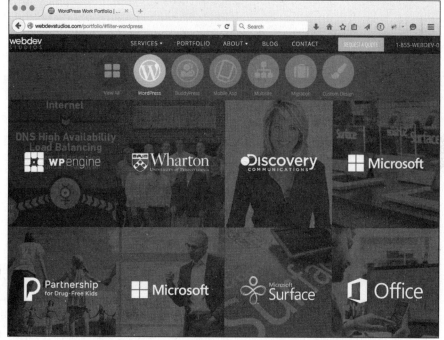

Figure 12-8:
My Portfolio
page layout.

To accomplish this display, create a specific template for the Design Portfolio category: `category-design-portfolio.php`. Every post you create that's assigned to the Design Portfolio category displays in the format that you've defined in the `category-design-portfolio.php` template in your theme folder.

If you want the Portfolio page to display a listing of images only, assign a featured image to each portfolio post; then in the `category-design-portfolio.php` template, follow these steps by using the code shown in Listing 12-2:

1. **Tell WordPress to display each post from the Design Portfolio category but display only the featured image.**

2. **Link that featured image to the individual post page.**

The code to create the Design Portfolio display looks like Listing 12-2.

Listing 12-2:   Category Page Template (category-design-portfolio.php)

```php
<?php get_header(); ?>
<div id="main" class="fullwidth">
<?php if (have_posts()) : while (have_posts()) : the_post(); ?>
<div id="post-<?php the_ID(); ?>" <?php post_class(); ?>>
<div class="entry">
<a href="<?php the_permalink(); ?>"><?php the_post_thumbnail( 'thumbnail' );
            ?></a></div>
<?php endwhile; else: ?>
<p><?php _e('Sorry, no posts matched your criteria.'); ?></p>
<?php endif; ?>
</div>
</div>
<?php get_footer(); ?>
```

Comparing two Page templates

The differences between the default Page template (refer to Listing 12-1) and the template used for the Category template (refer to Listing 12-2) are subtle and are explained in Table 12-1.

Table 12-1 Differences Between the Page and Category Templates

Element	In Page Template?	In Design Portfolio Template?
Call to the Header template `<?php get_header(); ?>`	Yes	Yes
Two-column layout	Yes. The `<div id="main">` styling is defined in CSS with a width of 600px.	No. The `<div id= "main" class= "full width">` is defined in CSS with a width of 900px.

Element	In Page Template?	In Design Portfolio Template?
Call to the post/page title `<?php the_title(); ?>`	Yes	No
Call to the post/page content `<?php the_content(); ?>`	Yes	No
Call to the featured image `<?php the_post_thumbnail(); ?>`	No	Yes
Call to the Sidebar template `<?php the_sidebar(); ?>`	Yes	No
Call to the Footer template `<?php the_footer(); ?>`	Yes	Yes

The differences between the standard, default page layout and the Portfolio category page layout are only one example of the power behind the WordPress theme engine. You use the theme engine to designate and define different types of looks, layouts, and designs for different types of content. This feature helps you create unique websites for you and your clients, and it's the true power behind using WordPress as a CMS.

Pulling in content from a single category

WordPress makes it possible to pull in specific types of content on your website through the `WP_Query();` template class. You place this template tag before The Loop, and it lets you specify which category you want to pull information from. If you have a category called WordPress, and you want to display the last three posts from that category on your front page, in your blog sidebar, or somewhere else on your site, you can use this template tag.

Looking at some of the parameters

The `WP_query();` template class has several parameters that let you display different types of content, such as posts in specific categories, content from specific pages/posts, or dates in your blog archives. Here's an example of two parameters you can use with the `WP_Query();` tag:

✔ **posts_per_page=X:** This parameter tells WordPress how many posts you want to display. If you want to display only three posts, for example, enter **posts_per_page=3**.

✔ `category_name=X`: This parameter tells WordPress that you want to pull posts from the category with this specific slug. If the category slug is `books-i-read`, for example, enter **category_name=books-i-read**. (Be aware that this parameter also pulls posts from any subcategories listed within the indicated category.)

The `WP_Query();` template class has several parameters that let you display different types of content, such as posts in specific categories, content from specific pages/posts, or dates in your blog archives. The `WP_Query();` class lets you pass many variables and parameters; it's not just limited to categories either, you can use it for pages, posts, tags, and more. Visit the WordPress Codex at `http://codex.wordpress.org/Class_Reference/WP_Query` and read about this feature.

Adding the WP_Query(); tag

Select which category you want to list posts from and locate the slug that belongs to the category. After you do that, you're ready to add the `WP_Query();` tag to your template. The category slug is usually the same as the category name, except in lowercase with words separated by dashes; for example, the Books category on my site has a `books` slug. To double-check, visit the Category page in your Dashboard by selecting Posts⇨Categories, click the name of the category you want to use, and find the category slug listed. The line of code to display five posts from the Books category looks like this:

```
<?php $the_query = new WP_Query( 'posts_per_page=5&category_name=books' ); ?>
```

It's not enough just to add that one line of code, however; the `WP_Query();` class needs to be used within The Loop in WordPress (see Chapter 9 for more information on The Loop). Follow these steps to include a `WP_Query` within The Loop in your template:

1. **In your Dashboard, select Appearance⇨Editor.**

   The Edit Themes page opens.

2. **In the Templates list on the right side of the page, click the template in which you want to display the content.**

   For example, if you want to display content in a sidebar, select the Sidebar template: `sidebar.php`.

   The template you select appears in the editor in the middle of the page.

3. **Locate the first closing `</ul>` or `</div>` tag in the Sidebar template for the theme you're using.**

   If you're using the Twenty Fifteen theme, for example, the ending `</div>` looks like this: `</div><!-- .widget-area -->` at line 42.

4. Type the following code directly above the ending </div> tag:

```php
<?php
    $the_query = WP_Query( 'posts_per_page=5&category_name=books' );
    while ($the_query->have_posts()) : $the_query->the_post();
?>
<a href="<?php the_permalink() ?>" rel="bookmark" title="Permanent Link to
<?php the_title_attribute(); ?>"><?php the_title(); ?></a>
<?php
    the_excerpt();
    endwhile;
?>
```

In the first line, I indicated the following: `posts_per_page=5&category_name=books`.

You can change these numbers to suit your specific needs. Just change 5 to whatever number of posts you want to display (there is no limit!), and change `books` to the specific category slug that you want to use.

5. Click the Update File button to save the changes to your template.

When you view your website now, you find a listing of the titles of the blog posts from the Books category displayed in your sidebar.

A lot of people still think of WordPress as simply a blogging platform on which you can have and display a typical blog on your domain. However, in the example I just demonstrated, you can see how you can have a blog but also have so much more on your website by making a few simple tweaks and adjustments to the templates that power your website theme.

Creating Different Sidebar and Footer Templates for Your Pages

You can create separate Sidebar templates for different pages of your site by using a simple `include` statement. When you write an `include` statement, you're telling WordPress that you want to include a specific file on a specific page.

The code that pulls the usual Sidebar template (`sidebar.php`) into all the other templates, such as the Main Index template (`index.php`), looks like this:

```php
<?php get_sidebar(); ?>
```

What if you create a page and want to use a sidebar that has different information from what you have in the Sidebar template (`sidebar.php`)? Follow these steps:

1. **Create a new Sidebar template in a text editor, such as Notepad (in Windows) or TextEdit (on the Mac).**

2. **Save the file on your computer as** `sidebar-second.php`.

3. **Upload** `sidebar-second.php` **to the folder containing your theme on your web server (for example:** `/wp-content/themes/your-theme-name`**).**

   See Chapter 3 for more on transferring files with FTP.

   The new Sidebar template is listed in your theme files on the Edit Themes page. You can open this page by selecting Appearance ➪ Editor in the Dashboard.

4. **To include the** `sidebar-second.php` **template in one of your Page templates, open the template on the Edit Themes page (Appearance ➪ Editor) and then find this code:**

   ```php
   <?php get_sidebar(); ?>
   ```

5. **Replace the preceding code with this** `include` **code:**

   ```php
   <?php get_template_part('sidebar', 'second'); ?>
   ```

With the `get_template_part();` function, you can include virtually any file in any of your WordPress templates. You can use this method to create Footer templates for pages on your site, for example. To do this, first create a new template with the filename `footer-second.php` and then locate the following code in your template:

```php
<?php get_footer(); ?>
```

Then replace the preceding code with this code:

```php
<?php get_template_part('footer,' 'second'); ?>
```

You can do multiple things with WordPress to extend it beyond the blog. This chapter gives you a few practical examples with the default Twenty Fifteen theme. The point is to show you how to use WordPress to create a fully functional website with a CMS platform — anything from the smallest personal site to a large business site. See Chapter 9 for a greater explanation of using template parts.

Creating Custom Styles for Sticky, Category, and Tag Posts

In Chapter 9, I discuss putting together a basic WordPress theme, which includes a Main Index template using The Loop. You can use a custom tag to display custom styles for *sticky posts* (posts that stay at the top of your blog at all times), categories, and tags on your blog. That special tag looks like this:

```
<div <?php post_class() ?> id="post-<?php the_ID(); ?>">
```

The part of that template tag that is so cool is the post_class() section. This template tag tells WordPress to insert specific HTML markup in your template that allows you to use CSS to make custom styles for sticky posts, categories, and tags.

To follow along easily in this section, you should read the earlier chapters in this book about the use of WordPress basic features so that you already know all about how to publish new posts to your blog, including the different options you can set for your blog posts, such as categories, tags, and publishing settings. One setting is the Stick This Post to the Front Page setting. In this section, I show you how to custom-style those sticky posts — it's not as messy as it sounds!

For example, I've published a post with the following options set for it:

- ✔ Stick This Post to the Front Page
- ✔ Filed in a Category Called WordPress
- ✔ Tagged with News

By having the post_class() tag in your template, WordPress inserts HTML markup that allows you to use CSS to style sticky posts or posts assigned to specific tags or categories, differently. WordPress inserted the following HTML markup for the post:

```
<div class="post sticky category-wordpress tag-news">
```

In Chapter 10, I talk about CSS selectors and HTML markup and how they work together to create a style and format for your WordPress theme. You can go to your CSS file and define styles for the following CSS selectors:

- ✔ .post: Use this as the generic style for all posts on your blog. The CSS for this tag is

  ```
  .post {background: #ffffff; border: 1px solid silver; padding: 10px;}
  ```

A style is created for all posts that have a white background with a thin, silver border and 10 pixels of padding space between the post text and the border of the post.

✔ `.sticky`: The concept of sticking a post to your front page is to call attention to that post, so you may want to use different CSS styling to make it stand out from the rest of the posts on your blog:

```
.sticky {background: #ffffff; border: 4px solid red; padding: 10px;}
```

This line creates a style for all sticky posts that display with a white background, a thicker red border, and 10 pixels of padding space between the post text and border of the post.

✔ `.category-wordpress`: If you blog a lot about WordPress, your readers may appreciate having a visual cue to which posts on your blog are about that topic. You can provide the cue through CSS by telling WordPress to display a small WordPress icon in the top-right corner of all your posts in the WordPress category:

```
.category-wordpress {background: url(wordpress-icon.jpg) top right
          no-repeat; height: 100px; width: 100px;}
```

This line of code inserts a graphic — `wordpress-icon.jpg` — that is 100 pixels in height and 100 pixels in width at the top-right corner of every post you've assigned to the WordPress category on your blog.

✔ `.tag-news`: You can style all posts tagged with news the same way you've styled the categories:

```
.tag-news {background: #f2f2f2; border: 1px solid black; padding: 10px;}
```

This CSS line styles all posts tagged with news with a light gray background and a thin, black border with 10 pixels of padding between the post text and border of the post.

Using the `post-class()` tag, combined with CSS, to create dynamic styles for the posts on your blog is fun and easy!

Adding Theme Support for Built-In Features

The WordPress core offers a number of helpful tools that can be easily added to a theme to give the theme more customization options. WordPress provides you with several built-in features that let you enhance your site and theme. This section covers three of the most popular features, including

✔ Custom post types

✔ Post formats

✔ Post thumbnails (or featured images)

Each of these features is part of the WordPress core; however, they aren't activated by default. By *adding theme support,* I mean that you're activating a built-in feature in your theme. When you're traveling around the WordPress community — whether on a support forum or at a WordCamp event — and you hear someone say, "That theme supports *a certain feature,*" you can smile because you know exactly what she's talking about.

You need to activate support for these features in the theme you're using:

✔ **Core function:** Adding support for the feature in your theme by including the core function in the Theme Functions (`functions.php`) file in your theme.

✔ **Template function:** Adding the necessary function tags in your theme template(s) to display the features on your website.

✔ **Templates:** In some cases, you can create feature-specific templates to create additional enhancement to display and include the feature on your site.

The following sections walk you through each feature, in this order: First, add the core function to your theme; second, add the function tags to your templates; and last, if indicated, create a feature-specific template in your theme that will handle added features.

Adding support for custom post types

Custom post types and custom taxonomies have expanded the content management system (CMS) capabilities of WordPress and are likely to be a major part of plugin and theme features as more developers become familiar with their use. *Custom post types* allow developers to create new content types, such as movie reviews or recipes, which are separate from posts and pages. *Custom taxonomies* allow developers to create new types of content groupings, such as genres for movie reviews or a season for recipes (for example, fall, spring, or winter recipes), which are separate from categories and tags.

Posts and pages are simple, generic containers of content. A *page* consists of timeless content that has a hierarchical structure because a page can have a parent (forming a nested, or hierarchical, structure of pages). A *post* consists of content that is listed in linear (not hierarchical) order based on when it was published, and a post can be organized into categories and tags. What happens when you want a hybrid of these features? What if you want content that doesn't appear in the post listings and has neither categories nor tags, but displays the posting date? Custom post types satisfy this desire to customize content types.

By default, WordPress already has different post types built in to the software, ready for you to use. These default post types include

- ✔ Blog posts
- ✔ Pages
- ✔ Menus
- ✔ Attachments
- ✔ Revisions

Custom post types let you create new and useful types of content on your website, including a smart and easier way to publish those content types to your site.

The possibilities for using custom post types are endless, but here are a few ideas to kick-start your imagination and to represent some of the more popular and useful ideas that others have implemented on sites:

- ✔ Photo galleries
- ✔ Podcasts or videos
- ✔ Book reviews
- ✔ Coupons and special offers
- ✔ Events calendars

Creating a custom post type

To create and use custom post types on your site, be sure that your WordPress theme contains the correct code and functions. In the following steps, you create a basic and generic Custom Post Type called Generic Content, and later in this section, you find detailed information on the different parameters you can use with custom post types to create different types to suit your needs:

1. In your Dashboard, select Appearance ⇨ Editor Link.

   The Edit Themes page opens.

2. **Click the Theme Functions template link to open the** `functions.php` **file.**

   The Theme Functions template opens in the text editor on the left side of the Edit Themes page.

3. **Add the custom post type code to the bottom of the theme functions template file.**

   Scroll down to the bottom of the `functions.php` file and include the following code to add a Generic Content custom post type to your site:

```
// ADD CUSTOM POST TYPE
add_action( 'init', 'create_post_type' );
function create_post_type() {
register_post_type( 'generic-content',
 array(
   'labels' => array(
    'name' => __( 'Generic Content' ),
    'singular_name' => __( 'Generic Content' )
   ),
   'public' => true
  )
);
}
```

The function `register_post_type();` can accept several arguments and parameters, which I detail in Table 12-2. You can use a variety and a combination of arguments and parameters to create a specific post type. You can find more information on custom post types and using the `register_post_type();` function on the WordPress Codex page at `http://codex.wordpress.org/Function_Reference/register_post_type`.

4. **Click the Update File button to save the changes made to the** `functions.php` **file.**

If you don't feel up to writing all this code in the theme functions file, the Custom Post Type UI plugin from WebDevStudios (`http://webdevstudios.com`) provides you with an easy interface in your WordPress Dashboard. This plugin also simplifies the creation of custom post types on your site and bypasses the need to create the code in the Theme Functions (`functions.php`) file. You can find the free plugin at `https://wordpress.org/plugins/custom-post-type-ui`.

After you complete the steps to add the Generic Content post type to your site, it's added to the left navigation menu in the Dashboard, as shown in Figure 12-9.

Table 12-2	Arguments and Parameters for register_post_types();		
Parameter	**Information**	**Arguments**	**Example**
`label`	The name of the post type.	None	`'label' => __ ( 'Generic Content' ),`
`singular_label`	Same as `label`, but in singular, not plural, format (posts become post, for example).	None	`'singular_label' => __ ( 'Generic Content' ),`
`description`	The description of the post type; displayed in the Dashboard to represent the post type.	None	`'description' => __ ( 'This is a description of the Generic Content type' ),`
`public` `show_ui` `publicly_queryable` `exclude_from_search`	`public` sets whether the post type is public. `show_ui` either shows or doesn't show admin screens. `publicly_queryable` allows this post type to be included in public queries within template code. `exclude_from_search` either shows or doesn't show the post type in search results.	`true` or `false` (default)	`'public' => true, 'show_ui' => true, 'publicly_queryable' => true, 'exclude_from_search' => false,`

Parameter	Information	Arguments	Example
`menu_ position`	Sets the position of the post type menu item in the Dashboard navigation menu; by default, custom post types appear after the Pages menu in the Dashboard.	Default is 25; sets integers in intervals of 5	`'menu_position' => 25,`
`menu_icon`	Defines a custom icon (or graphic) to the post type menu item in the Dashboard navigation menu; creates and uploads the image into the `images` directory of your theme folder.	None	`'menu_icon' => get_stylesheet_ directory_ uri() . '/ images/generic- content.png',`
`hierarchical`	Tells WordPress whether to display the post type content list in a hierarchical manner.	`true` or `false`; default is `false`	`'hierarchical' => true,`
`query_var`	Controls whether this post type can be used with a `query` variable, such as `query_ posts`.	`true` or `false`; default is `true`	`'query_var' => true,`
`capability_ type`	Defines permissions for users to edit, create, or read the custom post type.	`post` (default); gives the same capabilities for those who can edit, create, and read blog posts	`'query_var' => post,`

(continued)

Table 12-2 *(continued)*

Parameter	Information	Arguments	Example
supports	Defines what meta boxes, or *modules,* are available for this post type in the Dashboard.	`title` (text box for the post title); `editor` (text box for the post content); `comments` (check boxes to toggle comments on and off); `trackbacks` (check boxes to toggle trackbacks and pingbacks on and off); `revisions` (allows post revisions to be made); `author` (drop-down box to define post author); `excerpt` (text box for the post excerpt); `thumbnail` (featured image selection, see the section "Adding support for post thumbnails" later in this chapter); `custom-fields` (custom fields input area); `page-attributes` (page parent and Page template drop-down lists)	`'supports' => array( 'title', 'editor', 'excerpt', 'custom-fields', 'thumbnail' ),`
rewrite	Rewrites the permalink structure for the post type.	`true` or `false`; `slug` (permalink slug to prepend custom post types); `with_front` (if you've set your permalink structure with a specific prefix, such as `/blog`)	`'rewrite' => array( 'slug' => 'my-content', 'with_front' => false ),`
taxonomies	Uses existing WordPress taxonomies (category and tag).	Category `post_tag`	`'taxonomies' => array( 'post_tag', 'category'),`

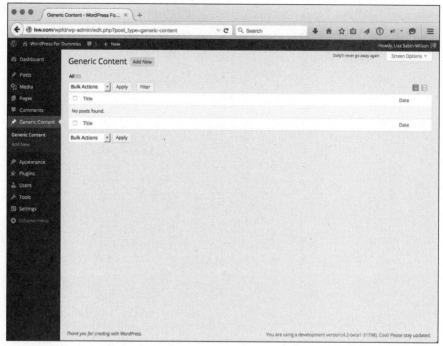

Figure 12-9:
The Generic
Content
post type is
added to the
Dashboard.

You add and publish new content using the new custom post type just as you would when you write and publish blog posts. The published content isn't added to the chronological listing of blog posts but is instead treated as separate content, just like static pages.

When you view the permalink for the custom post type, you see that it adopts the post type name, Generic Content, and uses it as part of the permalink structure. The permalink looks like this: `http://yourdomain.com/generic-content/new-article`.

Listing 12-3 gives you a real-life example that I use on the No Rules Theatre site I developed; see it at `http://norulestheatre.org`. This site uses a Shows custom post type to create custom content for the shows that the theatre produces each season. Reference the parameters and information in Table 12-2 while you read the lines of code in Listing 12-3 to see how the custom post types for the No Rules Theatre site were created and applied.

Listing 12-3:   Custom Post Types from the No Rules Theatre Site

```
// ADD CUSTOM POST TYPE: SHOWS
add_action( 'init', 'create_my_post_types' );
function create_my_post_types() {
                register_post_type( 'shows',
                array(
                'labels' => array(
                'name' => __( 'Shows' ),
                'singular_name' => __( 'Show' ),
                'add_new' => __( 'Add New Show' ),
                'add_new_item' => __( 'Add New Show' ),
                'edit' => __( 'Edit' ),
                'edit_item' => __( 'Edit Show' ),
                'new_item' => __( 'New Show' ),
                'view' => __( 'View Show' ),
                'view_item' => __( 'View Show' ),
                'search_items' => __( 'Search Shows' ),
                'not_found' => __( 'No shows found' ),
                'not_found_in_trash' => __( 'No shows found in Trash' ),
                'parent' => __( 'Parent Show' ),
                ),
                'public' => true,
                'show_ui' => true,
                'publicly_queryable' => true,
                'exclude_from_search' => false,
                'menu_position' => 10,
                'menu_icon' => get_stylesheet_directory_uri() . '/img/nrt-shows.
                png',
                'hierarchical' => true,
                'query_var' => true,
                'rewrite' => array( 'slug' => 'shows', 'with_front' => false ),
                'taxonomies' => array( 'post_tag', 'category'),
                'can_export' => true,
                'supports' => array(
                'post-thumbnails',
                'excerpts',
                'comments',
                'revisions',
                'title',
                'editor',
                'page-attributes',
                'custom-fields')
                )
                );
}
```

To add custom post types to the Menus options on the Menus page that are accessible from the Dashboard (select Appearance➪Menus), click the Screen Options tab in the top-right corner of that page. You see a check box next to Post Types that you can select to enable your custom post types in the menus you create. (The Post Types appear in the screen options only if you have custom post types enabled in your theme.)

Building a template for a custom post type

By default, custom post types use the `single.php` template in your theme — unless you create a specific template for your custom post type. You might find the regular WordPress `single.php` template limiting for your post type, depending on the type of content you want to include and whether you want to apply different formats and styles for your custom post type with HTML and CSS markup.

In the preceding section, I share the code to build a simple Generic Content custom post. After you add that, the Generic Content menu in the WordPress Dashboard appears (refer to Figure 12-9). Select Generic Content➪Add New and then publish a new post with some content for testing. For example, add a new Generic Content type with a `Test` title and a `test` slug. Because the Generic Content type has no specific template yet, it uses the `single.php` template, and resulting posts look no different from the standard.

If a Not Found page appears when you try to access a new custom post type entry, reset your permalink settings. Select Settings➪Permalinks in the WordPress Dashboard, and then click the Save Changes button. This forces WordPress to reset the permalinks for your site and adds the new, custom post type permalink formats.

To build a template specifically for the Generic Content post type, add a new `single-posttype.php` template (*posttype* is the first argument passed to the `register_post_type` function from the preceding section). In this example, the template file that's specific to the Generic Content post type is `single-generic-content.php`. Any modifications made to this template file are shown only for instances of the Generic Content post type.

The basic structure for `single-generic-content.php` for the Twenty Fifteen theme is

```php
<?php get_header(); ?>
<div id="primary" class="content-area">
<main id="main" class="site-main" role="main">
<?php // Start the loop.
    while ( have_posts() ) : the_post();

    // Include the page content template.
    get_template_part( 'content', 'generic' );
```

```
        // End the loop.
    endwhile;
?>


</main><!-- .site-main -->
</div><!-- .content-area -->


<?php get_footer(); ?>
```

By using the template part, creating a `content-generic.php` file allows for easy customization of The Loop for the Generic Content post type entry.

Adding support for post formats

Including the post formats in your theme allows you to designate a different content display and styling for certain types of designated posts. Unlike custom post types, you can't create different post formats, because WordPress has already assigned them for you; *you* decide which post format, if any, to use in your theme. You can, however, use one or all of them, depending on your needs.

This list describes the post formats that are designated in WordPress:

- ✔ **Standard:** Displays your blog posts in the default manner — as an ordinary blog post without special formats applied to it.

- ✔ **Aside:** A short post (but not a full post) to share a random thought or idea. Typically, an Aside is shared without a post title or category/tag designations. An Aside is simply a random, one-off thought shared on your blog.

- ✔ **Chat:** A transcript of an online chat conversation that can be formatted to look just like a chat (or instant messaging) window.

- ✔ **Gallery:** A gallery of images in which each image can be clicked to access a larger version. Often, these post formats contain no text and display only a gallery (but they may have a title).

- ✔ **Image:** Used for displaying one image, such as in a photo blog. The image may or may not have text or a caption to go along with the post.

- ✔ **Link:** Displays a short post that provides a link that you find useful and want to share with your readers. This post format often contains a title and sometimes a short bit of text that describes the link you're sharing.

- ✔ **Quote:** Displays a quotation on your blog. Often, users include the quotation along with a byline for its source.

✔ **Status:** Provides a short status update, usually limited to 140 characters or fewer (think Twitter!).

✔ **Video:** Displays a video, usually embedded within a handy video player (à la YouTube) so that your readers can simply click to play the video without leaving your site.

✔ **Audio:** The post format for sharing audio files, or podcasts. Usually, an Audio post has very little text included and instead includes items such as a built-in audio player that visitors can click to listen to audio files.

To see a helpful, real-world example of post formats in practice, see the website shown in Figure 12-10. The site separates the chosen formats to use, in the individual post styling and icons used to designate the different formats. (In Figure 12-10, you see the small post icon used to designate video posts.)

If your site needs a different type of a post format that isn't available, consider adding it as a custom post type instead. (See the earlier sections in this chapter for details.)

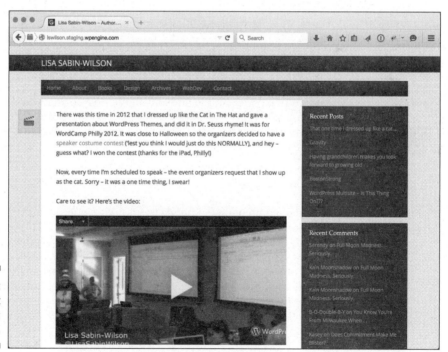

Figure 12-10: Video post formats in use.

Adding post formats to a theme

To add support for post formats in your theme (assuming it does not already have support for this features), you first need to add the function call to your Theme Functions (functions.php) template. After you follow these few steps to make that happen, I show you the magic that occurs on the Add New Post page in your WordPress Dashboard. But first follow these steps to add post formats support in your theme:

1. **From your Dashboard, select Appearance ⇨ Editor.**

2. **Click the Theme Functions (functions.php) file in the Templates list on the right to open the Theme Functions file.**

3. **In the text editor box, add the following function on a new line in front of the closing ?> tag:**

```
add_theme_support( 'post-formats', array(
    'aside',
    'chat',
    'gallery',
    'image',
    'link',
    'quote',
    'status',
    'video',
    'audio'
) );
```

The preceding code sample adds available post formats to the theme. You don't have to use all of them; you can simply include only those formats that you think you'll use in your theme and leave out the rest.

4. **Click the Update File button to save the changes made to the** functions.php **file.**

You don't notice an immediate change to your site when you save your new Theme Functions file with the post formats support added. To see what WordPress has added to your site, visit the Add New Post page by selecting Posts ⇨ Add New in the Dashboard. A Format item in the Publish section on the right side of the page appears and lists the different formats you added to your theme, as shown in Figure 12-11. Because I added all nine post format options, in the figure they're all listed as available formats that I can select. You also see a tenth format option — Standard — which is the format that's used if you don't select a specific format for your post.

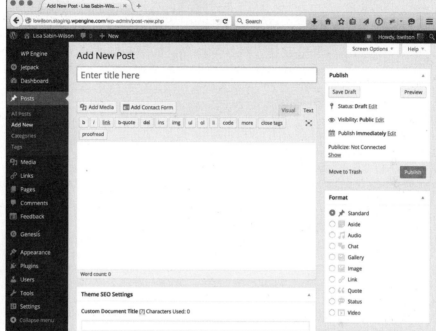

Figure 12-11:
Adding
post format
options on
the Add
New Post
page.

Using template tags for post formats

Adding post format support to your theme isn't enough. If you endure the hassle of adding post format support, you should provide some unique styling for each type of format. If you don't, your different post formats look just like the rest of your blog posts, and the point of adding them to your theme is lost.

You can provide a unique display for your post formats in two ways:

- ✔ **Content:** For each format, you can designate the content you want to display. For example, if you don't want to display a title for an Aside, leave out the template tag that calls it but leave in the template tag that calls the title for your Video post format.

- ✔ **Style:** Each of your formats has its own CSS class assigned to it. Use those CSS classes to provide unique styles for fonts, colors, backgrounds, and borders to your different post formats. In the following sidebar, "Post class defined," I discuss using the HTML markup that's provided by the `post_class();` tag.

Post class defined

In the default Twenty Fifteen theme, have a look at the `content.php` template by clicking it on the Edit Themes page. At the top of the template (line 13, specifically) is this line of code:

```
<article id="post-<?php the_ID(); ?>"
        <?php post_class(); ?>>
```

The `post_class();` section is the cool part of the template tag. This template tag tells WordPress to insert specific HTML markup in your template. This HTML markup allows you to use CSS to make custom styles for sticky posts, categories, tags, and post formats.

For example, you can set the following options for a post:

- ✔ Stick this post to the front page
- ✔ Filed in a WordPress category
- ✔ Tagged with News

For the preceding example, WordPress inserts the following HTML markup:

```
<article class="post sticky category-
        wordpress tag-news">
```

Likewise, for post formats, if you publish a post using the Image post format, the `post_class()` tag in the template contains the following HTML markup, indicating that this post should be formatted for an image display:

```
<article class="post type-post format-
        image">
```

Combine this information with the CSS and HTML information in Chapter 10, and you can see how you can use CSS along with the `post_class();` tag to provide custom styles for each of the post types, categories, and tags you've set up on your site.

Adding unique styles for your post formats starts with creating the content designations you want to display for each format. Earlier in this chapter, I describe the possible post formats and give you some ideas on what you can do to display them on your site. The possibilities are endless, and they're all up to you. See Chapter 9 for more information on the different content-related template tags you can use in these areas.

In the following steps, you create a simple, stripped-down Main Index (`index.php`) file to use on your site and include post format support. This template is only a sample for you to follow and refer to when you create your custom display for your post formats. There's no time like the present, so follow these steps:

1. **Open your favorite text editor, such as Notepad (PC) or TextEdit (Mac).**

2. **Enter the code in Listing 12-4 to create a simple template for post formats.**

   I describe the various lines in the code in Listing 12-4.

Listing 12-4:   A Simple Template for Post Formats

```php
<?php get_header(); ?>
            #1
<?php if (have_posts()) : ?>
            #2
<?php while (have_posts()) : the_post(); ?>
            #3
<div id="post-<?php the_ID(); ?>" <?php post_class(); ?>>
            #4
<?php
            #5
if ( has_post_format( 'aside' )) {
            #6
            echo the_content();
            #7
}
            #8

elseif ( has_post_format( 'chat' )) {
            #9
            echo '<h3>';
            #10
            echo the_title();
            #11
            echo '</h3>';
            #12
            echo the_content();
            #13
}
            #14

elseif ( has_post_format( 'gallery' )) {
            #15
            echo '<h3>';
            #16
            echo the_title();
            #17
            echo '</h3>';
            #18
            echo the_content();
            #19
}
            #20

elseif ( has_post_format( 'image' )) {
            #21
            echo '<h3>';
            #22
```

(continued)

Listing 12-4 *(continued)*

```
                    echo the_title();
            #23
                    echo '</h3>';
            #24
                    echo the_post_thumbnail('image-format');
            #25
                    echo the_content();
            #26
}
            #27

elseif ( has_post_format( 'link' )) {
            #28
                    echo '<h3>';
            #29
                    echo the_title();
            #30
                    echo '</h3>';
            #31
                    echo the_content();
            #32
}
            #33

elseif ( has_post_format( 'quote' )) {
            #34
echo the_content();
            #35
}
            #36

elseif ( has_post_format( 'status' )) {
            #37
                    echo the_content();
            #38
}
            #39

elseif ( has_post_format( 'video' )) {
            #40
                    echo '<h3>';
            #41
                    echo the_title();
            #42
                    echo '</h3>';
            #43
                    echo the_content();
            #44
}
            #45
```

```
elseif ( has_post_format( 'audio' )) {
                                                #46
                echo '<h3>';
                                                #47
                echo the_title();
                                                #48
                echo '</h3>';
                                                #49
                echo the_content();
                                                #50
}
                                                #51
else {
                                                #52

                echo '<h3>';
                                                #53
                echo the_title();
                                                #54
                echo '</h3>';
                                                #55
                echo the_content();
                                                #56
}
                                                #57

?>
                                                #58
</div>
                                                #59
<?php endwhile; else: ?>
                                                #60
<?php endif; ?>
                                                #61
<?php get_sidebar(); ?>
                                                #62
<?php get_footer(); ?>
                                                #63
```

3. **Save the file as** `index.php` **on your local computer.**

4. **Upload the file into your theme folder (located in the** `/wp-content/`
   `themes/`*your-theme-name* **directory), replacing the existing** `index.`
   `php` **file.**

   See Chapter 3 for details on transferring files by using FTP.

Here's a breakdown of the lines of code in Listing 12-4:

- ✔ **Line 1:** A function that includes all code from the `header.php` file of your theme.
- ✔ **Lines 2 and 3:** Indicates the beginning of The Loop (see Chapter 9).
- ✔ **Line 4:** Provides HTML and CSS markup using the `post_class();` function that provides you with unique CSS classes for each of your different post formats (see the earlier sidebar, "Post class defined").
- ✔ **Line 5:** Initiates the start of a PHP function.
- ✔ **Lines 6–8:** Provide content for the Aside post format.
- ✔ **Lines 9–14:** Provide content for the Chat post format.
- ✔ **Lines 15–20:** Provide content for the Gallery post format.
- ✔ **Lines 21–27:** Provide content for the Image post format.
- ✔ **Lines 28–33:** Provide content for the Link post format.
- ✔ **Lines 34–36:** Provide content for the Quote post format.
- ✔ **Lines 37–39:** Provide content for the Status post format.
- ✔ **Lines 40–45:** Provide content for the Video post format.
- ✔ **Lines 46–51:** Provide content for the Audio post format.
- ✔ **Lines 52–57:** Provide content for all other Default posts.
- ✔ **Line 58:** Ends the PHP function.
- ✔ **Line 59:** Closes the HTML div tag that was opened in Step 4.
- ✔ **Lines 60 and 61:** Close the `endwhile` and `if` statements that were opened in Lines 2 and 3.
- ✔ **Line 62:** This function calls in the code included in the `sidebar.php` file of your theme.
- ✔ **Line 63:** This function calls in the code included in the `footer.php` file of your theme.

Listing 12-4 is a simple example and doesn't include a lot of HTML markup or CSS classes. I made it this way on purpose to focus on the code bits that are required in order to designate and define different content displays for your post formats. You can see in Listing 12-4 that some formats contain the template tag to display the title — `the_title();` — and that others do not. However, they all contain the template tag to display the content of the post: `the_content();`. As I mention earlier, you can play with different content types and markup that you want to add to your post formats.

Couple your template additions for post formats with the `post_class();` that adds special CSS classes and markup for each post format type. You can truly customize the display of each individual post format to your heart's content.

Adding support for post thumbnails

Using post thumbnails (or featured images) takes a lot of the work out of associating an image with a post and using the correct size each time. A popular way to display content in WordPress themes includes a thumbnail image with a snippet (or an excerpt) of text; the thumbnail images all use the same size and placement within your theme.

Before the inclusion of post thumbnails in WordPress, users had to open an image in an image-editing program (such as Photoshop) and crop and resize the image. Or they had to use fancy scripts that would resize images on the fly; however, because this type of script tends to be resource intensive on web servers, it wasn't an optimal solution. How about a content management system that crops and resizes your images to the exact dimensions you specify? Yep — WordPress does that for you, with only a few adjustments.

By default, when you upload an image in WordPress, it creates three versions of the image based on dimensions that are set in your Dashboard's Media Settings page (select Settings ➪ Media):

- ✔ **Thumbnail size:** Default dimensions are 150px x 150px.
- ✔ **Medium size:** Default dimensions are 300px x 300px.
- ✔ **Large size:** Default dimensions are 1024px x 1024px.

So, when you upload one image, you end up with four sizes of that same image stored on your web server: thumbnail, medium, large, and the original (full size) image you uploaded. Images are cropped and resized proportionally, and when you use them in your posts, you can typically designate which size you want to use in the image options of the uploader (which I describe in more detail in Chapter 6). You can find the uploader on the Add New Post, Add New Page, and Add New Media pages in your WordPress Dashboard.

Within the WordPress image uploader, you can designate a particular image as the featured image of the post and then, using the Featured Images function that you add to your theme, include template tags to display your chosen featured image with your post. This is helpful for creating magazine- or news-style themes that are popular on WordPress sites. Figure 12-12 displays my personal blog, where I used post thumbnails and featured images

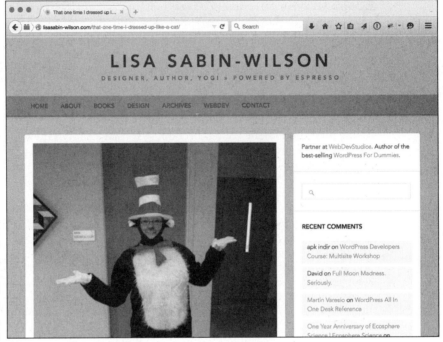

Figure 12-12:
A large featured image on my site.

to display a large featured image associated with each post excerpt on my home page. It's at `http://lisasabin-wilson.com`.

In Chapter 6, I cover the default image sizes that are set on the Media Settings page in your Dashboard. Having default image sizes is helpful when you have sections of your site in which you want to display a much smaller thumbnail or a larger version of the medium size but not as big as the large size.

Adding the post thumbnails to a theme

Adding support for post thumbnails includes a single line of code added to your theme functions (`functions.php`) file:

```
add_theme_support( 'post-thumbnails' );
```

Many themes, including the default themes that come packaged in WordPress, already have support for post thumbnails. If a theme you are using (or creating) does not, you can add it with the snippet previously provided.

After you add this line to your Theme Functions file, you can use the featured image for your posts because it requires the Post Thumbnails function to be activated. You can then start designating images as featured by using the built-in featured image found in the WordPress image uploader and on the Add New Post page, where you write and publish your posts.

After you start adding featured images to your posts, make sure that you add the correct tag in your template(s) so that the featured image displays on your site in the area you want it. Open your `index.php` template, for example, and add the following line of code to include the default thumbnail size version of your chosen featured image in your posts:

```
<?php if ( has_post_thumbnail() ) { the_post_thumbnail( 'thumbnail' ); ?>
```

The first part of this line of code checks to see whether a featured image is associated with the post; if one is, the image displays. If a featured image doesn't exist for the post, nothing returns. You can also include the other default image sizes (set in your Media Settings page in the Dashboard, as shown in Figure 12-13) for medium, large, and full-size images by using these tags:

```
<?php if ( has_post_thumbnail() ) { the_post_thumbnail( 'medium' ); ?>
<?php if ( has_post_thumbnail() ) { the_post_thumbnail( 'large' ); ?>
<?php if ( has_post_thumbnail() ) { the_post_thumbnail( 'full' ); ?>
```

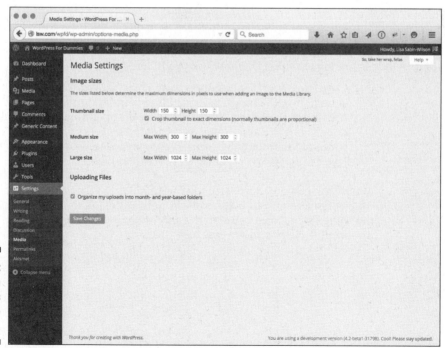

Figure 12-13:
The Media Settings page in the Dashboard.

Adding custom image sizes for post thumbnails

In case the predefined, default image sizes in WordPress (thumbnail, medium, large, and full) don't satisfy you and you have an area on your site in which you want to display images with dimensions that vary from the default, WordPress makes it relatively easy to add custom image sizes in your Theme Functions file. You then use the `the_post_thumbnail` function to display the featured image in your theme.

You aren't limited to sizes you can add for your images. Say that you want to add a new image size of 600px x 300px. Your Theme Functions file (`functions.php`) has the function `add_theme_support('post-thumbnails')`. (See the previous section, "Adding the post thumbnails to a theme.") Below that function, add this line of code:

```
add_image_size( 'custom', 600, 300, true);
```

This line tells WordPress that it needs to create an additional version of the images you upload and to crop and resize them to 600px wide and 300px tall. Notice the four parameters in the `add_image_size` function:

- ✔ **Name** (`$name`): Give the image size a unique name that you can use later in your template tag. In my example, I gave the new image size the name `'custom'`.

- ✔ **Width** (`$width`): Give the image size a width dimension in numbers. In my example, I defined the width as `600`.

- ✔ **Height** (`$height`): Give the image size a height dimension in numbers. In my example, I defined the height as `300`.

- ✔ **Crop** (`$crop`): This optional parameter tells WordPress whether it should crop the image to exact dimension or do a soft proportional resizing of the image. (Rather than be cropped to exact dimensions, dimensions are automatically corrected by WordPress based on the width of the thumbnails settings.) In my example, I set this to `true` (the accepted arguments are `true` or `false`).

Adding the custom image size to your template to display the image you've designated as featured is the same as adding default image sizes, except that the name of the image is set in the parentheses of the template tag. To add my example custom image size, use this tag:

```
<?php if ( has_post_thumbnail() ) { the_post_thumbnail( 'custom' ); ?>
```

Optimizing Your WordPress Site for Search Engines

Search engine optimization (SEO) is the practice of preparing your site to make it as easy as possible for the major search engines to crawl it and cache your data in their systems so that your site appears as high as possible in the search returns.

If you visit Google at www.google.com and search for *WordPress For Dummies author*, my personal blog at http://lisasabin-wilson.com is in the top-ten search results (at least, it is as I write this chapter). Those results can change from day to day, so by the time you read this book, someone else may well have taken over those coveted positions. The reality of chasing those high-ranking search engine positions is that they're here today, gone tomorrow. The goal of SEO is to make sure that *your* site ranks as high as possible for the keywords that you think people will use to find your site. After you attain those high-ranking positions, the next goal is to keep them.

Check out *Search Engine Optimization For Dummies,* 5th Edition, by Peter Kent (John Wiley & Sons, Inc.) for valuable information on keeping those high rankings through ongoing optimization of your site.

WordPress is equipped to create an environment that's friendly to search engines, giving them easy navigation through your archives, categories, and pages. This environment is provided by a clean code base, content that's easily updated via the WordPress interface, and a solid navigation structure.

To extend SEO even further, you can tweak these five elements of your WordPress posts, pages, and templates:

- ✔ **Custom permalinks:** Use custom permalinks, rather than the default WordPress permalinks, to fill your post and page URLs with valuable keywords.

- ✔ **Posts and page titles:** Create descriptive titles for your blog posts and pages to provide rich keywords in your site.

- ✔ **Text:** Fill your blog posts and pages with keywords for search engines to find and index. Keeping your site updated with descriptive text and phrases helps the search engines find keywords to associate with your site.

- ✔ **Category names:** Use descriptive names for the categories you create in WordPress to place helpful keywords directly in the URL for those category pages, if you use custom permalinks.

> ✔ **Images and alt tags:** Place `<ALT>` tags in your images to further define and describe the images on your site. You can accomplish this task easily by using the Alternate Text field in the WordPress image uploader, covered in Chapter 6.

Planting keywords in your website

If you're interested in a higher ranking for your site, I strongly recommend using custom permalinks. By using them, you automatically insert keywords into the URLs of your posts and pages, letting search engines include those posts and pages in their databases of information on those topics. If your site is hosted by a provider that has the Apache `mod_rewrite` module enabled, you can use the custom permalink structure for your WordPress-powered site.

Using keywords is the first step on your journey toward great search engine results. Search engines depend on keywords, and people use keywords to look for content.

The default permalink structure in WordPress is pretty ugly. When you're looking at the default permalink for any page, you see a URL that looks something like this:

```
http://yourdomain.com/?page_id=2
```

This URL contains no keywords of worth. If you change to a custom permalink structure, your post URLs automatically include the titles of your posts to provide keywords, which search engines absolutely love. A custom permalink may appear in this format:

```
http://yourdomain.com/the-page-title
```

I explain setting up and using custom permalinks in detail in Chapter 4.

Optimizing your post and page titles for search engine success

Search engine optimization doesn't completely depend on how you set up your site. SEO also depends on you, the site owner, and how you present your content.

One way to present your content in a way that lets search engines catalog your site easily is to give your blog posts and pages titles that make sense and coordinate with the actual content being presented. If you're creating a page on a certain topic, make sure that the title of the page contains at least one or two keywords about that particular topic. This practice gives the search engines even more ammunition to list your site in searches that are relevant to the topic of your page.

A page with the title "A Book I'm Reading" doesn't tell anyone what book it is, making it difficult for people searching for information on that particular book to find the page. If you give the page the title "WordPress Web Design For Dummies: My Review," you provide keywords in the title, and (if you're using custom permalinks) WordPress automatically inserts those keywords into the URL, giving the search engines this keyword triple play:

- ✔ Keywords exist in your page title.
- ✔ Keywords exist in your page URL.
- ✔ Keywords exist in the content of your page.

As your site's presence in the search engines grows, more people will find your site and your readership will increase as a result.

Writing content with readers in mind

When you write your posts and pages and you want to make sure that your content appears in the first page of search results so that people will find your site, you need to keep those people in mind when you compose the content.

When search engines visit your site to crawl through your content, they don't see how nicely designed it is — they look for words to grab and include in their databases. You, the site owner, should ensure that your posts and pages use the words and phrases that you want to include in search engines.

If your post is about a recipe for fried green tomatoes, for example, you need to add a keyword or phrase that you think people will use when they search for the topic. If you think people would use the phrase *recipe for fried green tomatoes* as a search term, you may want to include that phrase in the content and title of your post. Apply the same technique to pages you create on your website.

The title "A Recipe I Like" isn't as effective as the title "A Recipe for Fried Green Tomatoes," right? Including it in your post or page content gives the search engines a double keyword whammy.

Here's another example: I once wrote a post titled "Does Commitment Make Me Blister?" about a rash I developed on my finger, under my ring. I wrote that post in April 2006, not really meaning to attract a bunch of people to that particular post. However, it seems that many women around the world suffer from the same rash, because years later that post still attracts at least one comment a month. When people use Google to search for the keywords *commitment blister*, out of a possible 370,000+ results returned, my blog post appears in the top five slots.

This is how great blogs are! I was able to solve my problem of the rash under my finger because one woman from Australia found my blog through Google, visited my blog post, and left a comment with a solution that worked. Who says blogs aren't useful?

Creating categories that attract search engines

Here's one little-known SEO tip for WordPress users: The names you give the categories you've created for your blog provide rich keywords that attract search engines like bees to honey. A few services — Technorati is one of the biggest — treat categories in WordPress like tags. These services use those categories to classify recent blog posts on any given topic.

Search engines also see your categories as keywords that are relevant to the content on your site. In this regard, make sure that you're giving your categories names that are relevant to the content you provide on your site.

If you sometimes blog about your favorite recipes, you can make it easier for search engines to find your recipes if you create categories specific to the recipes you're blogging about. Rather than have one Favorite Recipes category, you can create multiple category names that correspond to the types of recipes you blog about — Casserole Recipes, Dessert Recipes, Beef Recipes, and Chicken Recipes, for example.

Creating specific category titles helps not only search engines, but also your readers.

You can also consider having one category — Favorite Recipes — and creating subcategories (or *child categories*) that give a few more details on the types of recipes you've written about.

Categories use the custom permalink structure as well. So, links to your WordPress categories also become keyword tools within your site to help the search engines — and ultimately, search engine users — find the content. Using custom permalinks gives you category page URLs that look something like this:

```
http://yourdomain.com/category/Category_Name
```

The `Category_Name` portion of that URL puts the keywords directly into the hands of search engines.

Using the <ALT> tag for images

When you use the WordPress image uploader to include an image in your post or page, you're given a Description text box in which you can enter a description of the image. This text automatically becomes the <ALT> tag.

The <ALT> tag's true purpose is to provide a description of the image for people who, for one reason or another, can't see the image. In a text-based browser that doesn't display images, for example, visitors see the description, or <ALT> text, telling them what image would be there if they could see it. Also, the tag helps people with impaired vision who rely on screen-reading technology, because the screen reader reads the <ALT> text from the image. You can read more about website accessibility for people with disabilities at `www.w3.org/WAI/intro/people-use-web/Overview.html`. (Capitalization in this URL matters.)

An extra benefit of <ALT> tags is that search engines gather data from them to further classify the content of your site. The following line of code inserts an image, with the <ALT> tag of the code in bold to demonstrate what I'm talking about:

```
<img src="http://yourdomain.com/image.jpg" alt="This is an ALT tag within an
             image" />
```

Search engines harvest those <ALT> tags as keywords. The WordPress image uploader gives you an easy way to include those <ALT> tags without worrying about inserting them into the image code yourself. Just fill out the Description text box before you upload and add the image to your post.

Chapter 13

Hosting Multiple Sites with WordPress

*I*n this chapter, I introduce you to the network feature that is built in to the WordPress software. The network feature allows you, the site owner, to add and maintain multiple blogs within one installation of WordPress. In this chapter, you discover how to set up the WordPress network feature, explore settings and configurations, gain an understanding of the Network Administrator role, determine which configuration is right for you (do you want subdirectories or subdomains?), and find some great resources to help you on your way.

With the network features enabled, users of your network can run their own sites within your installation of WordPress. They also have access to their own Dashboard with the same options and features as you've read about in the past 12 chapters. Heck, it would probably be a great idea to buy a copy of this book for every member within your network so everyone can become familiar with the WordPress Dashboard and features, too. At least have a copy on hand so people can borrow yours!

Considering Web-Hosting Services

This chapter assumes that you already have the WordPress software installed and running correctly on your web server, and that your web server meets the minimum requirements to run WordPress (see Chapter 2).

Before you enable the WordPress network feature, you need to determine how you are going to use the feature. You have a couple of options:

✔ Manage just a few of your own WordPress blogs or websites.

✔ Run a full-blown site network with several hundred different sites and multiple users.

If you are planning to run just a few of your own sites with the WordPress network feature, your current hosting situation is probably well suited (see Chapter 3 for information on web-hosting services). However, if your plans are to host a large network with hundreds of blogs and multiple users, you should consider contacting your host and increasing your bandwidth, as well as the disk space limitations on your account.

The best example of a large, multisite network with millions of websites and users is the hosted service at WordPress.com. At WordPress.com, people are invited to sign up for an account and start a website using the network feature within the WordPress.com platform on the WordPress.com server. When you enable this feature on your own domain and enable the user registration feature (covered later in this chapter), you are inviting users to:

✔ Create an account.

✔ Create a site on your WordPress installation (on your domain).

✔ Create content by publishing content.

✔ Upload media files such as photos, audio, and video.

✔ Invite their friends to view their site, or sign up for their own account.

In addition to the necessary security measures, time, and administrative tasks that go into running a community of websites, you've got a few other things to worry about. Creating a community will increase the resource use, bandwidth, and disk space on your web server. In many cases, if you go over your allotted limits given to you by your web host, you will incur great cost. Make sure you anticipate your bandwidth and disk space needs before running a large network on your website. (Don't say I didn't warn you!)

Many WordPress Network communities start with grand dreams of being a large and active community — be realistic about how your community will operate in order to make the right hosting choice for yourself, and your community.

Small multisite communities can be easily handled using a shared-server solution, whereas larger, more active communities should really consider a dedicated server solution for operation. The difference between the two lies in their names:

- ✔ **Shared-server solution:** You have one account on one server that has several other accounts on it. Think of this as apartment living. One apartment building has several apartments for multiple people to live, all under one roof.

- ✔ **Dedicated server:** You have one account. You have one server. That server is dedicated to your account, and your account is dedicated to the server. Think of this as owning a home and not sharing your living space with anyone else.

A dedicated server solution is a more expensive investment for your blog community, whereas a shared-server solution is the most economical. Your decision on which solution to go with for your WordPress Network blogging community will be based on your realistic estimates of how big and how active your community will be. You can move from a shared-server solution to a dedicated server solution if your community gets larger than you expected; however, it is easier to start with the right solution for your community from day one.

Enabling the WordPress Network Feature

WordPress makes it pretty easy to enable the network feature, but it does require opening a file on your web server called `wp-config.php` and making a small alteration. Follow these steps to get the process started:

1. **Download the file called** `wp-config.php` **from the WordPress installation on your web server.**

   It's easiest to use an FTP program to download a copy of this file from your web server to your computer. Chapter 3 covers the information you need about using FTP.

2. **Using your preferred text editor, open the** `wp-config.php` **file.**

   PC users can use Notepad to edit the file; Mac users can use TextEdit.

3. **Find the line that says** `define( 'DB_COLLATE', '' );` **and click at the end of that line. Press Enter to create a new blank line.**

4. **Type define ('WP_ALLOW_MULTISITE', true);**

   Save the file to your computer as `wp-config.php`. Your `wp-config.php` file should look similar to mine, shown in the code on line 37 in Figure 13-1. Save the `wp-config.php` file to your computer.

5. **Upload the new file to your web server in your WordPress installation directory.**

6. **Go to your WordPress Dashboard in your browser.**

   You now see a new item, labeled Network Setup, under the Tools menu.

7. **Click the Network Setup link in the Tools menu.**

   A page called Create a Network of WordPress Sites loads in your browser window, shown in Figure 13-2.

If you have any plugins installed and activated on your WordPress installation, deactivate them before you proceed with the network setup — WordPress won't allow you to continue until you deactivate all your plugins.

Before proceeding with the final steps in enabling the WordPress network feature, you need to get a few items in order on your web server. You also need to make a decision about how the multiple sites within your network will be handled. These configurations need to be in place so that you can run the WordPress Network successfully. If you can perform the configurations in this section yourself (and if you have access to the Apache configuration files), this section is for you. If you don't know how, are uncomfortable with adjusting these settings, or don't have access to change the configurations in your web server software, ask your hosting provider for help or hire a consultant to perform the configurations for you. You can hire a consultant that is local to your area, or several consultants are available worldwide who can work with you remotely. A listing of consultants can be found on the Code Poet (by Automattic) website: `http://directory.codepoet.com/`.

Figure 13-1:
The wp-config.php file with the network features enabled.

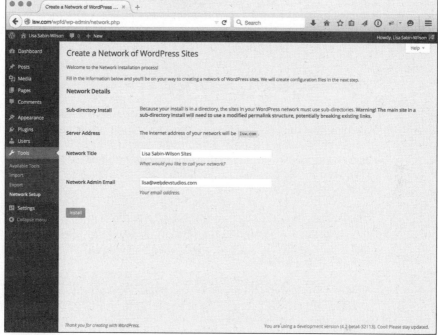

Figure 13-2:
The Create a
Network of
WordPress
Sites page
in your
WordPress
Dashboard.

DNS (domain name server)

The WordPress network feature gives you two different ways to run a network of sites on your domain, with one installation of WordPress. You can use the subdomain option or the subdirectory option. The most popular option (and recommended structure) sets up subdomains for the sites created by your WordPress Network. With the subdomain option, the username of the blog appears first, followed by your domain name. With the subdirectory option, your domain name appears first, followed by the username of the blog. Which one should you choose? The choice is yours. You can see the difference in the URLs of these two options by comparing the following examples:

  ✔ A **subdomain** looks like this: `http://username.yourdomain.com`.

  ✔ A **subdirectory** looks like this: `http://yourdomain.com/username`.

If you want to use a subdomain for each site in your WordPress Network, you must add a wildcard record to your DNS records. You need to add a hostname record pointing at your web server in the DNS configuration tool available in your web-server administration software (such as WebHost

Manager [WHM], a popular web-host administration tool). The hostname record looks like this: *.*yourdomain*.com (where *yourdomain*.com is replaced with your actual domain name).

Apache mod_rewrite

Apache (`http://httpd.apache.org`) is web-server software that's loaded and running on your web server. Not everyone has access to Apache files, however. Usually, the only person who has access to those files is the web-server administrator. (This is usually your web host.) Depending on your own web server account and configuration, you may or may not have access to the Apache software files.

The Apache module that's necessary for the WordPress Network to create nice permalink URLs (see Chapter 5 for information on pretty permalinks) is called `mod_rewrite`. This module must be configured so that it's active and installed on your server.

You or your web host can make sure that the Apache `mod_rewrite` module is activated on your server; open the `httpd.conf` file and verify that the following line is included within:

```
LoadModule rewrite_module /libexec/mod_rewrite.so
```

If it isn't, type that line on its own line and save the file. You will probably need to restart Apache before the change takes effect.

Virtual Host

In the same `httpd.conf` file that I discussed two paragraphs ago, you need to make some adjustments to the `<VirtualHost>` section of that file. Follow these steps:

1. **Find the `<VirtualHost>` section in the `httpd.conf` file.**

   This line of the `httpd.conf` file provides directives, or configurations, that apply to your website.

2. **Find a line in the `<VirtualHost>` section of the `httpd.conf` that looks like this:**

   ```
   AllowOverride None
   ```

3. **Replace that line with this line:**

   ```
   AllowOverride FileInfo Options
   ```

4. On a new line, type `ServerAlias *.`*yourdomain*`.com.`

Replace *yourdomain*.com with whatever your domain is. This line defines the host name for your Network site and is essential for the virtual host to work correctly.

5. Save the `httpd.conf` **file and close it.**

PHP (PHP Hypertext Processor)

In this section, you edit the PHP configuration on your web server. PHP needs to have the following configurations in place in the `php.ini` file on your web server to run WordPress Multisite on your server:

✔ Set your PHP to *not* display any error messages in the visitor's browser window. (This is usually already turned off by default; just double-check that to be sure.)

✔ Find out whether your PHP is compiled with memory limit checks. You can find this out by looking for the text `memory_limit` in the `php.ini` file. Usually, the default limit is 8MB. Increase the memory limit to at least 32MB, or even 64MB, to avoid PHP memory errors when running WordPress Multisite.

✔ Global variables should be set to Off. Usually, the default setting does have global variables turned off; double-check to be sure. An easy way to configure this is to open the `.htaccess` file (found on your web server in the same directory to which you installed the WordPress Multisite files) and add the following two lines to the very top of the `.htaccess` file:

```
php_flag register_globals 0
php_flag display_errors 0
```

Installing the Network on Your Site

The Network Details heading on the Create a Network of WordPress Sites page has options filled in automatically (refer to Figure 13-2). The server address, for example, is pulled from your installation and isn't editable. The network title and administrator email address are pulled from your installation database, too, because your initial WordPress site is the main site in the network.

Follow these steps to complete the installation of the Multisite Feature on the Create a Network of WordPress Sites page that appears after you install the Network in the previous section — be sure to have your preferred text editor program handy, as you will be editing files in the following steps:

1. **Click the Install button at the bottom of the Create a Network of WordPress Sites page in your WordPress Dashboard.**

   This opens the Enabling the Network page in the network Dashboard.

2. **Add the Network-related configuration lines to the** `wp-config.php`.

   On the Create a Network of WordPress Sites–Enabling the Network page, WordPress gives you up to six lines of configuration rules that need to be added to the `wp-config.php` file. The lines of code you add look something like this:

   ```
   define('MULTISITE', true);
   define('SUBDOMAIN_INSTALL', false);
   define('DOMAIN_CURRENT_SITE', 'localhost');
   define('PATH_CURRENT_SITE', '/');
   define('SITE_ID_CURRENT_SITE', 1);
   define('BLOG_ID_CURRENT_SITE', 1);
   ```

   These lines of code provide configuration settings for WordPress by telling it whether it is using subdomains, what the base URL of your website is, and your site's current path. This code also assigns a unique ID of 1 to your website and blog for the main installation site of your WordPress Multisite network. By default, WordPress sets up your network to use subdirectories, instead of subdomains. If you would like to use subdomains, change this line of code: `define('SUBDOMAIN_INSTALL', false);` to `define('SUBDOMAIN_INSTALL', true);`. Make sure that you have the VHost and Apache `mod_rewrite` configurations on your server in place before you do this.

   The lines of code that are given to you on the Create a Network of WordPress Sites page are unique to *your* installation of WordPress. Make sure that you copy the lines of code that are given to you on the Create a Network of WordPress Sites page on *your* installation because they are specific to your site's setup.

3. **Add the Rewrite Rules to the** `.htaccess` **file on your web server.**

   WordPress gives you several lines of code that you need to add to a file called `.htaccess` on your web server. You find that file in the WordPress installation directory. These lines look something like this:

   ```
   RewriteEngine On
   RewriteBase /wpfd/
   RewriteRule ^index\.php$ - [L]
   ```

```
# add a trailing slash to /wp-admin
RewriteRule ^([_0-9a-zA-Z-]+/)?wp-admin$ $1wp-admin/
    [R=301,L]

RewriteCond %{REQUEST_FILENAME} -f [OR]
RewriteCond %{REQUEST_FILENAME} -d
RewriteRule ^ - [L]
RewriteRule ^([_0-9a-zA-Z-]+/)?(wp-
    (content|admin|includes).*) $2 [L]
RewriteRule ^([_0-9a-zA-Z-]+/)?(.*\.php)$ $2 [L]
RewriteRule . index.php [L]
```

Earlier in this chapter, I discussed the required Apache module called
mod_rewrite and how you must have that installed on your web
server to run WordPress Multisite. The rules that you just added to the
.htaccess file on your web server are mod_rewrite rules, and they
need to be in place so that your web server tells WordPress how to
handle things like permalinks for blog posts, pages, media, and other
uploaded files. Without these rules in place, the WordPress multisite
feature will not work correctly.

4. **Copy the lines of code from the Create a Network of WordPress Sites:
   Enabling the Network page in Step 3. Then open the** .htaccess **file
   and paste the lines of code there.**

   Completely replace the rules that already exist in that file.

5. **Save the** .htaccess **file and upload it again to your web server.**

6. **Return to your WordPress Dashboard and click the Log In link at
   the bottom of the Create a Network of WordPress Sites: Enabling the
   Network page.**

   You are logged out of WordPress because by following these steps,
   you have changed some of the browser cookie-handling rules in the
   wp-config.php and .htaccess files.

7. **Log in to WordPress by entering your username and password in the
   login form displayed.**

Exploring the Network Admin Dashboard Menu

With the WordPress Network now fully enabled and configured, you see a
new link in the menu at the top right of your WordPress Dashboard called
My Sites. In this section, I show you how to become a Network Admin and
explain everything you need to know about being a Network Admin in your
new WordPress Network.

With the network (or multisite) feature enabled, you see the link to My Sites — if you hover your mouse pointer over that link, the Network Admin link displays in the drop-down menu on the upper-left side of the Dashboard, as shown in Figure 13-3. WordPress has separated the Network Admin menu features from the rest of the regular (Site Admin) Dashboard menu features to make it easier for you to know which part of your site you are managing. For example, if you are performing actions that maintain your main website — publishing posts or pages, creating or editing categories, and so on — you work on the regular Dashboard (Site Admin). However, if you are managing any one of the network sites, plugins, and themes for the network sites or registered users, you work in the Network Admin section of the Dashboard.

It is important to keep in mind the distinct difference between the Site Admin and Network Admin Dashboard, as well as subsequent menu features. WordPress tries its best to assume which features you are attempting to work with; however, if you find yourself getting lost in the Dashboard and not finding a menu or feature that you're used to seeing, double-check to make sure you're working in the correct section of the Dashboard.

Network Admin

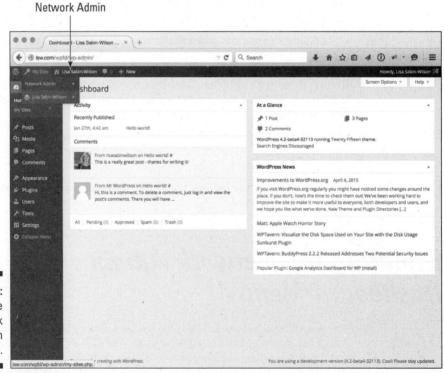

Figure 13-3:
Link to the
Network
Admin
Dashboard.

The Network Admin Dashboard (see Figure 13-4) looks similar to the regular WordPress Dashboard, but as you may notice, the modules shown on the Network Admin Dashboard pertain to the network of sites. Options there include letting you create a new site, create a new user, and search existing sites and users. Obviously, you won't perform this search if you don't have any users or sites yet. However, this function is extremely useful when you have a community of users and sites within your network.

The Network Admin Dashboard is configurable, just as the regular Dashboard is, and you can move the modules around and edit the settings of the modules. Refer to Chapter 4 for more information about arranging the Dashboard modules to suit your tastes.

The Search Users feature allows you to search usernames and user email addresses. If you search for the user *Lisa*, for instance, your results include any user whose username or email address contains *Lisa* — so you can receive multiple returns when using just one search word or phrase. The Search Sites feature returns any sites within your network that match the terms you've searched for.

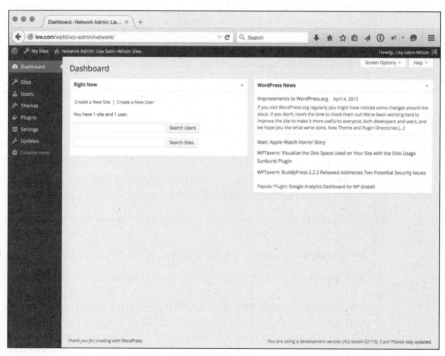

Figure 13-4:
The
Network
Admin
Dashboard.

The Network Admin page has two useful links near the top left of the page:

- ✔ **Create a New Site:** Click this link to create a new site within your network. After you click the link, the Sites page appears, on which you can add a new site. I cover how to do this in the upcoming "Sites" section.

- ✔ **Create a New User:** Click this link to create a new user account within your community. After you click the link, the Users page appears, on which you can add a new user to your community. I cover how to do this in the upcoming "Users" section.

Additionally, the WordPress Network Admin page gives you a real-time count of how many sites and users you have in your network, which is nice-to-know information for any Network Admin.

Managing Your Network

As mentioned, the Network Admin Dashboard has its own set of unique menus separate from the regular Site Admin Dashboard. Those menus are located on the left side of the Network Admin Dashboard. This section goes through each menu item and provides you with explanations and instructions on how to work with the different settings and configurations to help you manage your network, sites, and users.

The full list of menus available on the Network Admin Dashboard includes

- ✔ **Sites:** View a list of the sites in your network, along with details about them.

- ✔ **Users:** See detailed info about current users in your network.

- ✔ **Themes:** View all the currently available themes to enable or disable them for use in your network.

- ✔ **Plugins:** Manage (activate or deactivate) themes for use on all sites within your network.

- ✔ **Settings:** Configure global settings for your network.

- ✔ **Updates:** Upgrade all sites in your network with one click.

All the items in the Network Admin Dashboard are important, and you will use them all frequently throughout the life of your network. Typically, I would take you through each of the menu items in order so that you could easily follow along on your own Dashboard; however, you should set some important preliminary configurations for your network before you do anything else, so the following section starts with the Settings menu and then takes you through all the other menu items in order of appearance on the Network Admin Dashboard.

Settings

Click the Settings menu link on the Network Admin Dashboard. The Network Settings page loads in your browser window. The Network Settings page contains several sections of options for you to configure to set up your network the way you want.

Operational Settings

The Operational Settings section, shown in Figure 13-5, has Network Title and Network Admin Email:

- ✓ **Network Title:** This is the title of your overall network of sites. This name is included in all communications regarding your network, including emails that new users receive when they register a new site within your network. Type your desired Network Title in the text box provided here.

- ✓ **Network Admin Email:** This is the email address that all correspondence from your website is addressed from, including all registration and signup emails that new users receive when they register a new site and/or user account within your network. Type in the email that you would like to use for these purposes in the text box provided here.

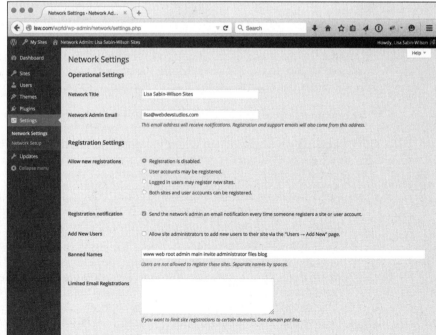

Figure 13-5:
The Operational Settings section on the Network Settings page.

Registration Settings

The Registration Settings section (see Figure 13-5) allows you to control aspects of allowing users to sign up to your network. The most important option is whether to allow open registration.

Decide how you want to handle registration on your network and select one of the following options by selecting the radio button to the left of each option:

- ✔ **Registration Is Disabled:** Disallows new user registration completely. When selected, this option prevents people who visit your site from registering for a user account.

- ✔ **User Accounts May Be Registered:** Gives people the ability to create only a user account; users will not be able to create a blog within your network.

- ✔ **Logged In Users May Register New Sites:** Allows only existing users — that is, those who are already logged in — to create a new blog within your network. This also disables new user registration completely. This is an option you would use if you didn't want just anyone registering for an account. Instead, you, as the site administrator, can add new users at your own discretion.

- ✔ **Both Sites and User Accounts Can Be Registered:** Gives users the ability to register an account and a site on your network during the registration process.

These options apply only to outside users. As a Network Admin, you're able to create new sites and users at any time you would like by using options available to you on the Network Admin Dashboard (see the information about creating new users in the "Users" section, later in this chapter).

The remaining options under the Registration Settings heading are as follows:

- ✔ **Registration Notification:** With this option selected, an email is sent to the Network Admin every time a user or a site is created on the system, even if it's the Network Admin who creates the new site.

- ✔ **Add New Users:** With this option selected, your community blog owners (individual site admins) have the ability to add new users to their own community blog via the Users page within their individual dashboards.

- ✔ **Banned Names:** By default, WordPress bans several usernames from being registered within your community, including *www, web, root, admin, main, invite,* and *administrator.* For good reason: You don't want a random user to register a username such as *admin* because you don't want that person misrepresenting himself as an administrator on your site. You can enter an unlimited amount of usernames that you do not want to allow on your site in the Banned Names text box.

✔ **Limited Email Registrations:** You can limit signups based on email domains by filling in this text box with one email per line. If you have open registrations but you've limited the email addresses, anyone who tries to sign up who doesn't match a domain on the list will be unable to register. This is an excellent option to use in a school or corporate environment in which students or employees get their own email addresses and you're providing them with their own sites.

✔ **Banned Email Domains:** This feature, the reverse of the preceding, blocks all signups from a particular domain, which can be useful in stopping spammers. For example, you can type **gmail.com** in the field, and anyone trying to sign up with a Gmail address will be denied.

New Site Settings

The New Site Settings section is a configurable list of items that populates default values when a new site is created. These include the values that appear in welcome emails, on a user's first post page, and on a new site's first page, as shown in Figure 13-6.

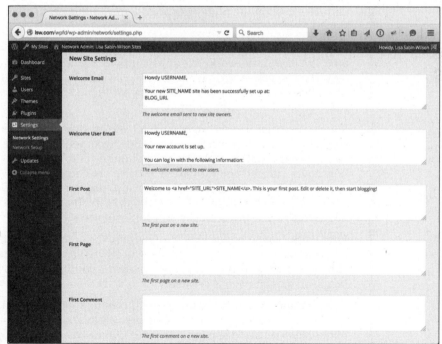

Figure 13-6:
New Site Settings on the Network Settings page.

✔ **Welcome Email:** This is the text of the email that owners of newly registered sites in your network receive after their registration is complete. You can leave the default message in place, if you'd like. Or you can type the text of the email you want new site owners to receive when they register a new site within your network.

A few variables you can use in this email aren't explained entirely on the Site Options page, including

- SITE_NAME: Inserts the name of your WordPress site

- BLOG_URL: Inserts the URL of the new member's blog

- USERNAME: Inserts the new member's username

- PASSWORD: Inserts the new member's password

- BLOG_URLwp-login.php: Inserts the hyperlinked login URL for the new member's blog

- SITE_URL: Inserts the hyperlinked URL for your WordPress site

✔ **Welcome User Email:** This is the text of the email that newly registered users receive after they've completed the registration process. The variables used in the preceding point apply to this email configuration as well.

✔ **First Post:** This is the first, default post displayed on every newly created site in your network. WordPress provides you with some default text that you can leave in place, or you can type your desired text in the provided text box that you want to appear in the first post on every site that's created in your community.

You can use this area to provide useful information about your site and services. This also serves as a nice guide for new users because they can view that post on their Dashboard, on the Edit Post page, and see how it was entered and formatted; it therefore can serve as a guide for creating their own blog posts. You can also use the variables described in the bullet points in the Welcome Email bullet (earlier in this list) to have WordPress automatically add some information for you.

✔ **First Page:** Similar to the First Post setting, this is the default text for a default page displayed on every newly created site in your network. (The First Page text box does not include default text; if you leave it blank, no default page is created.)

✔ **First Comment:** This is the first default comment displayed on the first default post on every newly created site within your network. Type the text that you want to appear in the first comment on every site that's created in your community.

✔ **First Comment Author:** Type the name of the author of the First Comment on new sites in your network.

✔ **First Comment URL:** Type the web address (URL) for the author of the First Comment; this will cause the First Comment Author's name to be hyperlinked to the URL you type here.

Upload Settings

The Upload Settings section (see Figure 13-7) defines global values pertaining to the type of files you will allow the site owners within your network to upload using the file upload feature in the WordPress Add Media window (see Chapter 6). The types of files that site owners can upload include

✔ Images

✔ Videos

✔ Documents

✔ Music

The first option in the Upload Settings section is Site Upload Space. The amount is in megabytes (MB), and the default storage space is 100MB. This amount of hard drive space is what you give users to store the files they upload to their blog. If you want to change the default storage space, type a number in the text box provided.

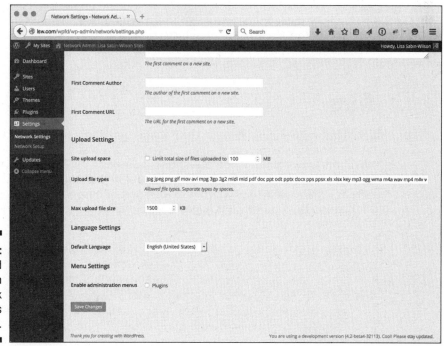

Figure 13-7:
Upload Settings on the Network Settings page.

The next text field is labeled Upload File Types, which defines the types of files that you, as the Network Admin, will allow the site owners to upload to their sites on their Dashboards. Users cannot upload any file types that do not appear in this text box. By default, WordPress includes the following file types: `.jpg`, `.jpeg`, `.png`, `.gif`, `.mp3`, `.mov`, `.avi`, `.wmv`, `.midi`, `.mid`, `.mt2s`, and `.pdf`. You can remove any default file types and add new ones.

The final option under Upload Settings defines the Max Upload File Size. This amount is in kilobytes (K), and the default file size is 1500K. This means that a user cannot upload a file that is larger than 1500K. Adjust this number as you see fit by typing a new number in the text box provided.

Menu Settings

The Plugins administration menu is disabled within the Dashboard of all network sites (except for the Network Admin). However, the Network Admin always has access to the Plugins menu. If you leave this option unselected, the Plugins page is visible to users on their own site's Dashboard. Select the box to enable the Plugins administration menu for your network users (see Figure 13-7). For more information about using plugins with WordPress, see Chapter 7.

When you have completely finished configuring the settings on the Network Settings page, don't forget to click the Save Changes button at the bottom of the page, underneath the final Menu Settings section (refer to Figure 13-7). If you navigate away from the Network Settings page without clicking the Save Changes button, none of your configurations will be saved, and you will need to go through the entire process again.

Sites

Clicking the Sites menu item on the Network Admin Dashboard takes you to the Sites page, where you can manage your individual sites. Although each site in the network has its own Dashboard for basic tasks, such as posting, changing themes, and so on, the Sites page is where you create and delete sites and make edits to properties of the sites within your network. Editing information from this page is handy when you have issues accessing a site's Dashboard.

The Sites page also lists all the sites within your network. The listing shows the following statistics about each community site:

✔ **Path:** The site's path in your network. For example, in Figure 13-8, you see a site listed with the path: `newsite`. This means that the site's domain is `newsite.yourdomain.com` if you are using a subdomain setup, or `yoursite.com/newsite` if you are using a subdirectory setup.

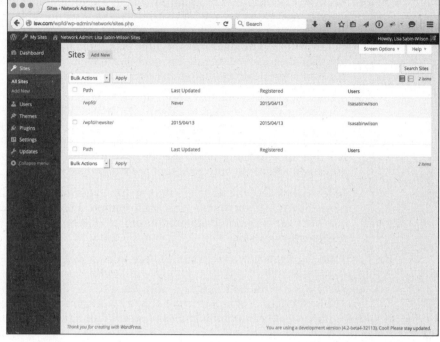

Figure 13-8:
Individual
site man-
agement
options on
the Sites
page.

✔ **Last Updated:** The date the site was last updated (or published to).

✔ **Registered:** The date the site was registered in your network.

✔ **Users:** The username and email address associated with the user(s) of that site.

When you hover your mouse pointer over the path name of a site in your network, you see a handy listing of links that help you manage the site. The options that appear underneath a site listing when you hover on a site name in the list include:

✔ **Edit:** A link to the Edit Site page (see Figure 13-9), where you can change aspects of each site.

✔ **Dashboard:** A link to the Dashboard of the site.

✔ **Deactivate:** Click this link to mark the site for deletion in your network. After clicking the Deactivate link, a message appears in a pop-up window that asks you to confirm your intention to deactivate the site. Click the Yes button to confirm. The user's site displays a message stating that the site has been deleted. This action can be reversed by revisiting the Sites page and clicking the Activate link that appears underneath the site pathname. (The Activate link appears underneath only sites that are marked as Deactivated.)

✔ **Archive:** Click this link to archive the site in your network, which prevents it from being viewed by visitors. The user's site displays a message stating `This site has been archived or suspended`. This action can be reversed by revisiting the Sites page and clicking the Unarchive link that appears underneath the site's pathname. (The Unarchive link appears underneath only sites that are marked as Archived.)

✔ **Spam:** Clicking this link marks the site as spam and blocks the users from being able to access the Dashboard. It also displays a message stating `This site has been archived or suspended`. This action can be reversed by revisiting the Sites page and clicking the Not Spam link that appears underneath the site's pathname. (The Not Spam link appears underneath only sites that are marked as Spam.)

✔ **Delete:** Click this link to delete the site from your network of sites permanently. Although you see a confirmation screen that asks you to confirm your intention to delete the site, after you've done it, you cannot reverse this decision.

✔ **Visit:** Click this link to visit the live site in your web browser.

Generally, you use the Edit Site page only when the settings are unavailable from the Dashboard of that particular site, by configuring the options that appear underneath each of the four tabs on the Edit Sites page, as shown in Figure 13-9:

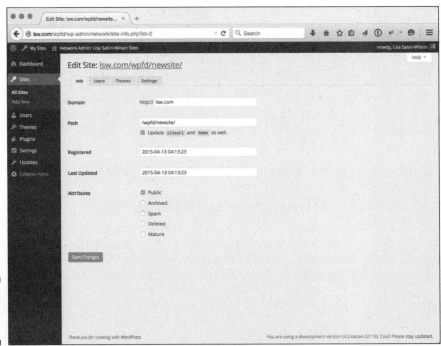

Figure 13-9:
The Edit Site
page.

✔ **Info:** Under this tab, you can edit the site's domain, path, registered date, updated date, and attributes (Public, Archived, Spam, Deleted, Mature).

✔ **Users:** Under this tab, you can manage the users that are assigned to the site, as well as add new users to the site under the Add New User section.

✔ **Themes:** Under this tab, you can enable themes for this site. This capability is particularly useful if you have themes that are not Network Enabled (see the "Themes" section later in this chapter) because all the themes that are not enabled within your network are listed under the Themes tab, which allows you to enable themes on a per-site basis.

✔ **Settings:** The settings under this tab cover all the database settings for the site that you are editing. You will rarely, if ever, need to edit these settings because as the Network Admin, you have access to each user's Dashboard and should be able to make any changes to the site's configuration settings there.

Also in the Sites menu on the Network Admin Dashboard, you see a link called Add New — click that link to load the Add New Site page on your Network Admin Dashboard. You can create a new site from the Add New Site page, shown in Figure 13-10. Fill in the Site Address, Site Title, and Admin Email fields and then click the Add Site button to add the new site to your network. If the Admin Email you entered is associated with an existing user, the new site is assigned to that user in your network. If the user doesn't exist, a new user is created and an email is sent with a notification. The site is immediately accessible. The user receives an email containing a link to his site, a login link, and his username and password.

Users

Clicking the Users menu link on the Network Admin Dashboard takes you to the Users page, where you see a full listing of members, or users, within your network. The Users page (see Figure 13-11) lists the following information about each user:

✔ **Username:** This is the login name the member uses when she logs in to her account in your community.

✔ **Name:** This is the user's real name, taken from her profile. If the user has not provided her name in her profile, this column is blank.

✔ **E-mail:** This is the email address the user entered when she registered on your site.

✔ **Registered:** This is the date when the user registered.

✔ **Sites:** If you enable sites within your WordPress Network, this lists any sites the user is a member of.

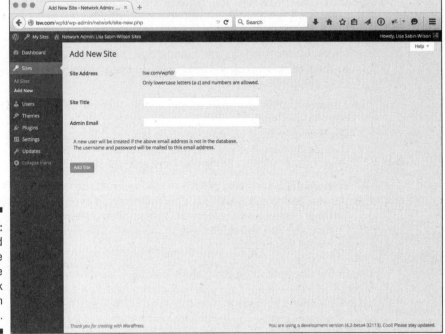

Figure 13-10:
The Add New Site page on the Network Admin Dashboard.

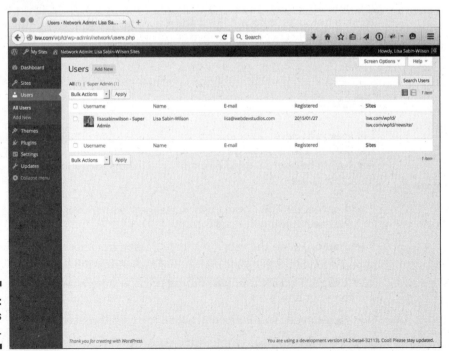

Figure 13-11:
The Users page.

Similarly to the Sites page, you can add and delete users to the network, as well as manage users by clicking either the Edit or Delete link that appears under their names when you hover over them with your mouse pointer (just as you do with sites on the Sites page).

To delete a user, simply hover over the username in the list that appears on the Users page. Click the Delete link and a new screen appears with a page telling you to transfer this user's posts and links to another user account (yours, most likely). Then click the Confirm Deletion button, and WordPress removes the user from the network, permanently. This action is irreversible, so be certain about your decision before you click that button!

You can also edit a user's profile information by clicking the Edit link that appears underneath his name when you hover your mouse pointer over it on the Users page. Clicking that link takes you to the Edit User profile page, shown in Figure 13-12, where you are presented with several options, which just happen to (mostly) be the very same options and settings that you configured for your own profile information in Chapter 4.

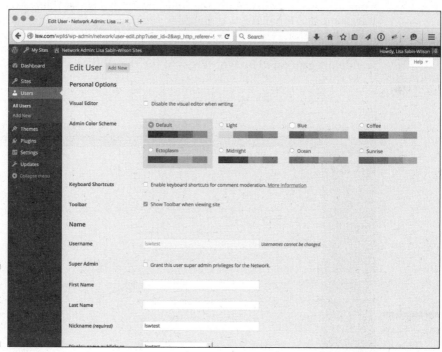

Figure 13-12:
The Edit User profile page.

The only difference with the Edit User profile page within the Network Admin Dashboard is one setting labeled Grant This User Super Admin Privileges for the Network. This setting is deselected by default; however, if you select this box, you grant this user Network Admin privileges for your network. Basically, this means that the user has the exact same access and permission as you do.

At the time of this writing, the terms *Super Admin* and *Network Admin* are interchangeable. When WordPress first merged the WordPress MU code base with the regular WordPress software, the term used to describe the Network Admin was Super Admin. Right now, Network Admin is the standard term; however, the term Super Admin is still used within some areas of both the Network Admin and the regular Dashboard. We will most likely see that change in the very near future when the folks at WordPress realize the discrepancy and make the updates in later versions of the software.

Also in the Users menu on the Network Admin Dashboard, you see a link called Add New; click that link to load the Add New User page on your Network Admin Dashboard (see Figure 13-13).

You can add a new user from the Add New User page by filling in the Username and Email fields of the user you'd like to add and then clicking the Add User button. The new user is sent an email notification alerting her of the new account, along with the site URL, her username, and her password (randomly generated by WordPress at the time the user account is created).

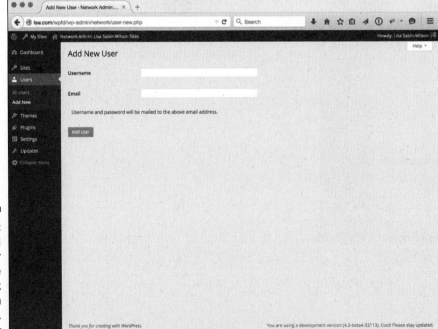

Figure 13-13:
The Add New User page on the Network Admin Dashboard.

Themes

When a network is enabled, only users with Network Admin access have permission to install themes, which are shared across the network. You can review details on how to find, install, and activate new themes with your WordPress installation in Chapter 8. After you install a theme, you must enable it in your network to have the theme appear in the Appearance menu of each site, where users in your network can activate it on their site. To access the network Themes page (shown in Figure 13-14), click the Themes link under the Themes menu on the Network Admin Dashboard.

Plugins

By and large, all WordPress plugins will work on your network. There are, however, some special plugins and some special considerations for using plugins with a network.

If you need a refresher on how to find, install, and activate plugins in WordPress, see Chapter 7.

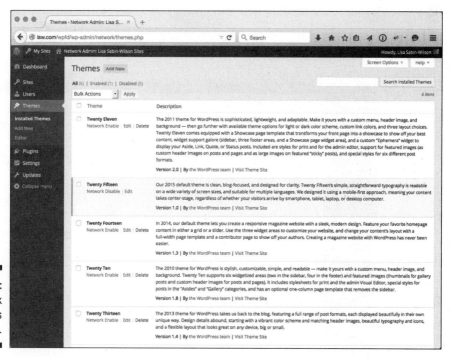

Figure 13-14: The network Themes page.

Browse to the Plugins page on your WordPress Network Admin Dashboard by clicking the Plugins link under the Plugins menu. You find that the Plugins page is just as described in Chapter 7, but if you don't know where to look, you can easily miss one very small, subtle difference. Check out Figure 13-15 and have a look below the name of the plugin. Do you see the Network Activate link? That is the big difference between plugins listed on the regular Dashboard and those on the Network Admin Dashboard. As the Network Admin, you can enable certain plugins to be activated globally, meaning across your entire network. This means that all sites in your network will have the network activated plugin features available on their site, in contrast to plugins that you activate on the regular Dashboard (under Site Admin), which are activated and available only for *your* main website.

If you select the Plugins administration menu (as I describe in the "Menu Settings" section, earlier in this chapter) on the Network Settings page, users see the plugins listed on their Plugins page on their Dashboard. In their list of plugins, they see only the plugins that you have not network activated; that is, they see a list of all the plugins you installed in your WordPress installation, but none of them are activated on that user's site. Users have the ability to activate and deactivate those plugins as they desire.

Only the Network Admins have access to install new plugins on the site; regular users within the network do not have that kind of access (unless you've made them Network Admins in their User settings).

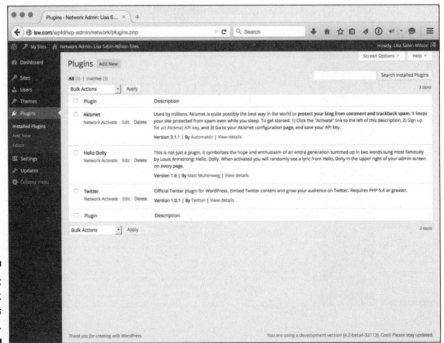

Figure 13-15:
The network Plugins page.

Also located in the Plugins menu on the Network Admin Dashboard are two other links: Add New and Editor. The Add New link lets you add and install new plugins by searching the WordPress Plugin Directory within your Dashboard, and the Editor link gives you access to the Plugin Editor. I cover these topics in more detail in Chapter 7.

Updates

Clicking the Updates link on the Network Admin Dashboard menu gives you access to the WordPress Updates page, which takes you through the same process of upgrading your WordPress installation software. WordPress takes the extra step of also upgrading all sites within your network so that they are all using the same, upgraded feature sets.

If the process of upgrading network sites stalls or stops, the URL of the last site upgraded appears on the WordPress Updates page. The Network Admin can access the Dashboard of the site where the upgrade stopped, which usually clears up the issue. A user accessing his site Dashboard after an upgrade also triggers the process of completing the upgrade.

Stopping Spam Signups and Splogs

If you choose to have open signups in which any member of the public can register and create a new site on your network, at some point, automated bots run by malicious users and spammers will visit your network signup page and attempt to create one, or multiple, sites in your network. They do so by automated means, hoping to create links to their sites or fill their site on your network with spam posts. This kind of spam blog or site is a *splog*.

Spam bloggers don't hack your system to take advantage of this; they call aspects of the signup page directly. You can do a few simple things to slow them down considerably or stop them altogether.

Diverting sploggers with settings and code

In the "Registration Settings" section earlier in this chapter, I go over a few options, including areas in which you can specify email addresses to allow or block. The Add New Users check box (refer to Figure 13-5) stops many spammers when it is deselected. When spammers access the system to set up a spam site, they often use the Add New Users feature to programmatically (through the use of programs built into the bots) create many other sites.

Spammers often find your site via Google Search, and that's where they find the link to the signup page. You can stop Google and other search engines from crawling your signup page by adding `rel=nofollow,noindex` on the signup page link. To do so, wherever you add a link to your signup page, inviting new users to sign up, the HTML code you use to add the `nofollow,noindex` looks like this:

```
<a href="http://yoursite.com/wp-signup.php" rel="nofollow,noindex ">Get your own
                  site here</a>
```

You can add this code to any page or widget area as a normal link to instruct legitimate visitors to sign up for a site in your network.

Plugins that help prevent spam

Plugins can help stop spam blogs, too. The Moderate New Blogs plugin interrupts the user signup process and sends you (the Network Admin) an email notification that a user has signed up for a site. You can then determine whether the site is legitimate. Download the plugin at `https://wordpress.org/plugins/moderate-new-blogs`.

The WangGuard plugin was written mainly to stop sploggers and prevent spam signups on a WordPress site — with or without the network feature activated. You can get the plugin at `https://wordpress.org/plugins/wangguard`. This plugin is free for personal use, or for sites with fewer than 500 daily user registrations.

The Cookies for Comments plugin (available at `https://wordpress.org/plugins/cookies-for-comments`) leaves a cookie in a visitor's browser. If the signup page is visited, the plugin checks for the cookie. If there isn't a cookie, the signup fails. Be sure to check the installation directions on this because it requires an `.htaccess` file edit.

Chapter 14

Upgrading, Backing Up, and Migrating

*Y*ou may, at some point, need to move your site to a different home on the web, either to a new web host or into a different account on your current hosting account. You may also be reading this book because you're moving your blog from a completely different platform to WordPress. You will also find that during your time as a WordPress user, upgrading the WordPress software is important, as is maintaining backups of your site so that you don't lose precious months or years of content.

In this chapter, you discover the WordPress upgrade notification system and what to do when WordPress notifies you that a new version of the software is available. This chapter also covers the best practices in upgrading the WordPress platform on your site to ensure the best possible outcome (that is, how not to break your website after a WordPress upgrade).

This chapter also covers how to migrate a blog that exists within a different blogging platform (such as Movable Type or TypePad) to WordPress. And finally, it takes you through how to back up your WordPress files, data, and content and move it to a new hosting provider or different domain.

Getting Notified of an Available Upgrade

When you install WordPress and have logged in for the first time, you can see the version number located at the bottom-right corner of the WordPress Dashboard. So, if anyone asks you what version you're using, you now know exactly where to look to find that information.

So, you have WordPress installed and you've been happily publishing content to your website with it for several weeks, maybe even months. Then one day, you log in and see a message at the top of your Dashboard screen that you've never seen before: `WordPress 4.1.1 is available! Please update now`. You can see such a message displayed in Figure 14-1.

Both the message at the top of the screen and the notification bubble on the Dashboard menu are visual indicators that you're using an outdated version of WordPress and that you can (and need to) upgrade the software.

Upgrade notification

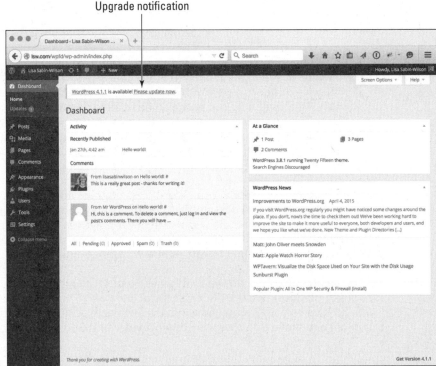

Figure 14-1: Alert notification of the available WordPress upgrade in the Dashboard.

The message at the top of your Dashboard has two links that you can click for more information. The first, in Figure 14-1, is a link called WordPress 4.1.1. Clicking it takes you to the WordPress Codex page titled Version 4.1.1 that's filled with information about the version upgrade, including

- ✔ Installation/upgrade information
- ✔ Summary of the development cycle for this version
- ✔ List of revised files

The second link, Please Update Now, takes you to the WordPress Updates page in the WordPress Dashboard, shown in Figure 14-2.

At the very top of the WordPress Updates page is another important message for you (see Figure 14-2): Important: before updating, please back up your database and files. For help with updates, visit the Updating WordPress Codex page. Both links in that message take you to the WordPress Codex pages that contain helpful information on creating backups and updating WordPress.

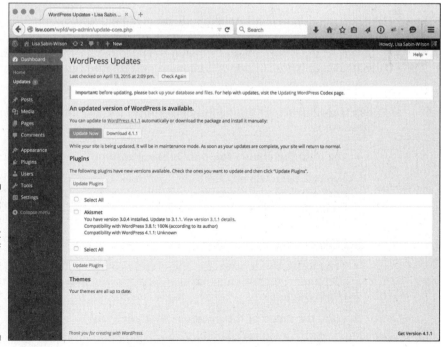

Figure 14-2: Get the latest version of WordPress through the WordPress Updates page.

The WordPress Updates page tells you that an updated version of WordPress is available and you have two different ways to update:

✔ **Automatically:** By using the built-in WordPress updater (this is the recommended method)

✔ **Manually:** By downloading the files and installing them on your server

Backing Up Your Database

One step I recommend you take before upgrading your WordPress software installation is to back up your database. This step isn't required, of course, but it's a smart step to take to safeguard your website and make absolutely sure that — should the upgrade go wrong for some reason — you have a complete copy of all your website data that can be restored if needed.

The best way to back up your database is to use the MySQL administration interface provided by your web-hosting provider.

 cPanel is a web-hosting interface provided by many web hosts as an account management tool containing phpMyAdmin as the preferred tool to manage and administer databases. Not all web hosts use cPanel or phpMyAdmin, however; so if yours doesn't, consult the user documentation for the tools that your web host provides. The instructions in this chapter are provided using cPanel and phpMyAdmin.

To create a database backup using the phpMyAdmin interface, follow these steps:

1. **Log in to the cPanel for your hosting account.**

   Typically, you will browse to `http://yourdomain.com/cpanel` to bring up the login screen for your cPanel. Enter your specific hosting account username and password in the login fields and click OK to log in.

2. **Click the phpMyAdmin icon.**

   The phpMyAdmin interface opens and displays your database. (Depending on your hosting environment, you may also have to log in to phpMyAdmin.)

3. **Click the name of the database that you want to back up.**

   If you have more than one database in your account, the left-side menu in phpMyAdmin displays the names of all of them. Click the one you want to back up, and that database loads in the main interface window on the side of the screen.

4. Click the Export tab at the top of the screen.

The page refreshes and displays the backup utility screen.

5. Select the Save as File check box.

6. Select the "zipped" option.

This compiles the database backup file in a `.zip` file and prepares it for download.

7. Click the Go button.

A pop-up window appears, allowing you to select a location on your computer to store the database backup file. Click Save to download it and save it to your computer.

With your WordPress website data safely backed up, you can proceed to upgrading the WordPress software. If anything happens to go wrong, you have a full copy of the content from your website, which can be restored at a future date if necessary.

Upgrading WordPress Automatically

To update WordPress automatically, follow these steps:

1. Back up your WordPress website; do not skip this step!

Backing up your website includes taking a backup of your database (covered in the previous section) and downloading the crucial elements via FTP (see Chapter 3). The crucial elements include the entirety of the `/wp-content` folder, which contains your plugins, themes, and all media (images, videos, documents, and so on) that you've uploaded to your website. Also download a backup of your `wp-config.php` file, located in the root install.

2. Deactivate all plugins.

This ensures that any plugin conflicts caused by the upgraded version of WordPress cannot affect the upgrade process. It also ensures that your website doesn't break after the upgrade is completed. You can find more information on working with and managing plugins in Chapter 7; for the purpose of this step, you can deactivate plugins by following these steps:

a. Click the Plugins link in the Plugins menu in the Dashboard.

This loads the Plugins page.

b. Select all plugins by selecting the box to the left of the Plugin column (see Figure 14-3).

c. In the drop-down menu at the top, select Deactivate.

d. Click the Apply button.

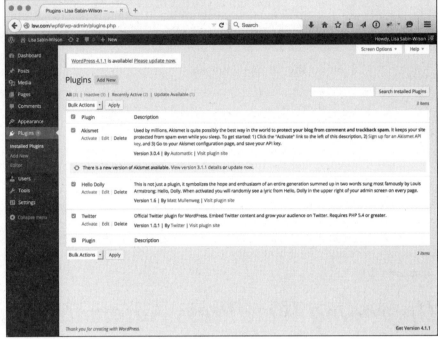

Figure 14-3:
The Plugins
page with
all plugins
selected,
ready to
deactivate.

3. Click the `Please Update Now` link on the WordPress Updates page.

This reloads the WordPress Updates page with the following messages:

- `Downloading update from http://wordpress.org/ wordpress-4.1.1.zip...`

- `Unpacking the update...`

- `Verifying the unpacked files...`

- `Installing the latest version...`

- `Upgrading database...`

- `WordPress updated successfully`

- `Welcome to WordPress 4.1.1. You will be redirected to the About WordPress screen. If not, click here.`

The Dashboard refreshes to display the welcome page for the latest version. This informational page (as shown in Figure 14-4) displays all of the important information about this upgrade, including version number and any major features that were added or bugs that were fixed.

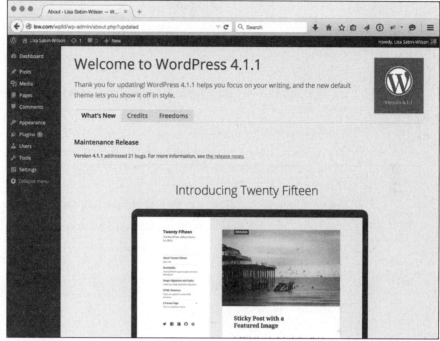

Figure 14-4:
The
welcome
page.

4. Wait until your screen redirects to the welcome page.

The welcome page loads in your web browser, and you can see that both the update alert message at the top of the site and the notification message on the Dashboard menu isn't there anymore. The welcome page displays a listing of new features in the version you just installed, shown in Figure 14-4. You're now using the latest version of WordPress.

Upgrading WordPress Manually

The second — and least used — method of upgrading WordPress is the manual method. It's the least-used method mainly because the automatic method, discussed in the previous section, is so easy, quick, and reliable. In some rare circumstances, you would manually upgrade WordPress because your web-hosting environment can't accommodate the automatic upgrade process, or maybe you just wanted to go through the experience of manually updating the software, for whatever weird reason.

The steps to manually upgrade WordPress are as follows:

1. **Back up your WordPress website and deactivate all plugins.**

   See Steps 1 and 2 in the previous section, "Upgrading WordPress Automatically."

2. **Navigate to the WordPress Updates page by clicking the Please Update Now link.**

3. **Click the Download button.**

   This opens a dialog box that allows you to save the .zip file of the latest WordPress download package to your local computer, shown in Figure 14-5.

4. **Select a location to store the download package and click Save.**

   The .zip file downloads to your selected location on your computer.

5. **Browse to the .zip file on your computer.**

6. **Unzip the file.**

   Use a program such as WinZip (www.winzip.com) to unzip files contained within a .zip file.

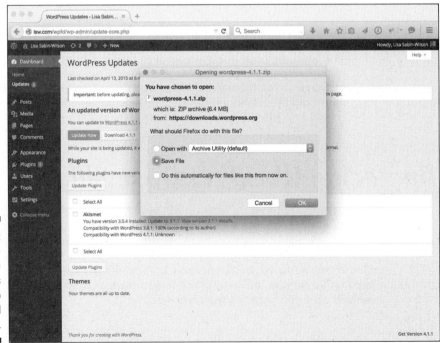

Figure 14-5: Downloading the WordPress files to your local computer.

7. **Connect to your web server via FTP.**

   See Chapter 3 for a refresher on how to use FTP.

8. **Delete all the files and folders in your existing WordPress installation directory *except* the following:**

   - /wp-content folder
   - .htaccess
   - wp-config.php

9. **Upload the contents of the**/wordpress **folder — not the folder itself — to your web server.**

   Most FTP client software lets you select all the files and drag and drop them to your web server. Other programs have you select the files and click a Transfer button.

10. **Navigate to the following URL on your website:** http: // *yourdomain*.com/wp-admin.

    Don't panic: Your database still needs to be upgraded to the latest version; so instead of seeing your website on your domain, you see a message telling you that a database upgrade is required, as shown in Figure 14-6.

11. **Click the Upgrade WordPress Database button.**

    This action causes WordPress to initiate the upgrade of the MySQL database associated with your website. When the database upgrade is complete, the page refreshes and displays a message saying so.

12. **Click the Continue button.**

    Your browser loads the WordPress login page. The upgrade is now complete, and you can continue using WordPress with all of its newly upgraded features.

Figure 14-6:
Press the
button to
upgrade
your
WordPress
database.

During your time as a WordPress user, you'll upgrade on a regular basis, at least three to four times per year. For some users, this is a frustrating reality of using WordPress; however, because of the very active development environment of the WordPress project, WordPress is the most popular platform available today. Because WordPress is always adding great new features and functions to the platform, upgrading always ensures that you're on top of the game and using the latest tools and features available.

If you're uncomfortable performing administrative tasks such as upgrading and creating database backups, you can hire someone to perform these tasks for you — either a member of your company, if you're a business, or a WordPress consultant skilled in these tasks.

Migrating Your Existing Site to WordPress

So you have a website on a different content management system and want to move your site to WordPress? This chapter helps you accomplish just that. WordPress makes it relatively easy to pack up your data and archives from one platform and move to a new WordPress site. WordPress lets you move your website from platforms such as Blogger, TypePad, and Movable Type. It also gives you a nifty way to migrate from any content management system via RSS feeds, as long as the platform you're importing from has an RSS feed available.

For some of the existing content management systems out there, the WordPress platform provides you with a quick and easy-to-install plugin that allows you to import and use your content right away. The importers are packaged in a plugin format because most people use an importer just once, and some people don't use the importer tools at all. The plugins are there for you to use if you need them. WordPress.com, on the other hand, has the importers built right into the software. Note the differences for the version you're using.

Movin' on up

Website owners have a variety of reasons to migrate away from one system to WordPress:

✔ **Simple curiosity:** The use of WordPress — and the whole community of WordPress users — is generating a *lot* of buzz. People are naturally curious to check out something that all the cool kids are doing.

✔ **More control of your website:** This reason applies particularly to those who have a site on Blogger, TypePad, or any other hosted service. Hosted programs limit what you can do, create, and mess with. When it comes to plugins, add-ons, and theme creation, hosting a WordPress blog on your own web server wins hands down. In addition, you have complete control of your data, archives, and backup capability when you host your blog on your own server.

✔ **Ease of use:** Many people find the WordPress interface easier to use, more understandable, and a great deal more user-friendly than many of the other blogging platforms available today.

 In the WordPress software, the importers are added to the installation as plugins. The importer plugins included in the previous list are the plugins packaged within the WordPress software, or they can be found by searching in the Plugin Directory at `https://wordpress.org/plugins/tags/importer`. You can import content from several other platforms by installing other plugins not available from the official WordPress Plugin Directory, but you may have to search on Google to find them.

Preparing for the big move

Depending on the size of your site (that is, how many posts and comments you have), the migration process can take anywhere from 5 to 30 minutes. As with any major change or update you make, no matter where your site is hosted, the very first thing you need to do is create a backup of your site. You should back up the following:

✔ **Archives:** Posts, pages, comments, and trackbacks; do this by taking a backup of your database.

✔ **Template:** Template files and image files; do this by transferring the `/wp-content/themes` folder from your hosting server to your local computer via FTP.

✔ **Plugins:** Plugin files; do this by transferring the `/wp-content/plugins` folder from your hosting server to your local computer via FTP.

✔ **Images:** Any images you use in your blog; do this by transferring from your hosting server to your local computer via FTP (images uploaded to blog posts are generally stored in `/wp-content/uploads`).

Table 14-1 gives you tips on creating the export data for your blog in a few major blogging platforms. *Note:* This table assumes that you're logged in to your blog software.

Table 14-1	Backing Up Your Blog Data on Major Platforms
Blogging Platform	**Backup Information**
Movable Type	Click the Import/Export button on the menu of your Movable Type Dashboard; then click the Export Entries From link. When the page stops loading, save it on your computer as a `.txt` file.
TypePad	Click the name of the blog you want to export; then click the Import/Export link in the Overview menu. Click the Export link at the bottom of the Import/Export page. When the page stops loading, save it on your computer as a `.txt` file.
Blogger	Back up your template by copying the text of your template to a text editor such as Notepad. Then save it on your computer as a `.txt` file.
WordPress	Click the Export link on the Tools menu in the Dashboard; the Export page opens. Choose your options on the Export page and then click the Download Export File button, then save this file on your computer.
RSS feed	Point your browser to the URL of the RSS feed you want to import. Wait until it loads fully (you may need to set your feed to display all posts). View the source code of the page, copy and paste that source code into a `.txt` file, and save the file on your computer.

This import script allows for a maximum file size of 128MB. If you get an "out of memory" error, try dividing the import file into pieces and uploading them separately. The import script is smart enough to ignore duplicate entries, so if you need to run the script a few times to get it to take everything, you can do so without worrying about duplicating your content.

Converting templates

Every blogging program has a unique way of delivering content and data to your blog. Template tags vary from program to program; no two are the same, and each template file requires conversion if you want to use *your* template with your new WordPress blog. In such a case, two options are available to you:

   ✔ **Convert the template yourself.** To accomplish this task, you need to know WordPress template tags and HTML. If you have a template that you're using on another blogging platform and want to convert it for use with WordPress, you need to swap the original platform tags for WordPress tags. The information provided in Chapters 8–11 gives you the rundown on working with themes as well as basic WordPress template tags; you may find that information useful if you plan to attempt a template conversion yourself.

✔ **Hire an experienced WordPress consultant to do the conversion for you.** You can find a list of available WordPress consultants, assembled by the folks at WPEngine (a premier managed hosting provider for WordPress) at `http://wpengine.com/consultants`.

To use your own template, make sure that you save *all* the template files, the images, and the stylesheet from your previous blog setup. You need them to convert the template(s) for use in WordPress.

Hundreds of free templates are available for use with WordPress, so it may be a lot easier to abandon the template you're currently working with and find a free WordPress template that you like. If you've paid to have a custom design done for your blog, contact the designer of your theme and hire him to perform the template conversion for you. Also, you can hire several WordPress consultants to perform the conversion for you — including yours truly.

Moving your website to WordPress

You've packed all your stuff and you have your new place prepared. Moving day has arrived! This section takes you through the steps for moving your site from one platform to WordPress. This section assumes that you already have the WordPress software installed and configured on your own domain.

Find the import function that you need by following these steps:

1. **In the Dashboard, click the Import link on the Tools menu.**

   The Import page opens, listing platforms from which you can import content (such as Blogger and Movable Type). Figure 14-7 shows the Import page in the WordPress Dashboard.

2. **Click the link for the blogging platform you're working with.**

   Click the Install Now button to install the importer plugin to begin using it.

The following sections provide some import directions for a few of the most popular content management systems (other than WordPress, that is). Each platform has its own content export methods, so be sure to check the documentation for the platform that you're using.

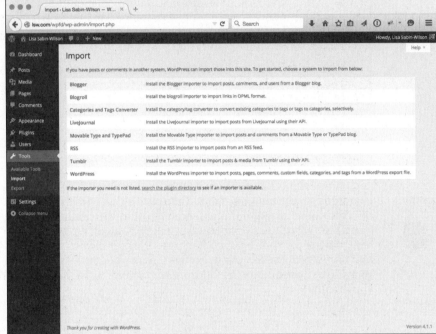

Figure 14-7:
The Import
page in the
WordPress
Dashboard.

Importing from Blogger

Blogger is the blogging application owned by Google (it's also called Blogspot).

To begin the import process, first complete the steps in the "Moving your website to WordPress" section, earlier in this chapter. Then follow these steps:

1. **Click the Blogger link on the Import page and install the plugin for importing from Blogger.**

   Click the Activate Plugin & Install Importer link, and the Import Blogger page loads with instructions to import your file, as shown in Figure 14-8.

2. **Click the Authorize button to tell WordPress to access your account.**

   A page from Google opens with a message that says your WordPress blog is trying to access your Google account.

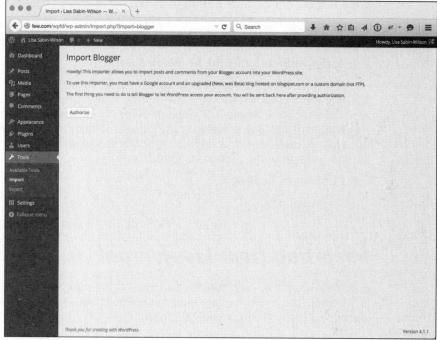

3. **Enter the email address and password you use for Google; then click the Sign In button.**

   The Access Request page in your Google Account opens. When you have successfully logged in, you receive a message from Google stating that your blog at WordPress is requesting access to your Blogger account so that it can post entries on your behalf.

4. **Give your permission by clicking the Allow Access button on the Access Request page.**

   If you have many posts and comments in your Blogger blog, the import can take 30 minutes or more.

   After the import script has performed its magic, you're redirected to your WordPress Dashboard, where the name of your Blogger blog is listed.

5. **To finish importing the data from Blogger, click the Import button (below the Magic Button header).**

   The text on the button changes to Importing ... while the import takes place. When the import is complete, the text on the button changes to Set Authors (no wonder it's called the Magic Button!).

6. **Click the Set Authors button to assign the authors to the posts.**

   The Blogger username appears on the left side of the page; a drop-down menu on the right side of the page displays the WordPress login name.

7. **Assign authors using the drop-down menu.**

   If you have just one author on each blog, the process is especially easy: Use the drop-down menu on the right to assign the WordPress login to your Blogger username. If you have multiple authors on both blogs, each Blogger username is listed on the left side with a drop-down menu to the right of each username. Select a WordPress login for each Blogger username to make the author assignments.

8. **Click Save Changes.**

   You're done!

Importing from LiveJournal

Both WordPress.com and WordPress.org offer an import script for LiveJournal users, and the process of importing from LiveJournal to WordPress is the same for each platform.

To export your blog content from LiveJournal, log in to your LiveJournal blog and then type this URL in your browser's address bar: `www.livejournal.com/login.bml?returnto=%2Fexport.bml`.

LiveJournal lets you export the XML files one month at a time, so if you have a blog with several months' worth of posts, be prepared to be at this process for a while. First, you have to export the entries one month at a time and then you have to import them into WordPress — yep, you guessed it — one month at a time.

 To speed up the process a little, you can save all the exported XML LiveJournal files in one text document by copying and pasting each month's XML file into one plain-text file (created in a text editor such as Notepad), thereby creating one long XML file with all the posts from your LiveJournal blog. You can then save the file as an XML file to prepare it for import into your WordPress blog.

After you export the XML file from LiveJournal, return to the Import page in your WordPress Dashboard and follow these steps:

1. **Click the LiveJournal link and install the plugin for installing from LiveJournal.**

   Click the Activate Plugin & Install Importer link, and the Import LiveJournal page loads with instructions to import your file, as shown in Figure 14-9.

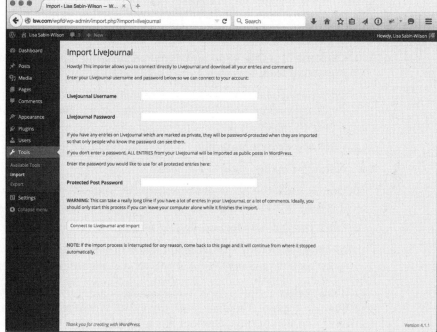

Figure 14-9:
The Import
LiveJournal
page in the
WordPress
Dashboard.

2. **Click the Browse button.**

   A window opens, listing files on your computer.

3. **Double-click the name of the XML file you saved earlier.**

4. **Click the Upload and Import button.**

   When the import script finishes, it reloads the page with a confirmation message that the process is complete. Then WordPress runs the import script and brings over all your posts from your LiveJournal blog.

Importing from Movable Type and TypePad

Movable Type and TypePad were created by the same company, Six Apart. These two blogging platforms run on essentially the same code base, so the import/export procedure is basically the same for both. Refer to Table 14-1 for details on how to run the export process in both Movable Type and TypePad. This import script moves all your blog posts, comments, and trackbacks to your WordPress blog.

Go to the Import page in your WordPress Dashboard by following Steps 1 and 2 in the "Moving your website to WordPress" section, earlier in this chapter. Then follow these steps:

1. **Click the Movable Type and TypePad link and install the plugin for importing from Movable Type and TypePad.**

   Click the Activate Plugin & Install Importer link, and the Import Movable Type or TypePad page loads with instructions to import your file, as shown in Figure 14-10.

2. **Click the Browse button.**

   A window opens, listing your files.

3. **Double-click the name of the export file you saved from your Movable Type or TypePad blog.**

4. **Click the Upload File and Import button.**

   Sit back and let the import script do its magic. When it's done, it reloads the page with a confirmation message that the process is complete.

When the import script is done, you can assign users to the posts, matching the Movable Type or TypePad usernames with WordPress usernames. If you have just one author on each blog, this process is easy; you simply assign

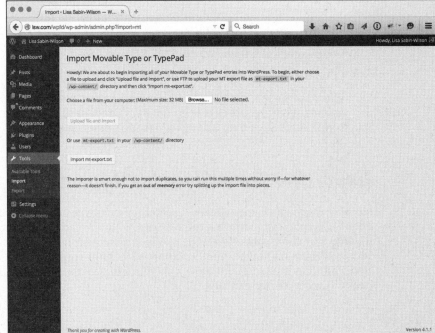

Figure 14-10:
The Import Movable Type or TypePad page in the WordPress Dashboard.

your WordPress login to the Movable Type or TypePad username using the drop-down menu. If you have multiple authors on both blogs, match the Movable Type or TypePad usernames with the correct WordPress login names and then click Save Changes. You're done!

Importing from WordPress

With this WordPress import script, you can import one WordPress blog into another, and this is true for both the hosted and self-hosted versions of WordPress. WordPress imports all your posts, pages, comments, custom fields, and categories into your website. Refer to Table 14-1 to find out how to use the export feature to obtain your blog data.

When you complete the exporting, follow these steps:

1. **Click the WordPress link on the Import page and install the plugin to import from WordPress.**

   Click the Activate Plugin & Install Importer link, and the Import WordPress page loads with instructions to import your file, as shown in Figure 14-11.

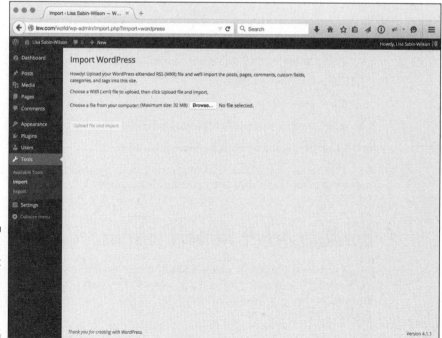

Figure 14-11:
The Import WordPress page in the WordPress Dashboard.

2. **Click the Browse button.**

   A window opens, listing the files on your computer.

3. **Double-click the export file you saved earlier from your WordPress blog.**

4. **Click the Upload File and Import button.**

   The import script gets to work and when it's done, it reloads the page with a confirmation message that the process is complete.

Importing from an RSS feed

If all else fails, or if WordPress doesn't provide an import script that you need for your current blog platform, you can import your blog data via the RSS feed for the blog you want to import. With the RSS import method, you can import only posts; you can't use this method to import comments, trackbacks, categories, or users. WordPress.com currently does not allow you to import blog data via an RSS feed; this function works only with the self-hosted WordPress.org platform.

Refer to Table 14-1 for information on creating the file you need to import via RSS. Then follow these steps:

1. **On the Import page in the WordPress Dashboard, click the RSS link and install the plugin to import from an RSS feed.**

   Click the Activate & Install link, and the Import RSS page loads with instructions to import your RSS file, as shown in Figure 14-12.

2. **Click the Browse button.**

   A window opens, listing the files on your computer.

3. **Double-click the export file you saved earlier from your RSS feed.**

4. **Click the Upload File and Import button.**

   The import script does its magic and then reloads the page with a confirmation message that the process is complete.

Finding other import resources

The WordPress Codex has a long list of other available scripts, plugins, workarounds, and outright hacks for importing from other platforms. You can find that information at `http://codex.wordpress.org/Importing_Content`.

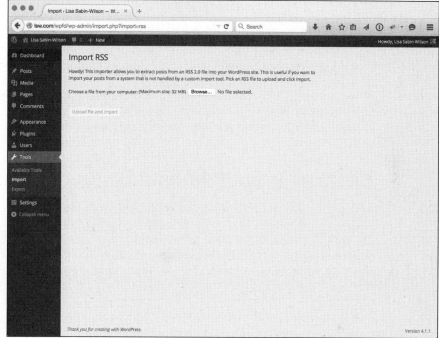

Figure 14-12:
The Import
RSS page
in the
WordPress
Dashboard.

Note: The WordPress Codex is run by a group of volunteers. When you refer to the Codex, be aware that not everything listed in it is necessarily up to date or accurate, including import information (or any other information about running your WordPress blog).

Moving Your Website to a Different Host

You may decide at some point that you need to switch from your current hosting provider to a new one. You may have to do this for several different reasons — maybe you're unhappy with your current provider and want to move to a new one, or your current provider is going out of business and you're forced to move.

Transferring from one host to another is a reality that some website owners must face, and transferring an existing website, with all its content, files, and data, from one host to another can seem a daunting task. This section of the chapter should make it easier for you to face.

You have two different ways to go about it:

- ✔ Manually, through backing up your database and downloading essential files
- ✔ Using a plugin to automate as much of the process as possible

Obviously, using a tool to automate the process is the easier and more desirable way to go, but just in case you need to do it manually, in the next section of this chapter, I provide you with the instructions for doing it both ways.

Creating a backup and moving manually

Earlier in this chapter, in "Backing Up Your Database," I provide you with step-by-step instructions on how to make a backup of your database using phpMyAdmin. Follow the steps in that section and you will have a backup of your database with all the recent content you've published to your blog. However, when I say "content," I mean the content that you (or others) have written or typed into your blog via the WordPress Dashboard, including

- ✔ Blog posts, pages, and custom post types
- ✔ Links, categories, and tags
- ✔ Post and page options, such as excerpts, time and date, custom fields, categories, tags, and passwords
- ✔ WordPress settings you configured under the Settings menu in the Dashboard
- ✔ All widgets that you've created and configured
- ✔ All plugin options that you configured for the plugins you installed

Other elements of your website aren't stored in the database, which you need to download, via FTP, from your web server. The following is a list of those elements, including instructions on where to find them and how to download them to your local computer:

- ✔ **Media files:** These are the files you uploaded using the WordPress media upload feature, including images, videos, audio files, and documents. Media files are located in the `/wp-content/uploads/` folder; connect to your web server via FTP and download that folder to your local computer.
- ✔ **Plugin files:** Although all the plugin settings are stored in the database, the actual plugin files that contain the programming code are not. The plugin files are located in the `/wp-content/plugins/` folder; connect to your web server via FTP and download that folder to your local computer.

✔ **Theme files:** Widgets and options you've set for your current theme are stored in the database; however, the theme template files, images, and stylesheets are not. They are stored in the `/wp-content/themes` folder; connect to your web server via FTP and download that folder to your local computer.

Now that you have your database and WordPress files stored safely on your local computer, moving them to a new host just involves reversing the process:

1. **Create a new database on your new hosting account.**

   You can find the steps for creating a database in Chapter 3.

2. **Import your database backup into the new database you just created:**

   a. Log in to the cPanel for your hosting account.

   b. Click the phpMyAdmin icon and click the name of your new database in the left menu.

   c. Click the Import tab at the top.

   d. Click the Browse button and select the database backup from your local computer.

   e. Click the Go button, and the old database imports into the new.

3. **Install WordPress on your new hosting account.**

   See Chapter 3 for the steps to install WordPress.

4. **Edit the** `wp-config.php` **file to include your new database name, username, password, and host.**

5. **Upload all that you downloaded from the** `/wp-content/` **folder to your new hosting account.**

6. **In your web browser, browse to your domain.**

   Your website should work, and you are able to log on to the WordPress Dashboard using the same username and password as before because that information is stored in the database you imported.

Using a plugin to back up and move to a new host

A plugin that I use on a regular basis to move a WordPress website from one hosting environment to another is aptly named BackupBuddy. This plugin isn't free or available in the WordPress Plugin Directory — you need to pay for it, but it's worth every single penny because it takes the entire backup and migration process and makes mincemeat out of it. This means that it's very easy, and you can be done in minutes instead of hours. You can purchase the BackupBuddy plugin from iThemes at `https://ithemes.com/purchase/backupbuddy` — currently pricing starts at $80 per year. Once you've purchased it, you can download the plugin and install it (see plugin installation instructions in Chapter 7) and follow the instructions given to you in the WordPress Dashboard to make a backup copy of your website and move it to another server.

Part V
The Part of Tens

Enjoy an additional WordPress Part of Tens chapter at www.dummies.com/
extras/wordpress.

In this part . . .

- ✔ Discover ten popular WordPress plugins that you can install today to extend the features and functionality of your existing WordPress site.

- ✔ Check out ten free themes for WordPress that you can use to add interest to the look and feel of your website.

Chapter 15

Ten Popular WordPress Plugins

In This Chapter

▶ Finding popular WordPress plugins

▶ Using plugins to enhance your website

*I*n this chapter, I list ten of the most popular plugins available for your WordPress site. This list isn't exhaustive by any means; hundreds of excellent WordPress plugins can, and do, provide multiple ways to extend the functionality of your blog. And if these ten plugins aren't enough for you, you can find many more at the official WordPress Plugin Directory (https://wordpress.org/plugins).

The greatest plugin of all is Akismet, which I describe in Chapter 7. Akismet is the answer to comment and trackback spam; it kills spam dead. It's installed with WordPress. Chapter 7 contains information on how to locate, download, unpack, install, activate, and manage plugins in your WordPress site.

AppPresser — Mobile App Framework

Developer: AppPresser

https://wordpress.org/plugins/apppresser

Introduced in January 2014, AppPresser is the very first plugin of its kind in that it allows users of the plugin to create native mobile applications using WordPress as the platform. Prior to AppPresser, if you wanted to develop a native mobile app, you needed to be an advanced programmer in languages like Objective C or Ruby. With the AppPresser plugin, if you know how to build a WordPress site, you can also build a mobile application.

AppPresser allows you to use a WordPress site as an app, including access to device features such as the camera, contacts, and more. You can create your app completely in WordPress, using themes, plugins, and all the stuff you already know.

The AppPresser core plugin is free to download from the WordPress Plugin Directory (`https://wordpress.org/plugins/apppresser/`), but you can also purchase nifty extensions to create your app from their website at `http://apppresser.com`. Some of the extensions that are available for $99 to $399 include:

- ✔ **AppCamera:** A native camera extension that hooks into your iPhone or Android device camera.

- ✔ **AppSwiper:** An extension that allows you to load images in an organized carousel gallery that supports touch and swiping on mobile devices and tablets.

- ✔ **AppGeo:** An extension that hooks into the GPS location features of your mobile device or tablet.

AppPresser also has bundled packages starting at $199/year (with a renewal rate of 50 percent of that cost) for special needs like Ecommerce or Agencies. Check it out at `http://apppresser.com`.

What the AppPresser plugin does:

- ✔ Integrates Phonegap with WordPress, which exposes the Phonegap API.

- ✔ Allows you to use JavaScript (using the Phonegap API) to use native device features.

- ✔ Allows you to use other AppPresser plugins and themes to create an app.

- ✔ Adds a settings page with an app-only home page, menus, and theme settings.

Follow these steps to use AppPresser:

1. Install and activate the plugin.

2. Add AppPresser themes or extensions to create your app.

3. Build your app yourself with Phonegap, or with its build service.

4. Distribute to the iOS/Android app stores.

Jetpack

Developer: Automattic

`https://wordpress.org/plugins/jetpack/`

Jetpack is not just one simple plugin; it's a suite of plugins that connects your self-hosted website running WordPress.org with the hosted WordPress.com service — and brings you many of the features that WordPress.com users enjoy. Jetpack bundles great features such as the following:

- **WordPress.com Stats:** This simple statistics program gives you easy-to-read statistics on your site visitors, such as how many visitors you have, where they're coming from, and what content they're viewing on your site.

- **Publicize:** Connect your site to popular social media networks like Twitter and Facebook.

- **Notifications:** Monitor and manage your site's activity with Notifications in the admin toolbar.

- **Jetpack Comments:** This feature is a comment system that integrates with social media login options like Facebook, Twitter, and Google.

- **Subscriptions:** With this feature, your site visitors can subscribe to your blog posts and/or comments via email.

- **Post by Email:** Publish posts to your blog directly from your email account.

- **Carousel:** Transform your standard image galleries into slideshows and carousels.

- **Likes:** Give your readers a way to show their appreciation for your content.

- **Sharing:** Your readers can easily share your content across different social networks like Facebook, Twitter, Google+, and Pinterest.

- **Spelling and Grammar:** Improve your grammar, spelling, and punctuation with this integrated proofreading service.

- **VaultPress:** This feature provides a real-time backup and security-scanning service for your site.

- **Omnisearch:** Use this single search box for everything on your WordPress-powered site.

- **Gravatar Hovercards:** Show a pop-up of your users' gravatar profiles in comments.

✔ **Contact Form:** Easily insert an email contact form anywhere on your WordPress site with one click of a button.

✔ **WP.me Shortlinks:** Create a short URL for easier social sharing with the WP.me service.

✔ **Google+ Profile:** Show a link to your Google+ profile in the sharing area of your posts and pages.

✔ **Tiled Galleries:** Easily create magazine-style image tile layouts for your photos.

✔ **Widget Visibility:** Easily control what pages your widgets are displayed on.

✔ **Mobile Theme:** Optimize your site for mobile devices.

✔ **Custom CSS:** Customize the appearance of your site using CSS, but without modifying your theme files.

✔ **Shortcode Embeds:** Easily embed videos and audio files with a WordPress shortcode.

✔ **Beautiful Math:** This feature uses the LaTeX markup language for complex mathematical equations within your posts — perfect for the real geeks out there.

✔ **Extra Sidebar Widgets:** Add widgets to your WordPress site like the Easy Image Widget and the RSS Widget.

✔ **Infinite Scroll:** Automatically pulls the next set of posts into the browser window when the visitor reaches the bottom of the page.

✔ **Photon:** Load images from the WordPress.com CDN (Content Delivery Network) service.

✔ **Jetpack Single Sign On:** Allow users to log in to your site using their credentials from WordPress.com.

✔ **Monitor:** Jetpack monitors your site for uptime and alerts you when your site is down.

✔ **Mobile Push Notifications:** Get updates on your mobile phone.

✔ **Enhanced Distribution:** Share your content with search engines and other services in real-time.

✔ **JSON API:** Allow applications to securely connect to your site through the cloud.

✔ **VideoPress:** Easily upload and insert videos on your site.

Because Jetpack runs and is hosted on the WordPress.com cloud server, updates to this suite of plugins happen automatically — giving you fast and ready access to the latest and greatest bundle of plugins that Automattic has to offer. In order to use Jetpack, you must have a WordPress.com account, and when you activate it in your Dashboard, it asks you to connect your site to your WordPress.com account (see Chapter 1).

Subscribe to Comments

Developer: Mark Jaquith

```
https://wordpress.org/plugins/subscribe-to-comments
```

The Subscribe to Comments plugin adds a very nice feature to your blog by letting your visitors subscribe to individual posts you've made to your blog. When your readers subscribe to individual posts on your blog, they receive notification via email whenever someone leaves a new comment on the post. This feature goes a long way toward keeping your readers informed and making the discussions lively and active!

The plugin includes a full-featured subscription manager that your commenters can use to unsubscribe to certain posts, block all notifications, or even change their notification email addresses.

Facebook

Developers: Facebook and Automattic

```
https://wordpress.org/plugins/facebook
```

This plugin was developed by Facebook for WordPress with a little help from the developers at Automattic. With the importance of a social media presence today, you'll want to make sure that all your content reaches the eyes of your friends and followers on social networks like Facebook. And that pursuit can be time-consuming. The goal of the Facebook plugin is to save you time by easily sharing your new content with your Facebook page and allowing your Facebook friends to discover that content and interact with your website seamlessly. The following great features allow you to

✔ Share new content from your WordPress site on your Facebook page automatically. After you connect your site to your Facebook account in the plugin settings, your new content is posted automatically to your Facebook page.

✔ Mention friends and favorite pages within the content of your posts and link those mentions directly to their Facebook pages.

✔ Include the Share, Like, and Subscribe Facebook buttons on your WordPress site, with easy customization.

✔ Display a recommendations box where Facebook makes additional content recommendations for your readers to discover, based on the content they're currently browsing on your site.

✔ Include Facebook commenting on your site to allow your Facebook friends to comment in both places at once.

✔ Include an Activity Feed Box Widget that allows Facebook friends to see what their friends are doing on your site.

✔ Determine how well your Facebook presence is doing in promoting your content through Facebook Insights integration.

The Facebook plugin installs easily, and after you connect your Facebook account to your WordPress site through the Facebook plugin settings, you're ready to go!

All in One SEO Pack

Developer: Michael Torbert

`https://wordpress.org/plugins/all-in-one-seo-pack/`

Almost everyone is concerned about search engine optimization (SEO) in blogs. Good SEO practices help the major search engines (such as Google, Yahoo!, and Bing) easily find and cache your blog content in their search databases so that when people search for keywords, they can find your blog in the search results. All in One SEO Pack helps you fine-tune your blog to make that happen. It automatically creates optimized titles and generates HTML keywords for your individual posts. If you're a beginner, this plugin works for you out of the box with no advanced configuration necessary. Woo-hoo! If you're an advanced user, you can fine-tune the All in One SEO settings to your liking.

BackupBuddy

Developer: iThemes Media

`https://ithemes.com/purchase/backupbuddy/`

Starting at $80 for the personal user and $297 for its entire development suite of plugins, the folks at iThemes have hit a home run with BackupBuddy, which lets you back up your entire WordPress website in minutes. With this plugin, you can also determine a schedule of automated backups of your site on a daily, weekly, or monthly basis. You can store those backups on your web server, email backups to a designated email address, FTP them to a designated FTP server, or store the backups in Amazon's Simple Storage Service, Dropbox, or the Rackspace Cloud, if you have an account there.

BackupBuddy not only backs up your WordPress data (posts, pages, comments, and so on), but it also backs up any theme and customized plugins you've installed (including all the settings for those plugins) and saves and backs up all WordPress settings and any widgets that you're currently using.

BackupBuddy also includes an import and migration script (`importbuddy.php`) that allows you to easily transfer an existing site to a new domain, or new host, within minutes. You simply download the backup file created by BackupBuddy from your Dashboard (choose BackupBuddy⇨Backups) and install the script on a new domain, follow the steps, and within minutes, your entire site is completely restored on a new domain, or web host, with minimal effort.

This plugin is invaluable for designers and developers who work with clients to design websites with WordPress. Using BackupBuddy, you can download a backup of the site and then use the import/migration script to transfer the completed site to your client's site within minutes — saving all the customizations you did to the theme and the plugins you installed, including the settings and data you've been working so hard on.

WP Super Cache

Developer: Donncha O'Caoimh

`https://wordpress.org/plugins/wp-super-cache`

WP Super Cache creates static HTML files from your dynamic WordPress content. Why is this useful? On a high-traffic site, having cached versions of your posts and pages can speed up the load time of your website considerably. A *cached* version simply means that the content is converted to static HTML pages (as opposed to dynamically created content pulled from your database through a series of PHP commands) that are then stored on the server. This process eases the efforts the web server must take to display the content in your visitors' browsers.

You can also read a very helpful article written by the plugin developer, Donncha O'Caoimh, on his website: `http://z9.io/wp-super-cache/`.

WooCommerce

Developer: WooThemes

`https://wordpress.org/plugins/woocommerce/`

eCommerce is the practice of selling products or services on your website. The WooCommerce plugin for WordPress gives you the ability to do just that. Whether you are selling products like t-shirts, posters, or art or selling services like consulting, WooCommerce has you covered in the ability to set up products and accept payment transactions on your website.

Here are some of the high-level features you enjoy with the WooCommerce plugin:

- **Accept payments:** You can accept payments from your customers from PayPal or any major credit card.
- **Configure shipping:** If you sell physical goods that require shipping, the WooCommerce shipping feature gives you several options, including configuring free shipping or flat-rate shipping.
- **Manage inventory:** Easily manage physical or digital goods (like music, for example); you can also assign store managers to handle day-to-day inventory for large online shops.
- **Run reports:** Keep track of your sales, reviews, stock levels, and overall store performance with WooCommerce reporting tools.
- **Run marketing campaigns:** You can run a multitude of marketing campaigns with a range of discounts, coupons, usage limits, and product and/or user restrictions — as well as free shipping.
- **Configure taxes:** No one likes to deal with taxes, but WooCommerce makes it relatively easy to configure tax settings with classes and local tax rates.

WooCommerce also has a variety of Add-Ons, called Extensions, that allow you to extend your e-commerce platform to your tastes. Its Extension library contains items such as Event Bookings, Membership subscriptions, Product Reviews, and Product Labels.

Overall, WooCommerce adds powerful shop options to your WordPress website — currently WooCommerce is powering 17 percent of all WordPress-based e-commerce websites.

Google XML Sitemaps

Developer: Arne Brachhold

```
https://wordpress.org/plugins/google-sitemap-generator
```

This plugin lets you create a Google-compliant site map of your entire blog. Every time you create a new post or page, the site map is updated and submitted to several major search engines, including Google, Yahoo!, and Bing. This plugin helps the search engines find and catalog new content from your site, so your new content appears in the search engines faster than it would if you didn't have a site map.

Sucuri Sitecheck Malware Scanner

Developers: Daniel Cid and Dre Armeda

```
https://wordpress.org/plugins/sucuri-scanner
```

With the rise in popularity of the WordPress software came a nefarious group of anonymous hackers trying to take advantage of the vast number of users in the WordPress community by attempting to inject malicious code and malware into themes, plugins, and insecure and outdated files within the WordPress core code.

Protect your website by using the Sucuri Sitecheck Malware Scanner — an easy-to-install-and-use plugin that enables full scan capabilities — for both malware and blacklisting — from Sucuri, right in your WordPress Dashboard. The plugin checks for malware, spam, blacklisting, and other security issues hidden inside code files. It's the best defense you have against malicious hackers and very easy to implement — and for the peace of mind that it provides you, the free price tag is worth every penny!

Chapter 16

Ten Free WordPress Themes

In This Chapter

▶ Finding good WordPress themes

▶ Using popular WordPress themes to style your website

The list I present here isn't exhaustive by any means. Chapters 8, 10, and 11 give you a few more resources to find a theme that suits your needs.

All the themes in this chapter meet the following criteria:

✔ **They're user-friendly.** You don't have to tinker with anything to get things to look the way you want them to.

✔ **They're compatible with widgets.** In a word, widgets are wonderful. I cover them in Chapter 9.

✔ **They're free.** Some very nice premium themes are out there, but why pay if you don't have to?

✔ **They use valid code.** Although you may not notice it, valid code that meets W3C (http://www.w3.org) standards won't cause errors in browsers.

Hybrid

Theme designer: Justin Tadlock

http://themehybrid.com

Hybrid is more of a theme *framework*, or parent theme that can be modified endlessly to create the perfect child theme, than a theme to use straight out of the box, but don't let that intimidate you! It's crazy-easy to use and very user-friendly.

By default, the Hybrid theme is very plain and simple, but it encompasses any and all of the WordPress features and functions that you would want:

- ✔ **It's SEO-ready:** Hybrid comes completely optimized for SEO (search engine optimization).

- ✔ **It's highly customizable:** Hybrid has 15 custom page templates for you to choose from. Each custom page is set up slightly differently, giving you an array of options.

- ✔ **It's widget-ready:** Hybrid has multiple widgetized areas for you to easily drop content into, making your WordPress theme experience easy and efficient.

You can read about the Hybrid theme at the developer's (Justin Tadlock) website at `http://themehybrid.com`. You can also download and install the theme directly into your WordPress website by using the automatic theme installer built in to your WordPress Dashboard.

Check out options for installing and tweaking WordPress themes in Chapters 9, 10, and 11. Those chapters give you information on CSS, HTML, and theme-tweaking, as well as guide you through working with parent/child themes.

designPile

Theme designer: Smashing Magazine

`http://demo.s5themes.com/?theme=designpile`

The highlights of this theme are the following:

- ✔ Three different color schemes: black and pink, black and green, and black and blue
- ✔ Sidebar and footer widgets
- ✔ Supports the WordPress post thumbnails/featured image feature
- ✔ Space for monetization with ads
- ✔ Built-in social networking links and sharing

The designPile theme, shown in Figure 16-1, is a sharp design and an easy-to-use, free WordPress theme for any new user.

Figure 16-1:
Try the
designPile
Theme by
Smashing
Magazine.

Responsive

Theme designer: CyberChimps

`https://wordpress.org/themes/responsive`

Responsive design is all the rage right now because of the emergence of mobile and tablet browsing. *Responsive design* ensures that a website looks perfect, no matter which device a reader is using to view it. The Responsive theme by Emil Uzelac features nine page templates including the Blog, Blog Summary, and other static page templates built on a fluid grid system that adapts to the user's browsing environment.

Theme options in this responsive design include webmaster tools, logo-management, social icons, and navigation menus, as well as multilingual support.

P2

Theme designer: Automattic

`https://wordpress.org/themes/p2`

You can easily see the Twitter-esque inspiration behind P2 by looking at the post text box displayed at the top of the theme. As with Twitter, users can post quick updates, and logged-in visitors can leave feedback on the updates. All this happens from the convenience of the front page of your site — without requiring anyone to click through to a different page on your site, locate the comment form, type, and submit the comment. The P2 theme also features the following:

- ✔ Live tag suggestions for your posts and updates
- ✔ Threaded comment display
- ✔ A show/hide feature for comments
- ✔ Real-time notification for posts, updates, and comments
- ✔ Keyboard shortcuts

Annotum Base

Theme designer: Annotum

`https://wordpress.org/themes/annotum-base`

Annotum Base is a scholar's blog theme providing a complete open-access journaling system including peer review, workflow, and advanced editing and formatting for blog posts and pages. The most interesting features in this theme include structured figures, equations, and cross referencing from PubMed and CrossRef (including reference importing).

Other theme options include the following:

- ✔ Customized color options
- ✔ Custom header image
- ✔ Custom background image/colors
- ✔ Navigation menus
- ✔ Featured images
- ✔ Microformats
- ✔ Multilingual support

Blackbird

Theme designer: InkThemes

`https://wordpress.org/themes/blackbird`

Blackbird, shown in Figure 16-2, is a responsive theme (mobile-ready) with extensive customization options, including the ability to

- ✔ Use your own logo.
- ✔ Include your analytics code.
- ✔ Customize featured text using an easy widget.
- ✔ Customize background colors and/or images.
- ✔ Incorporate post thumbnails using the WordPress featured image feature.
- ✔ Customize the header image.
- ✔ Use the navigation menu feature in WordPress.

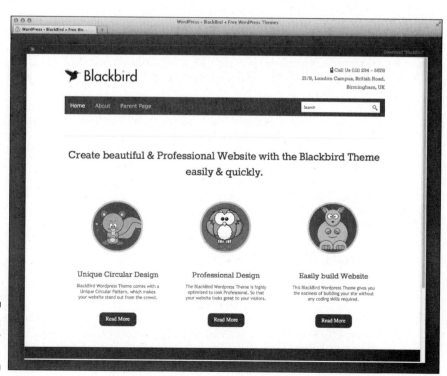

Figure 16-2:
Blackbird by
InkThemes.

iTheme2

Theme designer: Nick La

http://themify.me/themes/itheme2

iTheme2 is a WordPress theme designed with Mac lovers in mind. The theme emulates the design elements and features of the Mac operating system, with beautiful blue gradients and Mac-like menu headers and icons. This theme has a fully configurable sidebar that allows you to use WordPress widgets, and when they're in your blog, you can drag those widgets around in the sidebar.

Esquire

Theme designer: Automattic

https://wordpress.org/themes/esquire

Esquire is a free WordPress theme created by Automattic, the company behind the WordPress.com hosted service. It has a distinct visual design with creative typography (fonts), a two-column layout, and visually creative design elements that make it unique (such as the date format and content styling).

Esquire supports all of the expected default WordPress features such as featured images, custom background, custom header, navigation menus, and post formats. The theme design is inspired by the art direction of *Esquire Magazine*.

WP-Creativix

Theme designer: IWEBIX

https://wordpress.org/themes/wp-creativix

The WP-Creativix theme by IWEBIX is a very clean, professional-looking free theme for WordPress that you can begin using immediately after you install and activate it. This elegantly designed theme is well suited for a business, portfolio, or photoblogging website.

The WP-Creativix theme provides users with custom page templates (such as no-sidebar templates, portfolio, and blog) and allows you to use default WordPress features such as custom header, custom background, navigation menu, featured images, and threaded comments.

Gridline

Theme designer: Thad Allender

https://graphpaperpress.com/themes/gridline/

Gridline is a minimalist WordPress theme featuring a grid layout. The theme has clean, simple, light elements, which lets your design focus mainly on content rather than appearance. The theme uses black, white, and gray tones and a two-column layout, with content on the left and sidebar on the right.

This is a free theme offered by a commercial theme company, Graph Paper Press, and while it is free, to be able to download it, you need to register for a free account on the Graph Paper Press website.

Index

Notes

Notes

About the Author

Lisa Sabin-Wilson has worked with the WordPress software since its inception in 2003 and has built her career around providing technical support, hosting, and design solutions for bloggers who use WordPress. She reaches thousands of people worldwide with her WordPress services, skills, and knowledge regarding the product. Lisa is also the author of the best-selling *WordPress All In One For Dummies* and *WordPress Web Design For Dummies*.

Lisa operates a few blogs online, all of which are powered by WordPress. Her personal blog (`http://lisasabin-wilson.com`) has been online since February of 2002. She and her partners, Brad Williams and Brian Messenlehner, provide custom development and design services at her WordPress design and development business, WebDevStudios (`http://webdevstudios.com`).

When she can be persuaded away from her computer, where she is usually hard at work providing design solutions for her WordPress clients, she sometimes emerges for public speaking appearances on the topics of design, blogging, and WordPress. She has appeared at conferences such as the annual South By Southwest Interactive Conference, Blog World Expo, CMSExpo, Prestige Conference, and several WordCamp events across the country.

Lisa consults with bloggers both large and small. Bloggers come in thousands of different flavors, from business to personal, from creative to technical, and all points in between. Lisa is connected to thousands of them worldwide and appreciates the opportunity to share her knowledge with *WordPress For Dummies*. She hopes you find great value in it, as well!

When not designing or consulting with her clients, you can usually find her at her favorite coffee shop sipping espresso, on a mountaintop somewhere hitting the slopes with her family, or 100 feet beneath the ocean waters, scuba diving with her husband and swimming with the fishes.

You can find Lisa online at Twitter: @LisaSabinWilson.

Dedication

For my father, Donald Sabin — for him, his love, and his undying support and encouragement of my crazy choices in life. I miss you, Dad . . . rest in peace.

Author's Acknowledgments

Many, many thanks and kudos to Matt Mullenweg, the WordPress core development team, and every single person involved in making WordPress the best blogging platform available on the Internet today. To the volunteers and testers who destroy all those pesky pre-release bugs for every new version release, the WordPress community thanks you! And to each and every WordPress plugin developer and theme designer who donates his or her time, skills, and knowledge to provide the entire WordPress community of users with invaluable tools that help us create dynamic blogs, thank you a thousand times! Every person mentioned here is an invaluable asset to the overall WordPress experience; I wish I could name you all, individually, but there are literally thousands of you out there!

Extra special thanks to my friends and colleagues within the WordPress community who inspire and teach me every day.

Huge thanks to Amy Fandrei from Wiley and to Lynn Northrup for their support, assistance, and guidance during the course of this project. Just the mere fact they had to read every page of this book means that they deserve the Medal of Honor! Also, many thanks to the technical editor, Donna Baker, who worked hard to make sure that I look somewhat literate here.

Publisher's Acknowledgments

We're proud of this book; please send us your comments at http://dummies.custhelp.com. For other comments, please contact our Customer Care Department within the U.S. at 877-762-2974, outside the U.S. at 317-572-3993, or fax 317-572-4002.

Some of the people who helped bring this book to market include the following:

Acquisitions Editor: Amy Fandrei

Project Editor: Lynn Northrup

Copy Editor: Lynn Northrup

Technical Editor: Donna Baker

Editorial Assistant: Claire Brock

Sr. Editorial Assistant: Cherie Case

Cover Image: ©Getty Images/Vectorig

Apple & Mac

iPad For Dummies,
6th Edition
978-1-118-72306-7

iPhone For Dummies,
7th Edition
978-1-118-69083-3

Macs All-in-One
For Dummies, 4th Edition
978-1-118-82210-4

OS X Mavericks
For Dummies
978-1-118-69188-5

Blogging & Social Media

Facebook For Dummies,
5th Edition
978-1-118-63312-0

Social Media Engagement
For Dummies
978-1-118-53019-1

WordPress For Dummies,
6th Edition
978-1-118-79161-5

Business

Stock Investing
For Dummies, 4th Edition
978-1-118-37678-2

Investing For Dummies,
5th Edition
978-0-470-90545-6

Personal Finance

Personal Finance
For Dummies, 7th Edition
978-1-118-11785-9

QuickBooks 2014
For Dummies
978-1-118-72005-9

Small Business Marketing
Kit For Dummies,
3rd Edition
978-1-118-31183-7

Careers

Job Interviews
For Dummies, 4th Edition
978-1-118-11290-8

Job Searching with Social
Media For Dummies,
2nd Edition
978-1-118-67856-5

Personal Branding
For Dummies
978-1-118-11792-7

Resumes For Dummies,
6th Edition
978-0-470-87361-8

Starting an Etsy Business
For Dummies, 2nd Edition
978-1-118-59024-9

Diet & Nutrition

Belly Fat Diet For Dummies
978-1-118-34585-6

Mediterranean Diet
For Dummies
978-1-118-71525-3

Nutrition For Dummies,
5th Edition
978-0-470-93231-5

Digital Photography

Digital SLR Photography
All-in-One For Dummies,
2nd Edition
978-1-118-59082-9

Digital SLR Video &
Filmmaking For Dummies
978-1-118-36598-4

Photoshop Elements 12
For Dummies
978-1-118-72714-0

Gardening

Herb Gardening
For Dummies, 2nd Edition
978-0-470-61778-6

Gardening with Free-Range
Chickens For Dummies
978-1-118-54754-0

Health

Boosting Your Immunity
For Dummies
978-1-118-40200-9

Diabetes For Dummies

Diabetes For Dummies,
4th Edition
978-1-118-29447-5

Living Paleo For Dummies
978-1-118-29405-5

Big Data

Big Data For Dummies
978-1-118-50422-2

Data Visualization
For Dummies
978-1-118-50289-1

Hadoop For Dummies
978-1-118-60755-8

Language & Foreign Language

500 Spanish Verbs
For Dummies
978-1-118-02382-2

English Grammar
For Dummies, 2nd Edition
978-0-470-54664-2

French All-in-One
For Dummies
978-1-118-22815-9

German Essentials
For Dummies
978-1-118-18422-6

Italian For Dummies,
2nd Edition
978-1-118-00465-4

ⓔ Available in print and e-book formats.

Available wherever books are sold. **For more information or to order direct visit www.dummies.com**

Math & Science

Algebra I For Dummies,
2nd Edition
978-0-470-55964-2

Anatomy and Physiology
For Dummies, 2nd Edition
978-0-470-92326-9

Astronomy For Dummies,
3rd Edition
978-1-118-37697-3

Biology For Dummies,
2nd Edition
978-0-470-59875-7

Chemistry For Dummies,
2nd Edition
978-1-118-00730-3

1001 Algebra II Practice
Problems For Dummies
978-1-118-44662-1

Microsoft Office

Excel 2013 For Dummies
978-1-118-51012-4

Office 2013 All-in-One
For Dummies
978-1-118-51636-2

PowerPoint 2013
For Dummies
978-1-118-50253-2

Word 2013 For Dummies
978-1-118-49123-2

Music

Blues Harmonica
For Dummies
978-1-118-25269-7

Guitar For Dummies,
3rd Edition
978-1-118-11554-1

iPod & iTunes
For Dummies, 10th Edition
978-1-118-50864-0

Programming

Beginning Programming
with C For Dummies
978-1-118-73763-7

Excel VBA Programming
For Dummies, 3rd Edition
978-1-118-49037-2

Java For Dummies,
6th Edition
978-1-118-40780-6

Religion & Inspiration

The Bible For Dummies
978-0-7645-5296-0

Buddhism For Dummies,
2nd Edition
978-1-118-02379-2

Catholicism For Dummies,
2nd Edition
978-1-118-07778-8

Self-Help & Relationships

Beating Sugar Addiction
For Dummies
978-1-118-54645-1

Meditation For Dummies,
3rd Edition
978-1-118-29144-3

Seniors

Laptops For Seniors
For Dummies, 3rd Edition
978-1-118-71105-7

Computers For Seniors
For Dummies, 3rd Edition
978-1-118-11553-4

iPad For Seniors
For Dummies, 6th Edition
978-1-118-72826-0

Social Security
For Dummies
978-1-118-20573-0

Smartphones & Tablets

Android Phones
For Dummies, 2nd Edition
978-1-118-72030-1

Nexus Tablets
For Dummies
978-1-118-77243-0

Samsung Galaxy S 4
For Dummies
978-1-118-64222-1

Samsung Galaxy Tabs
For Dummies
978-1-118-77294-2

Test Prep

ACT For Dummies,
5th Edition
978-1-118-01259-8

ASVAB For Dummies,
3rd Edition
978-0-470-63760-9

GRE For Dummies,
7th Edition
978-0-470-88921-3

Officer Candidate Tests
For Dummies
978-0-470-59876-4

Physician's Assistant Exam
For Dummies
978-1-118-11556-5

Series 7 Exam For Dummies
978-0-470-09932-2

Windows 8

Windows 8.1 All-in-One
For Dummies
978-1-118-82087-2

Windows 8.1 For Dummies
978-1-118-82121-3

Windows 8.1 For Dummies,
Book + DVD Bundle
978-1-118-82107-7

Available in print and e-book formats.

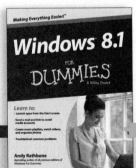

Available wherever books are sold. **For more information or to order direct visit www.dummies.com**

Take Dummies with you everywhere you go!

Whether you are excited about e-books, want more from the web, must have your mobile apps, or are swept up in social media, Dummies makes everything easier.

Leverage the Power

For Dummies is the global leader in the reference category and one of the most trusted and highly regarded brands in the world. No longer just focused on books, customers now have access to the For Dummies content they need in the format they want. Let us help you develop a solution that will fit your brand and help you connect with your customers.

Advertising & Sponsorships

Connect with an engaged audience on a powerful multimedia site, and position your message alongside expert how-to content.

Targeted ads • Video • Email marketing • Microsites • Sweepstakes sponsorship

21 Million Monthly Page Views & 13 Million Unique Visitors

# of For Dummies

Custom Publishing

Reach a global audience in any language by creating a solution that will differentiate you from competitors, amplify your message, and encourage customers to make a buying decision.

Apps • Books • eBooks • Video • Audio • Webinars

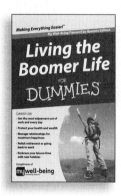   

Brand Licensing & Content

Leverage the strength of the world's most popular reference brand to reach new audiences and channels of distribution.

For more information, visit www.Dummies.com/biz

Dummies products make life easier!

- DIY
- Consumer Electronics
- Crafts
- Software
- Cookware
- Hobbies
- Videos
- Music
- Games
- and More!

For more information, go to **Dummies.com** and search the store by category.

FOR
DUMMIES

A Wiley Bran